# *Reader's Guide*
# *to*
# ERNEST HEMINGWAY

# *Reader's Guide*
# *to*
# ERNEST HEMINGWAY

**Rudolf Eisler**

**CENTRUM PRESS**
NEW DELHI-110002 (INDIA)

**CENTRUM PRESS**
**H.O.:** 4360/4, Ansari Road, Daryaganj,
New Delhi-110 002 (India)
Ph.: 23278000, 23261597

**B.O.:** No. 1015, Ist Main Road, BSK IIIrd Stage
IIIrd Phase, IIIrd Block,
Bangalore - 560 085 (India)
Tel.: 080-41723429
*Visit us at*: www.centrumpress.com

*Reader's Guide to Ernest Hemingway*



First Edition, 2009

ISBN 978-93-80106-63-2

PRINTED IN INDIA

*Printed at* Salasar Imaging Systems, Delhi-110035 (India)

# Contents

# Preface

Ernest Hemingway, born in Oak Park, Illinois, started his career as a writer in a newspaper office in Kansas City at the age of seventeen. After the United States entered the First World War, he joined a volunteer ambulance unit in the Italian army. Serving at the front, he was wounded, was decorated by the Italian Government, and spent considerable time in hospitals. After his return to the United States, he became a reporter for Canadian and American newspapers and was soon sent back to Europe to cover such events as the Greek Revolution.

During the twenties, Hemingway became a member of the group of expatriate Americans in Paris, which he described in his first important work, *The Sun Also Rises* (1926).

Equally successful was *A Farewell to Arms* (1929), the study of an American ambulance officer's disillusionment in the war and his role as a deserter. Hemingway used his experiences as a reporter during the civil war in Spain as the background for his most ambitious novel, *For Whom the Bell Tolls* (1940). Among his later works, the most outstanding is the short novel, *The Old Man and the Sea* (1952), the story of an old fisherman's journey, his long and lonely struggle with a fish and the sea, and his victory in defeat.

Author

## Chapter 1

# Introduction

Ernest Hemingway was born in Oak Park, Illinois, in the summer of 1899. He later portrayed his middle-class parents rather harshly, condemning them for their conventional morality and values. As a young man, he left home to become a newspaper writer in Kansas City. Early in 1918, he joined the Italian Red Cross and served as an ambulance driver in Italy during World War I, in which the Italians allied with the British, French, and Americans against Germany and Austria-Hungary.

During his time abroad, Hemingway had two experiences that affected him profoundly and that would later inspire one of his most celebrated novels, A Farewell to Arms. The first occurred on July 8, 1918, when a trench mortar shell struck him while he crouched beyond the front lines with three Italian soldiers. Though Hemingway embellished the story over the years, it is certain that he was transferred to a hospital in Milan, where he fell in love with a Red Cross nurse named Agnes von Kurowsky.

Scholars are divided over Agnes's role in Hemingway's life and writing, but there is little doubt that his relationship with her informed the relationship between Lieutenant Henry and Catherine Barkley in A Farewell to Arms. After his recovery, Hemingway spent several years as a reporter, during which time he honed the clear, concise, and emotionally evocative writing style that generations of authors after him would imitate. In September 1921, he married his first of four wives and settled in Paris, where he made valuable connections with American expatriate writers like Gertrude

Stein and Ezra Pound. Hemingway's landmark collection of stories, In Our Time, introduced Nick Adams, one of the author's favourite protagonists, whose difficult road from youth into maturity he chronicled. Hemingway's reputation as a writer, however, was most firmly established by the publication of The Sun Also Rises in 1926 and A Farewell to Arms in 1929.

Critics generally agree that A Farewell to Arms is Hemingway's most accomplished novel. It offers powerful descriptions of life during and immediately following World War I and brilliantly maps the psychological complexities of its characters using a revolutionary, pared-down prose style. Furthermore, the novel, like much of Hemingway's writing during what were to be his golden years, helped to establish the author's myth of himself as a master of many trades: writing, soldiering, boxing, bullfighting, big-game hunting. Hemingway was skilled, to a greater or lesser extent, in each of these arts, but most critics maintain that his writing fizzled after World War II, when his physical and mental health declined.

Despite fantastic bouts of depression, Hemingway did muster enough energy to write The Old Man and the Sea, one of his most beloved stories, in 1952. This novella earned him a Pulitzer Prize, and three years later Hemingway was awarded the Nobel Prize in Literature. Still, not even these accolades could soothe the devastating effects of a lifetime of debilitating depression. On July 2, 1961, Hemingway killed himself in his home in Ketchum, Idaho. Lieutenant Frederic Henry is a young American ambulance driver serving in the Italian army during World War I.

At the beginning of the novel, the war is winding down with the onset of winter, and Henry arranges to tour Italy. The following spring, upon his return to the front, Henry meets Catherine Barkley, an English nurse's aide at the nearby British hospital and the love interest of his friend Rinaldi. Rinaldi, however, quickly fades from the picture as Catherine and Henry become involved in an elaborate game of seduction. Grieving the recent death of her fiancé, Catherine longs for love so deeply that she will settle for the illusion of it. Her passion, even though pretended, wakens a desire for emotional interaction in Henry, whom the war has left coolly detached and numb.

When Henry is wounded on the battlefield, he is brought to a hospital in Milan to recover. Several doctors recommend that he stay in bed for six months and then undergo a necessary operation on his knee. Unable to accept such a long period of recovery, Henry finds a bold, garrulous surgeon named Dr. Valentini who agrees to operate immediately. Henry learns happily that Catherine has been transferred to Milan and begins his recuperation under her care. During the following months, his relationship with Catherine intensifies. No longer simply a game in which they exchange empty promises and playful kisses, their love becomes powerful and real. As the lines between scripted and genuine emotions begin to blur, Henry and Catherine become tangled in their love for each other.

Once Henry's damaged leg has healed, the army grants him three weeks convalescence leave, after which he is scheduled to return to the front. He tries to plan a trip with Catherine, who reveals to him that she is pregnant. The following day, Henry is diagnosed with jaundice, and Miss Van Campen, the superintendent of the hospital, accuses him of bringing the disease on himself through excessive drinking. Believing Henry's illness to be an attempt to avoid his duty as a serviceman, Miss Van Campen has Henry's leave revoked, and he is sent to the front once the jaundice has cleared. As they part, Catherine and Henry pledge their mutual devotion.

Henry travels to the front, where Italian forces are losing ground and manpower daily. Soon after Henry's arrival, a bombardment begins. When word comes that German troops are breaking through the Italian lines, the Allied forces prepare to retreat. Henry leads his team of ambulance drivers into the great column of evacuating troops. The men pick up two engineering sergeants and two frightened young girls on their way. Henry and his drivers then decide to leave the column and take secondary roads, which they assume will be faster.

When one of their vehicles bogs down in the mud, Henry orders the two engineers to help in the effort to free the vehicle. When they refuse, he shoots one of them. The drivers continue in the other trucks until they get stuck again. They send off the young girls and continue on foot toward Udine.

As they march, one of the drivers is shot dead by the easily frightened rear guard of the Italian army. Another driver marches off to surrender himself, while Henry and the remaining driver seek refuge at a farmhouse. When they rejoin the retreat the following day, chaos has broken out: soldiers, angered by the Italian defeat, pull commanding officers from the melee and execute them on sight. The battle police seize Henry, who, at a crucial moment, breaks away and dives into the river. After swimming a safe distance downstream, Henry boards a train bound for Milan. He hides beneath a tarp that covers stockpiled artillery, thinking that his obligations to the war effort are over and dreaming of his return to Catherine.

Henry reunites with Catherine in the town of Stresa. From there, the two escape to safety in Switzerland, rowing all night in a tiny borrowed boat. They settle happily in a lovely alpine town called Montreux and agree to put the war behind them forever. Although Henry is sometimes plagued by guilt for abandoning the men on the front, the two succeed in living a beautiful, peaceful life. When spring arrives, the couple moves to Lausanne so that they can be closer to the hospital. Early one morning, Catherine goes into labour. The delivery is exceptionally painful and complicated. Catherine delivers a stillborn baby boy and, later that night, dies of a hemorrhage. Henry stays at her side until she is gone. He attempts to say goodbye but cannot. He walks back to his hotel in the rain.

## CAREER

Upon graduation from high school, Hemingway left Oak Park for a stint as a reporter at the highly respected daily newspaper the Kansas City Star. Shortly afterward, he enlisted in a Red Cross ambulance corps stationed on the Austrian front in Italy during the last year of the First World War. Hemingway was wounded almost immediately (he was delivering cigarettes and chocolate to Italian soldiers beyond the front lines) and sent to an American hospital in Milan, where he fell in love with an American nurse named Agnes von Kurowsky; these events would inspire A Farewell to Arms. After the war, Hemingway returned to the States in hopes of beginning a career of one kind or another that would support him and Agnes, whom he planned to marry. That plan was shattered when she wrote from Europe to say that she'd fallen in love with another man.

Instead, Hemingway married Hadley Richardson in 1921; shortly thereafter, the couple moved to Paris, where the first of the writer's three sons was born. All the while, Hemingway was reading as much as he could, writing stories and poems, and trying to find his voice as a writer—a process that suffered a devastating setback when a suitcase containing all the copies of all the stories he had written to date (four years' work) was stolen from Hadley on a train to Switzerland. Hemingway's formal education did not extend beyond high school in Oak Park, where he edited the school paper. His training as a writer continued, however, during his time as a reporter in Kansas City and as a foreign correspondent for the Toronto Star.

He covered the Greek-Turkish War of 1920, and the experience would inspire some of the most striking and effective of the inter-chapter vignettes in Hemingway's groundbreaking debut story collection, In Our Time. Even more influential, perhaps, were the writers Hemingway met while living in Paris during the 1920s: the Irishman James Joyce and the American expatriates Ezra Pound, F. Scott Fitzgerald, and especially Gertrude Stein. Hemingway liked to claim that he learned about writing from the post-Impressionist paintings of Cezanne—an intriguing notion, though he never made it clear exactly what Cezanne taught him. Any discussion of Hemingway's education would be incomplete without a mention of the attention and energy he devoted to the subject matter of his books.

Just as he learned to write from the most talented contemporary practitioners of the craft, he apprenticed himself to acknowledged experts in warfare and the "blood sports" with which his work is so often concerned. He learned about military tactics from career soldiers met in World War I, bullfighting from Spanish matadors, big-game hunting from a British guide in East Africa, and deep-sea fishing from a native of the Bahamas. Hemingway loved mastering the abstruse terminology and complex procedures of each of these activities. As any reader of his work knows, he also was fascinated by food and drink; the pages of Hemingway's fiction and nonfiction are filled to overflowing with references to foreign dishes and obscure wines and liqueurs. Finally, he was a quick study at languages and was relatively fluent in quite a few.

Hemingway's first book published in the United States, In Our Time (1925), was a collection of stories (like "Indian Camp" and "Big Two-Hearted River") linked by the character of Nick Adams, who appears in many of them; by the short vignettes between the stories that tell a story of their own; by the theme of behaviour in the face of life-threatening violence; and by the now-famous Hemingway style.

The book was acclaimed upon its publication, and it remains a classic. The Torrents of Spring, a novella that attempts in a rather belabored fashion to satirize the work of the American writer Sherwood Anderson, followed in 1926, as did Hemingway's The Sun Also Rises, a novel about expatriate life in Paris and Spain after World War I. In both subject and style, the latter book is a genuinely radical work of Modern art. (The specifics of its central conflict are never explicitly stated, for instance.)

The Sun Also Rises is probably the most-admired of all the writer's books. Men Without Women (1927) comprises stories of boxers and bullfighters, including "The Undefeated," "The Killers," and "Fifty Grand." Men Without Women also contains "Hills Like White Elephants," a story told almost entirely in dialogue.

Published in 1929, A Farewell to Arms toned down Hemingway's revolutionary style to yield a more conventional—and a more moving—book than the writer had produced up to that time. The result was the novel's widespread popular success as well as worldwide fame for the author himself. The story collection Winner Take Nothing followed in 1933. Less consistently satisfying than the two collections that preceded it, Winner Take Nothing nevertheless contained more formal experimentation, like the verbatim foreign dialogue in "Wine of Wyoming."

At this point in his career, Hemingway seems to have become distracted by his own celebrity. Eight years would pass between A Farewell to Arms and the writer's next novel, the slight and poorly received To Have and Have Not (1937) which is really a collection of linked short stories that share a setting (Cuba and Key West) rather than a true novel. In the interim, Hemingway wrote two books of nonfiction: a loose, baggy treatise on bullfighting called Death in the Afternoon (1932) and The Green Hills of Africa (1935), which was about big-game hunting. All the while, the Hemingway legend was growing thanks in no small part to the author's own embellishments (and sometimes out-and-out lies) about his past.

Finally, in 1940, For Whom the Bell Tolls appeared. The book is a big novel about the Spanish Civil War, which Hemingway had covered as a correspondent and documentary filmmaker. Critics accused it, and him, of self-parody—and indeed, the novel's style is often unbearably mannered. Still, the best-selling For Whom the Bell Tolls stands among the early stories and his first two novels as Hemingway's main storytelling achievements.

During the Second World War, Hemingway occupied himself by reporting from Europe. In 1950, he published another book, the critically lambasted Across the River and Into the Trees. He recovered somewhat with The Old Man and the Sea (1952), a novella about a Cuban fisherman's struggle with a great marlin, which might be Hemingway's answer to Moby-Dick. His most popular work, The Old Man and the Sea was the last Ernest Hemingway book to be published before the author's suicide in Ketchum, Idaho, on July 2, 1961. A Moveable Feast, his charming memoir of the years spent with other expatriates in Paris during the 1920s, appeared three years later. Hemingway's fame, and the public's desire for more of his work, continues to be so formidable that his executors have brought out a number of books since his death that the writer himself had not considered fit for publication. Islands in the Stream (1970) reprises To Have and Have Not's Caribbean setting. The Garden of Eden (1986), about a menage a trois, dramatizes the author's fascination with androgyny hinted at in The Sun Also Rises and near the end of A Farewell to Arms, as well as in stories like "The Sea Change."

The Complete Short Stories: The Finca Vigia Edition (1987) contains some of the author's unpublished short fiction. And 1999's True at First Light either reports on or imagines an affair between a Hemingway-like hero and an African girl. The most influential American writer of the twentieth century, Ernest Hemingway was rewarded throughout his life for his achievements. Upon the appearance of his first published stories, he received the kudos of his literary peers, giants like James Joyce and Ezra Pound. With the publication of A Farewell to Arms, he achieved bestsellerdom.

By the time For Whom the Bell Tolls appeared, "Papa" Hemingway was recognized worldwide by millions who had never read a word of his prose; he had achieved a degree of celebrity that had never been approached by a literary writer and has not been matched since. Near the end of his life, the adulation was made explicit, as The Old Man and the Sea was awarded the Pulitzer Prize in 1953.

The following year, Hemingway won the Nobel Prize for Literature "for his powerful, style-forming mastery of the art of narration." Though his popularity has diminished somewhat in the past quarter-century due to charges of sexism and brutality in his life and work, Ernest Hemingway's influence lives on. Whether consciously or not, any writing teacher who advises students to "show, don't tell" is paying Hemingway tribute.

## Chapter 2

# The Most Influential Writer

Ernest Hemingway has been called the twentieth century's most influential writer. With the publication of A Farewell to Arms in 1929, he achieved widespread fame, and despite a steady decline in the quality of his work thereafter, his fame continued to grow until his suicide in 1961 and beyond. Striking evidence of this is the 1958 movie of The Old Man and the Sea; it's hard to imagine a book less suited to the big screen, and yet Hemingway's celebrity at the time of its publication was so massive that Hollywood had virtually no choice but to film the novella. The publication of recovered fragments from the writer's unpublished oeuvre has never failed to make headlines worldwide, from A Moveable Feast in 1964 to the so-called "fictional memoir" True at First Light, in 1999. Like those of Shakespeare and Einstein, Hemingway's face is recognized by millions who have never read a word he wrote.

Hemingway achieved more than celebrity, however. If imitation is the sincerest form of flattery, then he was a great writer indeed. Especially after reading A Farewell to Arms, Hemingway's influence is easy to discern in an enormous number of the writers who have followed him. This influence has taken three forms: thematic, stylistic, and the "Papa" Hemingway lifestyle.

### THE HEMINGWAY CHARACTER

As the literary critic Leslie Fiedler argues in his study Love and Death in the American Novel, the classic American literary hero is a soldier, sailor, or cowboy who is brave, laconic, and (ultimately) alone. From Hawkeye in James Fenimore Cooper's Last of the Mohicans through Moby-Dick's Ishmael and Mark Twain's Huckleberry Finn, these characters "light out for the territories" because they don't quite fit in polite society, and they quickly learn self-sufficiency in the wilderness, at sea, or in combat. Hemingway, who identified Adventures of Huckleberry Finn as the source of all American literature, recognized this archetype, then updated and refined it. The overriding theme of his stories and books was "grace under pressure"—specifically, the ability of "men without women" (the title of an early story collection) to remain calm and competent in the face of life-threatening violence.

Thus, Hemingway heroes like Frederic Henry stoically accept not only war wounds, but the pain of losing whom they love, as well. (Think of Henry walking into the rain after the agonizing death of his lover and child at the conclusion of A Farewell to Arms.) Whether handling firearms, betting on horses, or ordering wine, they are almost scarily adept at what they do, and when the universe conspires to defeat them, they never complain. The influence of the Hemingway hero can therefore be seen in many of the literary soldiers who followed in Henry's footsteps: for instance, the protagonist of James Salter's The Hunters, an account of the exploits of a Korean War jet pilot squadron. It is even more evident in the archetypal tough-talking detectives of Raymond Chandler (The Big Sleep) and James Ellroy (L.A. Confidential). The cowboys in Cormac McCarthy's Border Trilogy are essentially. Hemingway characters, too.

## THE HEMINGWAY STYLE

Hemingway's influence has been even more pronounced in the realm of prose style. In his first collection of stories and thereafter, he combined elements from Gertrude Stein, James Joyce, and journalism to create a radically modern approach to the writing of sentences and paragraphs distinguished by the following hallmarks:

- An emphasis on nouns and verbs rather than adjectives and adverbs. This is closely related to

Hemingway's preference for the actual versus the abstract. "I was always embarrassed by the words sacred, glorious, and sacrifice and the expression in vain," Frederic Henry tells us in A Farewell to Arms. "Abstract words such as glory, honour, courage or hallow were obscene beside the concrete names of villages, the numbers of roads, the names of rivers, the numbers of regiments and the dates."

- A limited word-palette. Hemingway was fluent in three romance languages: French, Spanish, and Italian. Each has a much smaller vocabulary than English, and yet each manages to be richly expressive. Hemingway may have been inspired by this phenomenon.
- Frequent repetition of the same words and phrases a technique learned from Gertrude Stein. (The best known sentences she ever wrote were "A rose is a rose is a rose" and "When you get there, there's no there there.")
- Short sentences ("The next year there were many victories.") or long sentences consisting of short phrases and clauses connected by conjunctions: "The mountain that was beyond the valley and the hillside where the chestnut forest grew was captured and there were victories beyond the plain on the plateau to the south and we crossed the river in August and lived in a house in Gorizia that had a fountain and many thick shady trees in a walled garden and a wistaria vine purple on the side of the house." (A Farewell to Arms, Chapter II)
- A lack of clarity in the relationship between one sentence and the next. Instead of writing "I drank much wine because it was good," Hemingway writes "The wine was good. I drank much of it," merely implying the relationship. He thus forces us to be active readers, connecting the dots and filling in the blanks.

Many storytellers (Salter, Chandler, McCarthy, and

others) have attempted to recapitulate Hemingway's themes while mimicking his prose style. During the 1970s and 1980s, however, a group of American writers known as the Minimalists adopted the Hemingway style but rejected "grace under pressure" and so forth as distasteful and perhaps permanently outdated.

In her earliest stories, Ann Beattie wrote in the Hemingway style about well-off Baby Boomers paralyzed by the challenges of adulthood. (Like Chandler and so many others, Beattie has specifically mentioned Hemingway as an inspiration, specifically the inter-chapter vignettes from In Our Time.) Raymond Carver's down-and-out drunks could hardly be less heroic, and yet the use of diction and syntax in his masterly short stories is profoundly indebted to Hemingway. Frederick Barthelme continues to craft stories and novels in an intentionally flat, unadorned voice about largely ineffectual men (and sexy, aggressive women) living in the so-called New South. All these writers jettisoned the sometimes embarrassing excesses associated with Hemingway's value system while retaining the lessons he taught them as a writer of prose.

## THE HEMINGWAY LIFESTYLE

Finally, in many ways Ernest Hemingway exemplified for the Twentieth Century what it means to live like a writer. The most visible example of his influence in this area has been Norman Mailer. Though Mailer's often baroque style could hardly be more different from Hemingway's (an exception is the laconic "non-fiction novel" The Executioner's Song, which many critics consider Mailer's best book), he seems to have modeled his life after Hemingway's, seeking fistfights, serial wives (Hemingway had four, Mailer six), and "Papa"-like celebrity in general. And the career of the George Plimpton has been a kind of parody of Hemingway's: Plimpton lived in Paris as a young man, but founded a magazine rather than writing stories and novels.

Since then he has engaged in a number of stunts that seem actually to mock Hemingway's vigorous lifestyle while attempting to pay it tribute: briefly fighting a champion boxer and playing professional football, for instance, then writing books about the experiences. Prior to the publication of A Farewell to Arms, the Romantic poets probably served as our primary model for the writing life. A writer was a tortured soul recollecting his or her experiences in tranquility, a la Wordsworth, Shelley, and Keats. Hemingway changed all that. Proust composed Remembrance of Things Past in bed; Hemingway wrote standing up. Then he went big-game hunting or deep-sea fishing, or to the bullfights.

Today, Hemingway's thematic influence is a victim of its own success. The tough-talking private investigator is such a pervasive figure in our culture that is seems always to have existed. As his death recedes further into the past, the "Papa" lifestyle becomes harder to recall—and therefore tougher to emulate than when Hemingway's exploits were a fixture in newsreels and the pages of Life magazine. Regarding the influence of his prose itself, however, the Nobel Prize committee was correct when it rewarded Ernest Hemingway "for his powerful, style-forming mastery of the art of narration."

He changed the way we write and read literature, and he changed it forever. One attempts to kiss her, and is quickly slapped by an offended Catherine. Later in the story, Frederic is wounded and sent to the American hospital where Catherine works. Here he finds a part of him he has never had before, the ability to love. This is where his feelings for Catherine become extremely evident. Their relationship progresses and they begin a passionate love affair. After his stay in the hospital, Frederic returns to the war front.

During this period, Hemmingway heavily indicates the love Frederic has for Catherine. It is evident that Frederic is distracted by his love for Catherine. During a massive retreat from the Austrians and the Germans, the Italian forces become disordered and chaotic. Frederic is forced to shoot an engineer sergeant under his command, and in the confusion is arrested by the Italian military police for the crime of not being Italian.

Disgusted with the Army and facing death, Frederic decides he has had enough of the war; he dives in to the river to escape. After swimming to safety, Frederic boards a train and reunites with Catherine. She is pregnant with their baby. With the help of an Italian bartender, Catherine and Frederic escape to Switzerland, and plan to marry after the baby is born. When Catherine goes into labour, the doctor suddenly discovers that her pelvis is too narrow to deliver the baby. He attempts an unsuccessful Cesarean section, and she dies in childbirth with the baby. To Frederic, her dead body is like a statue; he walks back to his hotel without finding a way to say goodbye, seemingly lost forever.

I found it to be evident that there was a lot of foreshadowing and symbolism in this story, especially concerning the rain. The rain always seemed to be around when something bad was happening and when Catherine and Frederic were apart. When they were together the rain suddenly disappeared. It seemed that Hemingway was using the rain as a vehicle to show Frederic's generally hidden emotions. I liked this book very much but there were a lot of things I was uncertain of at the end of this story. Did Catherine really love Frederic? Did he really love her? Were they both just looking for closure at a hard time in their lives? I do truly believe that they did love each other but Hemingway makes some things unclear.

## Chapter 3

# An Assessment of the Author's Reputation

It's always a gamble to reread the books one loved in youth. Most of Fitzgerald still holds up, but Thomas Wolfe is virtually unreadable. J. D. Salinger's Catcher in the Rye turns out to be as good as I remembered it, but Franny and Zooey is unbearably cute. Scribner has recently reissued in hardcover Ernest Hemingway's four major works. The Sun Also Rises, A Farewell to Arms, For Whom the Bell Tolls, and The Old Man and the Sea — and I made my way through them again, mesmerized by Hemingway's genius as a storyteller and alarmed by the vicissitudes of his prose.

The discrepancy between eloquence and maudlin self-indulgence was often visible and never knew when he would soar and when he would lapse into the fabled macho pose that has proved so irresistible to parody. (I especially recommend Dwight Macdonald's essay in Against the American Grain, which begins: "He was a big man with a bushy beard and everybody knew him.") But there is something moving about this uneven achievement; Hemingway's tremendous vulnerability and his dogged efforts to master it, to push on at whatever cost, gave his life and work a terrible pathos.

Hemingway's apprenticeship, like everything else about him, constitutes a legend. By his early twenties he had found a style, the crisp declarative sentences and willfully simple diction of In Our Time; and with The Sun Also Rises, begun just after his return from Pamplona in 1925, he found his narrative voice. The dissolute expatriate scene he depicts may seem overly familiar to us now, the spare dialogue mannered, but Hemingway never sentimentalizes Jake Barnes's obsession with Lady Brett; the story's action, from Paris to Pamplona, unfolds with calculated simplicity.

He had already mastered a technique of leaving things out that gave special emphasis to what he left in. Here is Jake Barnes looking over a whore: "She grinned and I saw why she made a point of not laughing. With her mouth closed she was a rather pretty girl." The only thing we're told about one Harvey Stone is that he "had a pile of saucers in front of him, and he needed a shave" enough to convey his situation and the shabbiness of the whole boulevard scene. In a Montmartre nightclub, Jake glances over at the count who has become his latest rival for Brett and notices that "there were three girls at his table," establishing the count's decadence in a single image.

Everything is understated, compressed evidence of how confident Hemingway was of his material. I wasn't surprised to learn from Bernice Kert's gossipy new book, The Hemingway Women, that he wrote the first draft of The Sun Also Rises in two months; it has a concentrated fluency that no amount of revision can achieve, and that comes from having something definite to say. Some novelists confess their weaknesses in their work; Hemingway confessed his strengths. He made his central characters men who stood apart from the terrible things they saw and studied life with cold detachment. Even when they got hurt, they were stoical about it. Jake suffers his rejection at Brett's hands without complaint, just as Lieutenant Frederic Henry, in A Farewell to Arms, endures the death of his lover, the English nurse Catherine Barkley.

That Hemingway's marriage was falling apart in Pamplona, that the nurse he fell in love with while recovering from a wound received while driving an ambulance during World War I eventually ditched him for someone else, are facts of more than biographical interest: the only way he could deal with them in his work was by omission (Jake is unmarried) or by having the woman who betrayed him die in childbirth. He could never allow his protagonists to be confused or weak. They're shadowy figures, so well defended that they nearly forfeit our sympathy. One feels that these guys can take care of themselves.

It seems fair to say that Hemingway never really understood himself. His well-publicized front of bravado and he-man feats masked a nature that was somehow empty. What comes through in the huge volume of letters edited by Carlos Baker is the portrait of a man utterly deluded about the extent and sources of his pain, a malicious bully whose exploits served to fill up a life in which something love, empathy, genuine interest in others was missing.

He could never seem to hit upon the right tone, addressing his correspondents in a garrulous, swaggering voice that always came off sounding hollow ("Hadley and I have been very tight and having a swell time"). He dwelled with sentimental enthusiasm on the joys of domestic life while going through four wives; praised his contemporaries to their faces and dismissed them after they died; disparaged and celebrated himself in the same breath ("I am truly, and I say this in all humility, very brave; that is brave enough to sell it as a commodity."). He laid bare his confusion, his resentment, his doubt, in everything he wrote, but never seemed to know it. Hemingway's literary versions of himself reflect this self-deception.

Jake, Frederic Henry, Robert Jordan in For Whom the Bell Tolls, are men without qualities, bleak-hearted adventurers obsessed with proving themselves. Jake has to show off how much he knows about bullfights, and Lieutenant Henry is annoyingly competitive, putting down the doctor who doesn't drink and admiring the one who does; ridiculing a boxing instructor who "went all to pieces if you started after him"; boasting of his sexual prowess, his bravery, his taste in wine. Robert Jordan is another virile guy, an unreal exemplar of Hemingway's motto, "Grace under pressure."

Vain about his ability to identify types of guns and planes ("Now, as they moved out of sight toward Segovia, they did not look to be the green, red wing-tipped, low flying Russian conversion of the Boeing P32 that the Spaniards called Moscas"), and patronizing toward the guerrillas he's working with behind the fascist lines ("give the men tobacco and leave the women alone"), Jordan is too courageous to be believed. He can ride, shoot, wire a bridge with explosives, even face his own death with equanimity. Fear is just another obstacle to be mastered.

Whenever Hemingway leaves his heroes to themselves (usually during some lull in the action), he gets in trouble. They can't seem to reminisce without becoming sentimental. Frederic Henry recalling the joys of whoring in the Abruzzi ("Suddenly to care very much and to sleep to wake with it sometimes morning and all that had been there gone and everything sharp and hard and clear.") sounds like a bad imitation of Molly Bloom. Jordan goes on at tedious length about the good old days, musing reverentially on his grandfather's heroic deeds in the Civil War ("Aw hell, I wish Grandfather was here, he thought") and dismissing his father, a suicide like Hemingway's, as "that other one that misused the gun." This is the closest Hemingway ever gets to writing about what must have been one of the most traumatic episodes of his life.

A bitter loneliness afflicts these characters. The only love Hemingway ever convincingly describes is between various "buddies" Jake and his fishing companions, Henry and his roommate who provide the special kind of fellowship that harks back to boyhood, sharing stuff girls don't know about. Women seem to exist wholly for the pleasure of his protagonists, like the good whiskey they're always extolling. The dialogue between Henry and his lover, Catherine, is enough to make one wince:

"We won't fight."

"We mustn't. Because there's only us two and in the world there's all the rest of them. If anything comes between us we're gone and then they have us."

"They won't get us," I said. "Because you're too brave. Nothing ever happens to the brave."

And so on. Henry is gruff but tender-hearted, Catherine utterly passive an "adolescent daydream," in Macdonald's pitiless estimate. And the love scenes in For Whom the Bell

Tolls are even worse; Robert Jordan can't look at Maria without feeling "a thickness in his throat" (I counted four such thickenings within as many pages). The lovers' notorious talk about how "the earth moved" when they made love is more ludicrous than I remembered.

Hemingway was obviously fond of the phrase; they resort to it three times on a single page, and then Maria tries it out on the wise old woman Pilar, vying with her for the distinction of who has known the earth to move most times. Nothing is harder to write than sex scenes, but Hemingway's stream-of-consciousness rendering of this geological phenomenon ("Come now, now, for there is no now but now. Yes, now. Now, please now.") isn't one of the more notable attempts.

Faced with the technical problem of how to put into English a novel whose entire cast speaks in Spanish, Hemingway hit upon the curious method of literally translating Spanish grammar, diction, and idiom to convey the language's character. (A case of imitative fallacy, if there ever was one.) Thus we have, repeated again and again, such peculiar curses as "I obscenity in the milk of thy mother," and "Take your bad milk out of here, you horse exhausted máricón."

Pilar, in a highly implausible flashback that goes on for some thirty pages, speaks in a kind of stylized poetry that no one has ever spoken and only Hemingway ever wrote:

And as we stood there the sun rose over the far hills and shone now on the road where we stood and on the white wall of the barracks and the dust in the air was golden in that first sun and the peasant who was beside me looked at the wall of the barracks and what lay there and then looked at us and then at the sun and said, "Vaya, a day that commences."

This from a writer noted for his command of idiom. Hemingway couldn't not write in this style. It was "his way of life," Harry Levin noted, in a brilliant anatomy of its features, a reflection of his remorseless will to see, and to register what he saw with as little elaboration as possible.

The linked, run-on sentences, the plain vocabulary, the internal monologues, are pared down to give the narrative momentum. Among their many virtues, Hemingway's novels are exciting to read; they course with rapid action. What gives his novels such heightened urgency is the succession of brisk images. Hemingway can sustain a breathless pace for chapters at a time, piling image upon image, scene upon scene, until the need to know what happens next submerges every other consideration. He isn't a leisurely read.

One of the most powerful impressions one gets from The Sun Also Rises is of how desolate Hemingway felt by the time he was in his twenties. The novel is saturated with details that convey an overpowering sense of depression:

The flags in the square hung wet from the white poles and the banners were wet and hung damp against the front of the houses, and in between the steady drizzle the rain came down and drove every one under the arcades and made pools of water in the square, and the streets wet and dark and deserted; yet the fiesta kept up without any pause. It was only driven under cover.

For all the devoted attention he lavishes on the world the sad beauty of Paris, the pristine clarity of a trout stream high up in the mountains an aura of profound melancholy clings to Jake and his crowd. The fiesta in Pamplona is evoked with a detached exactitude that points up the characters' desperation: the incessant piping of fifes; the drunken men in the cafés "singing the hard-voiced singing"; the "wine-shops with light coming out from their doors onto the wet, black street" in the town at night. Against this somber backdrop, the deceptions of Lady Brett and her thwarted, quarreling lovers seem even more heartbreaking.

When Brett confesses to Jake that she's fallen for the matador, and pleads with him to arrange a tryst, Hemingway manages to write the entire scene without a single reference to how Jake felt except that "it was not pleasant." After Brett and the matador go off, he returns to the café and notices their three empty cognac glasses on the table: "A waiter came with a cloth and picked up the glasses and mopped off the table. "There the chapter ends.

The cinematic quality of this style, its immediacy and

urgent pace, made it a perfect vehicle for the war scenes that were Hemingway's great achievement. His ability to chronicle the experience of combat was unequalled an astonishing accomplishment for someone who never actually fought in either World War I or the Spanish Civil War. The logistics of troop movements, the panic of soldiers and fleeing peasants, the contrast between the natural beauty of the countryside and the ruin war inflicts: it was when Hemingway was working with a large canvas that he was most effective.

The shelling, the wounded on stretchers, the caravans of trucks moving through the mountains in A Farewell to Arms, have a lurid, Goyaesque clarity:

The wounded were coming into the post, some were carried on stretchers, some walking and some were brought on the backs of men that came across the field. They were wet to the skin and all were scared. We filled two cars with stretcher cases as they came up from the cellar of the post and as I shut the door of the second car and fastened it I felt the rain on my face turn to snow. The flakes were coming heavy and fast in the rain.

Here the syntax spills forward with scarcely a qualifying adjective, depending for its effect on repetition and on strong monosyllabic verbs. Henry's portentous musings on the futility of war seem fatuous beside his clear-eyed account of how war looks. A Farewell to Arms is narrated in the first person; For Whom the Bell Tolls, published eleven years later, is told by a whole cast of characters Robert Jordan, Jordan's lover, Maria, the peasants enlisted to help Jordan blow a bridge, a famous revolutionary, various Loyalist officers, even a fascist lieutenant. The novel shifts effortlessly from voice to voice, enabling Hemingway to portray the war from every side. Jordan's is the least plausible of these voices; it's the peasants who bring home the courage and terror latent in every skirmish.

The meanspiritedness that spoils Hemingway's letters and his memoir, A Moveable Feast, is nowhere in evidence. For those who were no threat soldiers, peasants, doomed revolutionaries Hemingway was capable of unaffected sympathy, and his intuitions about what they must have gone through constitute a radical imaginative feat. The scene where a few guerrillas make their last stand on a hilltop, fending off a battalion of fascists only to perish when planes are brought in to bomb them from above, is nearly unbearable to read.

Praying madly, firing at the strafing planes, they're caught at the very moment of death:

Then, through the hammering of the gun, there was the whistle of the air splitting apart and then in the red black roar the earth rolled under his knees and then waved up to hit him in the face and then dirt and bits of rock were falling all over and Ignacio was lying on him and the gun was lying on him. But he was not dead because the whistle came again and the earth rolled under him with the roar. Then it came again and the earth lurched under his belly and one side of the hilltop rose into the air and then fell slowly over them where they lay. Hemingway's terse valediction is a masterpiece of indirect summary:

"The planes came back three times and bombed the hilltop but no one on the hilltop knew it."

For Whom the Bell Tolls made Hemingway a hero of the left in Spain, but he was too shrewd an artist to write a partisan book. The fascist lieutenant who storms the hill is given equal time to brood about how war is hell, and when, on the last page, Jordan lies dying behind a tree, submachine gun at the ready to take a few fascists with him, who should ride into view but this same lieutenant. Men are men, and both sides suffer equally: a hackneyed truth, perhaps, but a profound one.

The end of Hemingway's career was a sad business. The last novels were self-parodies, none more so than The Old Man and the Sea. The internal monologues of Hemingway's crusty fisherman are unwittingly comical ("My head is not that clear. But I think the great Dimaggio would be proud of me today"); and the message, that fish are "more noble and more able" than men, is fine if you're a seventh grader. "The sea is the sea. The old man is an old man. The boy is a boy and the fish is a fish," Hemingway explained to Bernard Berenson. "All the symbolism that people say is shit." He was right about that. Why do so many American writers have disastrous final years? I suspect the public attention devoted to their careers has something to do with it. Hemingway claimed to have nothing but contempt for the journalistic creation known as "Papa," but the safari-suited, marlin-hunting tough whose exploits filled the pages of Life magazine was a persona he created himself. The vow of unworldliness demanded as a condition of belonging to the order of artists wasn't for him, and he made sure everyone knew it. Hemingway resisted the narrowness of the writer's life in America as strenuously as he could – hunting, fishing, covering wars – but he was always haunted by that next book.

Like Fitzgerald and Faulkner, Dos Passos and James T. Farrell, he had done his best work by the time he reached his forties but he forced himself to go on, toting up the number of words he produced each morning until he killed himself. Maybe if he'd found some other way to live his life, some role that honored his achievement without demanding that he exceed it, he wouldn't have felt compelled to keep on writing when he had nothing more to say. Even so, he managed to produce since we must keep score three novels and an imposing opus of stories that have lasted, as he knew they would.

For all his bluster, his conspicuous roistering in far-off lands, his stubborn production of bad books, he was an obsessive craftsman who created through sheer hard work one of the most distinctive prose styles in the English language. To read through these handsome, plainly designed editions of his best-known works is to be reminded that whether or not he "beat Mr. de Maupassant" or "fought two draws with Mr. Stendhal," as he once boasted to a reporter, Hemingway could go the distance with any novelist of the twentieth century.

## Chapter 4

# Analyzing "A Farewell to Arms"

Although there were several themes in this book, a major theme seemed to dominate the story. This theme is the importance of love and loss in a male female relationship. These two lovers were so absorbed in each other that they needed no one else in their life. "'Wouldn't you like to go on a trip somewhere by yourself, darling, and be with men and ski?' 'No. Why should I?' 'I should think sometimes you would want to see other people besides me.' 'Do you want to see other people?' 'No.' 'Neither do I.'" p.297. This conversation shows that Catherine loves him so much that she is willing to be alone just so he can be happy. At the same time, Mr. Henry would probably like to go skiing but would never dream of leaving Catherine alone. Death wins out over love. "It is very dangerous.'

The nurse went into the room and shut the door. I sat outside in the hall. Everything was gone inside of me. I did not think. I could no think. I knew she was going to die and I prayed that she would not. Don't let her die. Oh, God, please don't let her die. I'll do anything for you if you won't let her die ". Hemingway went on for an entire paragraph of him pleading with God. This is how he is able to show that Mr. Henry loves her more than anything, more than life its self. In a way, I think that they loved each other too much. They did not go out often or do anything that was with other people. They were always together.

This is an unhealthy life style. They were creating their own fortress and isolating themselves from the world. "'My life used to be full of everything,' I said. 'Now if you aren't with me I haven't a thing in the world.'" This quote further supports the idea that they are isolating themselves from the world. Since they were so cut off from the outside world, Mr. Henry has even a more difficult time going back into the reality of life after her death. This theme of man and woman isolated in love and finally their loss to dark death is universal. The most profound aspect of this book would be its ageless symbolism.

The free-living, heavy-drinking life that Catherine and Mr. Henry shared could be compared to the heavy investing, speculating and consequence-free life of the 20's. The product that came from Catherine and Mr. Henry's lifestyle was a dead child. The result of the over- investing of the 20's was the great depression. So the baby symbolizes the depression. Another point to consider was that Mr. Henry was a deserter. He left the army to be with Catherine. Desertion was illegal and he paid for it by loosing that which he loved the most, Catherine. Rain was connected with pain or grief. He drank to dull this grief or pain. Rain is wet and "wet" is connected with alcohol. "We had each been drinking out of one of the bottles and I took my bottle with me and went over and lay flat on the hay and looked out the narrow window at the wet country." p.217.

In this scene, he has been thinking of Cat and he decided that it would be best to drink his troubles away. When Hemingway said that the land was "wet", it usually meant that Mr. Henry was drunk. After Catherine and the baby died at the hospital, Mr. Henry walked home in the rain. "After a while I went out and left the hospital and walked back to the hotel in the rain." He had just suffered a major loss and dealt with it in the only way that he knew; through alcohol.

Although drinking at this point was not actually mentioned directly, we can nevertheless assume that he was going to make this connection just because of the setting in the rain. This book had many examples of symbolism and they all point to the fact that there is always a terrible price to pay for weak actions or for blind love. The word choice and ordering of detail of this book also leads one to believe that they are reading a classic. Hemingway's style is one of simple, straightforward dialogue with the absence of slang. Many generations of readers can read and understand the story. An example of this simplicity of dialogue is as follows: "'Where do you want to go, Cat?' 'Montreux.' 'It is a very nice place,' the official said. 'I think you will like that place.' 'Here at Locarno is a very nice place,' another official said." Although this simple dialogue is very easy to read, it is also very powerful in it's directness and simplicity.

On the other hand, his use of language when describing scenery is very elaborate. "The next year there were many victories. The mountain that was beyond the valley and the hillside where the chestnut forest grew was captured and there were victories beyond the plain on the plateau to the south and we crossed the river in August and lived in a house in Gorizia that had a fountain and many thick shady trees in a walled garden and a wisteria vine purple on the side of the house."

When describing these scenes, not only does he do it in an elaborate and detailed way, but he also runs his thoughts and sentences together as if it were all being spoken in one long drawn-out breath. The ordering of detail of this book was in a straight-forward, well-organized way. It was very linear and the story did not jump around between the present and flash-backs to the protagonist's past. This kept the story from becoming confusing. Hemingway's style is that of a classic author.

## THE WRITING STYLE

Hemingway became a newspaper writer in Kansas City as a young man and, in 1918, he joined the Red Cross to become an ambulance driver just like the character, Frederick Henry. This partially autobiographical novel is a combination of Hemingway's personal experiences in war and writing. Hemingway's life gave him the refinement that he needed for the inspirational language of the novel. He inspires us with his journalistic directness, sensory detail and his different writing styles that reflect the moods of the characters.

Critics usually describe Hemingway's style as simple,

spare, and journalistic. These are all good words; they all apply. Perhaps because of his training as a newspaperman, Hemingway is a master of the declarative, subject-verb-object sentence. His writing has been likened to a boxer's punches—combinations of lefts and rights coming at us without pause. Take the following passage: "We were all cooked. The thing was not to recognize it. The last country to realise they were cooked would win the war. We had another drink. Was I on somebody's staff? No. He was. It was all balls".

The style gains power because it is so full of sensory detail.

There was an inn in the trees at the Bains de l'Allaiz where the woodcutters stopped to drink, and we sat inside warmed by the stove and drank hot red wine with spices and lemon in it. They called it gluhwein and it was a good thing to warm you and to celebrate with. The inn was dark and smoky inside and afterward when you went out the cold air came sharply into your lungs and numbed the edge of your nose as you inhaled.

The simplicity and the sensory richness flow directly from Hemingway's and his characters' beliefs. The punchy, vivid language has the immediacy of a news bulletin: these are facts, Hemingway is telling us, and they can't be ignored. And just as Frederic Henry comes to distrust abstractions like "patriotism," so does Hemingway distrust them. Instead he seeks the concrete, the tangible: "hot red wine with spices, cold air that numbs your nose." A simple "good" becomes higher praise than another writer's string of decorative adjectives.

Though Hemingway is best known for the tough simplicity of style as seen in the first passage cited above, if we take a close look at A Farewell to Arms, we will often find another Hemingway at work. A writer who is aiming for certain complex effects, who is experimenting with language, and who is often self-consciously manipulating words. Some sentences are clause-filled and eighty or more words long. Take for example the description in Chapter 1 that begins, "There were mists over the river and clouds on the mountain"; it paints an entire dreary wartime autumn and foreshadows the deaths not only of many of the soldiers but of Catherine.

Hemingway's style changes, too, when it reflects his characters' changing states of mind. Writing from Frederic Henry's point of view, he sometimes uses a modified stream-of-consciousness technique, a method for spilling out on paper the inner thoughts of a character. Usually Henry's thoughts are choppy, staccato, but when he becomes drunk the language does too, as in the passage in Chapter 3:

I had gone to no such place but to the smoke of cafes and nights when the room whirled and you needed to look at the wall to make it stop, nights in bed, drunk, when you knew that that was all there was, and the strange excitement of waking and not knowing who it was with you, and the world all unreal in the dark and so exciting that you must resume again unknowing and not caring in the night, sure that this was all and all and all and not caring.

The rhythm and the repetition have us reeling with Henry. Thus, Hemingway's prose is in fact an instrument finely tuned to reflect his characters and their world. As we read A Farewell to Arms, we must try to understand the thoughts and feelings Hemingway seeks to inspire in us by the way he uses language. Although the book, A Farewell To Arms by Ernest Hemingway was not the type of book that had an exciting page-turning story, it can nevertheless be called a classic.

A classic has been defined as "a book that lasts through generations because of its universality of theme, ageless symbolism, word choice and the ordering of detail." This book has a universal theme, several ageless symbols, and a classic style that is as easily read today as it was 50 years ago. Although there were several themes in this book, a major theme seemed to dominate the story. This theme is the importance of love and loss in a male female relationship.

These two lovers were so absorbed in each other that they needed no one else in their life. "'Wouldn't you like to go on a trip somewhere by yourself, darling, and be with men and ski?' 'No. Why should I?' 'I should think sometimes you would want to see other people besides me.' 'Do you want to see other people?' 'No.' 'Neither do I.'" p.297. This conversation shows that Catherine loves him so much that she is willing to be alone just so he can be happy. At the same time, Mr. Henry would probably like to go skiing but would never dream of leaving Catherine alone. Death wins out over love. "'It is very dangerous.' The nurse went into the room and shut the door. I sat outside in the hall. Everything was gone inside of me. I did not think.

I could no think. I knew she was going to die and I prayed that she would not. Don't let her die. Oh, God, please don't let her die. I'll do anything for you if you won't let her die " p.330. Hemingway went on for an entire paragraph of him pleading with God. This is how he is able to show that Mr. Henry loves her more than anything, more than life its self. In a way, I think that they loved each other too much. They did not go out often or do anything that was with other people. They were always together. This is an unhealthy life style. They were creating their own fortress and isolating themselves from the world. '"My life used to be full of everything,' I said. 'Now if you aren't with me I haven't a thing in the world.'" p. 257.

This quote further supports the idea that they are isolating themselves from the world. Since they were so cut off from the outside world, Mr. Henry has even a more difficult time going back into the reality of life after her death. This theme of man and woman isolated in love and finally their loss to dark death is universal. The most profound aspect of this book would be its ageless symbolism. The free-living, heavy-drinking life that Catherine and Mr. Henery shared could be compared to the heavy investing, speculating and consequence-free life of the 20's. The product that came from Catherine and Mr. Henry's lifestyle was a dead child.

The result of the over- investing of the 20's was the great depression. So the baby symbolizes the depression. Another point to consider was that Mr. Henry was a deserter. He left the army to be with Catherine. Desertion was illegal and he paid for it by loosing that which he loved the most, Catherine. Rain was connected with pain or grief. He drank to dull this grief or pain.

Rain is wet and "wet" is connected with alcohol. "We had each been drinking out of one of the bottles and I took my bottle with me and went over and lay flat on the hay and looked out the narrow window at the wet country." p.217.

In this scene, he has been thinking of Cat and he decided that it would be best to drink his troubles away. When Hemingway said that the land was "wet", it usually meant that Mr. Henry was drunk. After Catherine and the baby died at the hospital, Mr. Henry walked home in the rain. "After a while I went out and left the hospital and walked back to the hotel in the rain." He had just suffered a major loss and dealt with it in the only way that he knew; through alcohol. Although drinking at this point was not actually mentioned directly, we can nevertheless assume that he was going to make this connection just because of the setting in the rain. This book had many examples of symbolism and they all point to the fact that there is always a terrible price to pay for weak actions or for blind love.

The word choice and ordering of detail of this book also leads one to believe that they are reading a classic. Hemingway's style is one of simple, straightforward dialogue with the absence of slang. Many generations of readers can read and understand the story. An example of this simplicity of dialogue is as follows: "'Where do you want to go, Cat?' 'Montreux.' 'It is a very nice place,' the official said. 'I think you will like that place.' 'Here at Locarno is a very nice place,' another official said." Although this simple dialogue is very easy to read, it is also very powerful in its directness and simplicity. On the other hand, his use of language when describing scenery is very elaborate.

"The next year there were many victories. The mountain that was beyond the valley and the hillside where the chestnut forest grew was captured and there were victories beyond the plain on the plateau to the south and we crossed the river in August and lived in a house in Gorizia that had a fountain and many thick shady trees in a walled garden and a wisteria vine purple on the side of the house." When describing these scenes, not only does he do it in an elaborate and detailed way, but he also runs his thoughts and sentences together as if it were all being spoken in one long drawn-out breath.

The ordering of detail of this book was in a straight-forward, well-organized way. It was very linear and the story did not jump around between the present and flash-backs to the protagonist's past. This kept the story from becoming confusing. Hemingway's style is that of a classic author. Because of the universal themes, ageless symbolism, and style of word choice and story detail, A Farewell to Arms, by Ernest Hemingway can indeed be considered a classic literary work. The theme of love between a man and woman so self-absorbed that all else is ignored and the theme of life bringing them to a breaking point is a human story that all can sympathize with.

The ageless symbolism that compares the loss of a baby, or hope, with the beginning of the American economic depression is profound. The alcoholism in the story reflects the careless attitudes toward life by the people living at this time. The irresponsible attitudes, such as the decision to desert the army, only lead to heartache. Life is nothing but a game to these characters, until the reality finally smacks them in the face. Hemingway's simple and straight-forward dialogue and story line makes this an easy to read and understandable ageless story.

A Farewell to Arms, by Ernest Hemingway, is a typical love story. A Romeo and his Juliet placed against the odds. In this novel, Romeo is Frederick Henry and Juliet is Catherine Barkley. Their love affair must survive the obstacles of World War I. The background of war-torn Italy adds to the tragedy of the love story. The war affects the emotions and values of each character. The love between Catherine and Frederick must outlast long separations, life-threatening war-time situations, and the uncertainty of each other's whereabouts or condition. This novel is a beautiful love story of two people who need each other in a period of upheaval.

Frederick Henry is an American who serves as a lieutenant in the Italian army to a group of ambulance drivers. Hemingway portrays Frederick as a lost man searching for order and value in his life.

Frederick disagrees with the war he is fighting. It is too chaotic and immoral for him to rationalize its cause. He fights anyway, because the army puts some form of discipline in his life. At the start of the novel, Frederick drinks and travels from one house of prostitution to another and yet he is discontent because his life is very unsettled. He befriends a priest because he admires the fact that the priest lives his life by a set of values that give him an orderly lifestyle.

Further into the novel, Frederick becomes involved with Catherine Barkley. He slowly falls in love with her and, in his love for her, he finds commitment. Their relationship brings some order and value to his life. Compared to this new form of order in his life, Frederick sees the losing Italian army as total chaos and disorder where he had previously seen discipline and control. He can no longer remain a part of something that is so disorderly and so, he deserts the Italian army. Frederick's desertion from the Italian army is the turning point of the novel.

This is the significance of the title, A Farewell to Arms. When Frederick puts aside his involvement in the war, he realizes that Catherine is the order and value in his life and that he does not need anything else to give meaning to his life. At the conclusion of this novel, Frederick realizes that he cannot base his life on another person or thing because, ultimately, they will leave or disappoint him. He realizes that the order and values necessary to face the world must come from within himself. Catherine Barkley is an English volunteer nurse who serves in Italy.

She is considered very experienced when it comes to love and loss since she has already been confronted with the death of a loved one when her fiance was killed earlier in the war. The reader is not as well acquainted with Catherine's inner thoughts and feelings as we are with those of Frederick. The story is told through Frederick's eyes and the reader only meets Catherine through the dialogue between her and Frederick or through his personal interpretations of her actions. Catherine already possesses the knowledge that her own life cannot be dependent on another. She learned this lesson through the death of her fiance. Her love for Frederick is what her life revolves around, yet she knows not to rely on him to be the order in her life. Had she been dependent on Frederick for the order in her life, she would not have been able to allow him to participate in the war for fear of losing her own stability with his death.

The theme that Hemingway emphasizes throughout the novel is the search for order in a chaotic world. Hemingway conveys this through Frederick's own personal search during the chaos of World War I. Catherine has found strength within herself to lead her through life. This is what Frederick must come to realise. Through his involvement with Catherine, Frederick slowly finds his own inner strength. Frederick's affair with Catherine prompts him to leave his wild life of prostitutes and drink. He becomes aware of an element of stability in their affair and realizes that the war that he was involved in was too chaotic, so he deserts the army. He and Catherine make a life for themselves totally isolated from everything and everyone else.

Frederick believes that his life is now completely in order and that his values are in perspective, yet he still seems discontented. He continuously has to convince himself that he has "a fine life." He has not yet reached Catherine's level that enables her to be perfectly happy in their love and yet not dependent on it for all comfort and support. Frederick still has to find that within himself. Until the conclusion of the novel, Frederick still relies on Catherine as the source of order in his life. With the end of their affair when Catherine dies giving birth to their stillborn love-child, Frederick realizes that he cannot depend on any one person, such as Catherine, or any thing, such as religion, war, or frivolity, for order and discipline.

Hemingway describes Frederick's enlightenment best in the final paragraph of the novel when Frederick sees Catherine's corpse for the first and last time. Frederick's reaction was that "it was like saying good-by to a statue." Frederick realizes that Catherine was only a symbol of the order and strength in his life. Strength to face life must come from within him and only he will be able to get himself through his own life. He will have to learn to depend on himself.

Frederick realizes this and is able to get on with his life on his own. "After a while [he] went out and left the hospital and walked back to the hotel in the rain." He did not mourn or feel like his own life had ended with her death, rather he was able to continue on with his newfound inner strength and face his world alone.

This novel succeeds in getting Hemingway's message across. Frederick's realization causes the reader to reflect on his/her own life and on what institutions they depend on in their own lives. I enjoyed this novel because I learned along with Frederick that I must face my life on my own. The strength to face my problems cannot come from any other source because no other source can ever be as permanent as the strength that I can find within myself.

## CHARACTERS, TONE, AND SETTING

Throughout the world many individuals believe love is the cure for everything. In the novel, A Farewell to Arms, by Ernest Hemingway, is a typical love story between a nurse and a war soldier. Their love affair must survive the obstacles of World War one. Hemingway develops this theme by means of characters, tone, and setting. Hemingway expresses the theme through the use of two main characters, Frederick Henry and Catherine Barkley. Frederick Henry is a young American ambulance driver in the Italian army during World War one. At the beginning of the novel Henry never experienced love he believed it was an elaborate game. When he is wounded and sent back to the American hospital where Catherine works their relationship progresses. Frederick slowly falls in love with her and in his love for her, he finds commitment.

At the conclusion of the novel, Frederick realizes that he cannot base his life on another person or thing because it will eventually leave him. Catherine Barkley is an English nurse who serves in Italy. On the other hand Catherine is experienced when it comes to love since she has already lost a loved one which was killed earlier in the war. Hemingway also lets us know Catherine already has the knowledge that her life cannot be dependent on another through her husband's death. This all sets the tone for the novel. Hemingway also develops the theme through tone. The tone of this novel is a tragic one. Throughout the novel Hemingway foreshadows Catherine's death. When Catherine is brought into the delivering room, the doctor tells her he has concerns about her narrow hips. Therefore, they had to get a caesarean, and the baby dies.

Then Catherine starts to hemorrhage and Henry realizes why he did not want to become involved with love and now he must suffer the consequences. Frederick then states "it was like saying goodbye to a statue," he walks back to his hotel without finding a way to say good-bye. Frederick realizes that Catherine was just a symbol of strength in his life. Evidently, Hemingway conveys this novel as a tragic one. One last ingredient the author expresses to develop the theme is the novel's setting. The story takes place during World War one. However, the plot is always active.

The characters were never staying in one place too long. This makes the novel more exciting and allows the reader to meet new characters and witness new events such as the army base and the hospital. In addition, when Henry escapes from the Army, the clean water he jumps into symbolizes the new clean life that he was going to live from now on. Nevertheless, Ernest Hemingway uses many aspects to develop the theme of this novel. Through means of characters, tone, and setting, the author is able to express how individuals must learn to cope with love and the consequences love may bring upon an individual's life.

## SYMBOLISM AND PLOT

The book A Farewell to Arms, written by Ernest Hemingway, is a classic about the love story of a nurse and a war ridden soldier. The story starts as Frederick Henry is serving in the Italian Army. He meets his future love in the hospital that he gets put in for various reasons. I thought that A Farewell to Arms was a good book because of the symbolism, the exciting plot, and the constant moving of the main character. The symbolism in A Farewell to Arms is very much apparent. Ernest Hemingway has always been one who is big on the symbolism of night as being bad. To the main character in Hemingway's novels, nights have always been a sign of death, or something negative to happen.

Another one of the symbolisms in A Farewell to Arms is when Henry tries to escape from the Italian army by jumping off one of the ships the army was traveling on and running away from the army. This symbolism was the water that he jumped into was a symbolism of the new, clean life that he was going to live from now on. At this time, Henry goes off and finds his wife to be.

The plot in A Farewell to Arms was always active. They were never staying in one place too long. It had a very good story line, which was a love story that ended up in a tragedy. The main character's wife got pregnant and she was off to have her baby when problems started occurring. They had to have a caesarean, and the baby dies, and when the mother of the child starts to hemorrhage Henry knows that it was over for his wife and he was right.

From the beginning of the book until the end, the action was up. Ever since the front page Henry was traveling around to different towns so it was not boring for the reader. That made it very interesting for the reader because it was always a new town coming up so they were being introduced in the new characters quite often.

As the story goes on, the reader is not introducing as many new people, but they are still traveling around quite a bit. Hemingway has a way with arranging the plots of all his stories. They all have that right timing to them. He always introduces only people that will affect the story, he does not introduce someone who will be in the scene for five minutes and then leave. I felt that the author's planning on putting this novel together was very good.

Ernest Hemingway has always been one of the world's best known classic writers. His style and technique of symbolism is much different than others. He uses then in very strong ways that you the reader does not always pick up. I am sure that I missed some of the symbolism that went on in the book. I picked up a few though and they were very interesting. I recommend this to anyone who is interested in a love story that does not get too intimate.

## DEALING WITH DEATH

"I'm afraid of the rain because sometimes I picture myself dead in it" (P 126). This is a short quotation from, A Farewell to Arms, (1929), by Ernest Hemingway. A Farewell to Arms has a very unexpected death in the end. The reader sympathizes with the main character as he matures from the beginning to the conclusion of the novel. A Farewell to Arms is a love story during World War I. The novel is centered on Lieutenant Fredric Henry, an American who has volunteered for the Italian army driving ambulances in Europe because the United States has not yet entered the war.

Fredric is known as being a lost man searching for order and value in his life. He is very subdued and does not care about himself or about the war. In the first book of the novel, Fredric is characterized, along with the other characters. Throughout the first book, Fredric takes a leave of absence from the war and travels the country looking for his purpose in life. During the second book, Fredric returns to the warfront town and meets with his closest friend, Rinaldi, who introduces Fredric to Catherine Barkely. Catherine is a French nurse with whom Fredric falls in love immediately.

Fredric finds commitment with her, and they start to spend time together. Their relationship brings order and value to his life. He starts to care more about himself and Catherine. Being away from the war, Fredric feels safe with Catherine. When they are together, the war seems to not exist. "The war seemed as far away as the football games of someone else's college," says Fredric (P 63).

Catherine is experienced when it comes to love and loss since she lost her fiancé in an earlier war. She cannot depend on another person so she tries not to depend on Fredric to bring order to her life and less chaos. This then allows her to be emotionally stronger when Fredric has to go off to war again. While off at war, Fredric and his other driver friends are sitting in a cave, when the Austrians attack. Fredric is hit in the knee while trying to help his friend, who dies. Fredric is taken to the hospital in Milan. When he arrives at the hospital, Rinaldi and Catherine come to visit him. During his recuperation from having knee surgery, Catherine becomes one of his nurses. Fredric and Catherine's love affair starts again. They now get to spend more time together and isolate themselves from everything and everyone else.

Book three is when Fredric realizes he doesn't want to be part of the war, but only with Catherine. Fredric convinces himself that he has a "fine life" (P 298). Catherine then finds out that she is pregnant with Fredric's baby. After a few months, Fredric is sent back to the warfront and has to leave Catherine. While at war, Fredric leaves his troops because they did not follow his orders. German troops are looking for Fredric for leaving his troops. "Along the top of the stone bridge, I could see German helmets moving". Floating down the Taglimento River, Fredric goes through the Venetian fields and then rides a train to safety.

Returning to Milan, in the fifth book, Catherine is not at the hospital and has gone to Stresa for time off.

They stay in a motel and find out that Fredric will be arrested if they stay there. Leaving during the middle of the night, they travel to Switzerland to find safety. There they live in the mountains above Montreaux until Catherine gets closer to having the child, and then they move into a hotel in Lausanne. Until the end of the novel, Henry relies on Catherine for order in his life. Catherine's and Fredric's love ends when Catherine dies of hemorrhages while giving birth to their stillborn baby. When Fredric sees his baby boy, he feels no sense of fatherhood and only wants to be with Catherine.

During the last paragraph, Hemingway characterizes Fredric, when he sees Catherine's dead body lying on the hospital bed for the first and last time. Henry's response was, "it was like saying good-bye to a statue" (P 332). Fredric then realizes that Catherine was the only symbol of the order and strength in his life. "If people bring so much courage to this world the world has to kill them to break them, so of course it kills them. The world breaks every one and afterward many are strong at the broken places. But those that will not break it kills. It kills the very good and the very gentle and the very brace impartially. If you are none of these you can be sure it will kill you too but there will be no special hurry."

Hemingway describes the separation between Catherine and Fredric, in this quotation. People deal with death in very different ways. In this novel, Fredric has to learn how to live without Catherine in his life. Finding strength from within will allow Fredric to go on with his life. "After a while I went out and left the hospital and walked back to the hotel in the rain".

## PORTRAYAL OF FEAR AND SUFFERING

The protagonist, Frederick Henry faces fear when he is injured where he admits his own fear. He shows courage without second thought when he helps injured men coming from the front. Individual suffering is shown through the eyes of Frederick Henry having to face the death of his wife and child. Physical suffering is obviously shown by the men that get injured in the war. This physical suffering provides the context in which courage can take place. Comradery, surprisingly, doesn't seem to be as obvious in the novel as the other themes; it is mainly shown by the nurses' commitment to one another and the 'male bonding' at the mess.

There also seems to be more of an individual comradery within friendships and with individuals rather than a whole group. In fact, there doesn't seem to be a sense of people working together for a common cause. These four themes contribute to the many decisions that Frederick Henry has to make. That is in regards to the war and his relationship with Catherine, he has an inner conflict with himself with external forces pulling him in opposite directions which the protagonist must sort out which is more important to follow.

Frederick Henry is an American who serves as a lieutenant in the Italian army to a group of ambulance drivers, whom is portrayed by Hemmingway as a 'lost man' searching for order and value in his life. The fear and suffering the Frederick Henry has in his life which he experiences by the war, shows him how pointless the war is, he disagrees with the war because it is too chaotic and immoral for him to rationalize its cause. However, he fights anyway, in order to achieve the discipline which the army forces into his life. The courage he has in the war and comradeship or the individual comradeship he has with various people such as Catherine and the priest gives him a sense of order and value in his life that the war does not give him.

Frederick Henry befriends the priest because he admires the fact that the priest lives his life by a set of values that give him an orderly lifestyle. He has a special bond with the priest and when he stops going to the mess as much as he used to, the Priest says: "I miss you at the mess". His relationship and bond that he has with the Priest also brings some order and value in his life. However this order is different from the sort of order found in the army. His comradeship that seems forced upon him by the other men at the mess where he is forced to fit in by drinking and traveling from one house of prostitution, he is discontent by this is because his life is already unsettled and lacking any order.

Frederick Henry mentions this earlier in the novel:

"They talked too much at the mess and I drank wine because tonight we were not all brothers unless I drank a little and talked with the priest". This individual comradeship that has been mentioned is shown by his personal relationships with the other men in the army, they all share one common thing, in that they are trying to survive while depending on others and showing commitment to do this.

Rinaldi shows the bond that they have:

"We are war brothers."

The comradery that the men have is also made so by the amount of courage Frederick Henry shows, he puts other people before him, where he isn't trying to be a hero yet just being himself. Henry is a man who thinks about others and this is shown when he is injured:

"There are much worse wounded than me"

Not only does he show courage at this point but he experiences fear and also expresses this:

"I looked at my leg and I was very afraid"

It is here, that we realise that his acts of courage are not intentional for him to get recognition. We know this because when Frederick Henry is told that he is to receive a medal for his courage he doesn't think he deserves it. The main character does not do things to be a 'hero'.

Catherine also shows her fear of the rain mainly because she associates it with death and suffering:

"I've always been afraid of the rain-and sometimes I see you dead in it."

This morbid image that Catherine associates of the rain to death and suffering shows that rain can be just as unpredictable as the war, which is what Catherine has a fear of, loosing Frederick Henry to the unpredictability of the war. Another prominent theme is Frederick Henry's personal suffering. This is shown by the death of Catherine and his child. When he meets Catherine he finds a new form of order in his life. When Frederick puts aside his involvement in the war, he realises that Catherine is the order and value in his life and that he does not need anything else to give meaning to his life. However, at the conclusion of the novel Frederick Henry suffers because he comes to the realisation that cannot base his life on another person or thing, because, ultimately, they will leave or disappoint him.

With the end of their affair when Catherine dies giving birth to their stillborn love child, Frederick experiences suffering as his order and values in his life have been completely shattered. He cannot depend on any one person, such as Catherine, or any thing, such as religion, war, order or discipline. He suffers because he realises that Catherine and the child that he was going to have would give him that order and real meaning to his life that he has been searching for.

He doesn't really show any suffering through his grief, in fact his reaction to Catherine's death is rather unemotional, Frederick reaction was that:

"It was like saying good-by to a statue."

It is at this point that he knows Catherine was a symbol of the order and strength in his life, and he suffers as his strength and order have been diminished by her death. In conclusion it can be shown that Hemmingway does have a balanced portrayal of fear and suffering as when he writes of courage and comradeship. With the war that Frederick Henry is involved in it causes him to evaluate the chaos and disorder that he is living in.

Through these external forces of fear, suffering, courage and comradeship which are important in making the decision of whether he should stay obligated with the army in the war or follow his love for Catherine Barkley, he discovers that both choices have their consequences. Frederick Henry realises that the strength that he needs to face this chaotic life needs to come from within and he must learn from his past experiences. Along with Henry's disagreement of the war, he is forced to face his own fear, suffering, deal with courage as if it were instinctive and show commradery with his men and the people that he has a special bond with.

## NATURAL SYMBOLISM, DEATH, AND LANGUAGE

Ernest Hemingway's novel A Farewell to Arms (1929) uses nature to structure the novel and provide symbols that replace human emotions. Nature serves as a basic structure for the plot and the actions that occur. It also emerges as a source of symbols that replace human sentiment or feelings. Characters die and there is no mention of sadness or pain. Instead, Hemingway writes that it is raining, that it is autumn, or that peace has occurred when people are still at war.

The replacement of emotions with symbols allows Hemingway to frequently understate what is really going on in the action. He further uses symbols to completely omit references to sentiments or feelings. Even more unsettling is the fact that these symbols often ironically represent the opposite of their meanings in common parlance. Not only symbols, but also individual words, come to be used in this way. This undermines the use of technical language throughout the novel and causes the breakdown of that language. Thus, symbols and words provide a basis for the structure of the novel and for the loss of the technical language.

The structure of the novel occurs largely through natural symbolism, i.e. symbols drawn from nature. This is set up in the first chapter, which shows the rapid progression of the seasons from summer into autumn. Summer is identified with dryness and abundance, a plain "rich with crops". This is immediately contrasted with autumn, where "the branches were bare and the trunks black with rain. This miniature transition of the seasons relates to the larger transitions in the novel as a whole. For example, the first part of the novel takes place in relative dryness up until when Catherine informs Henry that she is going to have a baby.

No sooner has she told him this news than the rains start, ending the dry part of the novel: "It turned cold that night and the next day it was raining". Thus the novel is separated into two segments in the same manner that the first chapter is separated into summer and fall. This separation of the seasons helps to set up the transition in the plot from good to bad. "Good" is represented by the dry season, "bad" by the wet season. Thus, the opening scenes describe the bed of the river as being "dry and white", an image that changes drastically by the end, where the river has turned into a raging torrent. This contrast is explicated by the events that occur on hard versus soft surfaces.

For instance, the first military operation (in which Henry is wounded) is fast paced, with the wounded are rushed away in trucks, and everything is described as being hard, including the road and operating table. This contrasts with the second military operation, a defeat that takes place on wet roads, with vehicles stuck in the mud, and where rivers have to be crossed instead of river beds. Thus the world of the first half of the novel is a dry, sterile version of the wet and sickly world that follows it. Within this world, the dry part is the world of success; Henry wins Catherine and the army wins some battles. The wet world is the exact opposite: the army loses and is forced to retreat and Henry loses Catherine.

The natural world thereby provides the setting within which Henry's personal and military experiences can take place. Natural changes from dryness to wetness are paralleled in the plot by both Catherine's pregnancy and the corrupt horse races. These scenes are juxtaposed onto each other through their side-by-side placement. They define the transition from love to "marriage" and advancement to retreat, respectively. Thus, after Catherine announces that she is pregnant, she and Henry consider themselves "married," thereby catapulting their relationship from casual to serious. Similarly, the war with Austria goes well for the Italians until Henry describes the corruption of the horse races, a corruption that permeates every level of the Italian army and political machine.

After the horse races, the Italian army no longer is able to win battles; instead, the war turns into a retreat and becomes far more serious and deadly. This structure is complemented by natural symbols that substitute for emotions or feelings. The most important of these symbols is that of rain. Rain represents death and all the accompanying emotions of grief, pain, and despair. Death is both brought by rain and can be considered analogous to it. Catherine is the first person to make this analogy explicit when she tells Henry that she is afraid of the rain. "I am afraid of the rain because sometimes I see me dead in it".

Although Henry dismisses her words at the time, they continue to haunt the novel up until she dies. Indeed, immediately after Henry visits her dead body in the hospital, the novel ends with the passage: "I walked back to the hotel in the rain". The novel thus ends with rain being used as a substitute for Catherine's death. Rain is also symbolically used by Hemingway to understate the obvious. For instance, when Catherine dies, there is no emotional outpouring. Instead, the novel ends with the word "rain" as the only hint of the emotional stress that Henry is experiencing.

This form of understatement is ironically introduced right at the beginning of the novel:

At the start of the winter came the permanent rain and with the rain came the cholera. But it was checked and in the end only seven thousand died of it in the army.

In this passage, rain and death are linked for the first time, yet there is no emotional content connected to the fact that seven thousand men have died. This understatement is a key feature of the novel and will be used every time a death occurs. For instance, when Aymo dies after being shot, Henry informs the reader that, "He looked very dead. It was raining." Those two lines embody the full extent of the emotion that Henry shows. This form of understatement, where a symbol substitutes for emotions, allows Hemingway to omit key facts. A good example of omission occurs right after Henry has been wounded.

He is placed in an ambulance and driven to the hospital while the man above him bleeds to death. "The drops fell very slowly, as they fall from an icicle after the sun has gone". This simple description omits all the pain and suffering and replaces them with the image of "drops" from an icicle. Using symbols to replace death or emotions allows foreshadowing. Rain, for example, is frequently used to foreshadow death. Before getting killed, Aymo states, "We drink [barbera] now. Tomorrow maybe we drink rainwater".

Catherine's death is foreshadowed in similar manner: she is terrified of the rain and states that she sometimes sees herself dead in the rain. Henry comforts her and stops her crying. However, Hemingway shows that this is a false comfort; in one of the very infrequent uses of the word "but", the chapter ends with the sentence, "But outside it kept on raining". Thus symbols are used to foreshadow the things they substitute for. An unsettling aspect of the novel is that symbols stand for the opposite of what they mean in common parlance.

For example, rain is normally associated with growth, healthy crops, and a cleansing of the outside world. Instead, Hemingway uses it to mean death. He does the same thing with autumn and spring, seasons traditionally thought of as abundant in harvest and fecund, respectively. In the novel they come to stand for the rainy season, a time of death, retreat, and loss. The same inversion takes place with language; Hemingway uses words like "peace" to denote someone deserting the army. By using the words and symbols in the opposite context of what they are expected to mean, uncertainties are introduced. These uncertainties are caused by the fact that symbols and words do not have an inherent meaning that can be relied upon. This causes Henry to slowly start to mistrust language, and language as a whole is thus slowly undermined as the novel progresses.

This causes the language of the novel to retreat away from simple technical language to a more abstract, questioning language. For example, the second half of the novel introduces questions into the text.

This has the effect of undermining the manual-like nature of much of the novel, in which skills are constantly taught to others (such as how to eat spaghetti on or how to fish). These skills help to make the world understandable and uncomplicated; if there is a problem, someone can teach the other person how to fix it.

Questions destroy the purity of this world because they introduce uncertainty into it. This uncertainty results in chaos, both for the army and for Henry's love affair. The first time a question is asked where no one has an answer is when Henry decides to take his cars off of the main road. One of the Sergeants asks, "You know the road?" and forces Henry to say, "No". This uncertainty quickly takes over the text of the novel, causing Henry to insert his own questions, such as "Which side did [Catherine] sleep on?", or "If you did not go forward what happened?" This climaxes in the hospital scene where Henry almost goes insane with uncertainty:

Yes, but what if she should die? She can't die. Why would she die? What reason is there for her to die? There's just a child that has to be born, the by-product of good nights in Milan. It makes trouble and is born and then you look after it and get fond of it maybe. But what if she should die? She won't die. But what if she should die? She won't. She's all right. But what if she should die? She can't die. But what if she should die? Hey, what about that? What if she should die?

The repetition of the questions in this paragraph hides the fact that this is actually an inversion of a manual. Instead of providing the answers to the questions, as he has throughout the novel, Henry is now posing the questions. This transition is mirrored by the brief but uncharacteristic moments of sentimentality that occur near the end (which I will spare the reader by not quoting), in which Henry "whines" about the fact that everyone eventually dies. The breakdown of language that occurs in the novel eventually leads Henry to state that he has "made a separate peace" This oft quoted line embodies many of the fundamental themes of the novel. Foremost, it relates to the title, "A Farewell to Arms", a phrase the can be interpreted as running away or deserting the army.

Running away is exactly what Henry is doing when he makes his "peace"; after changing clothes, he refuses to read about the war in the newspapers, thus choosing "peace" by ignoring the war. This is a false peace, however, since Henry is soon caught up in fleeing to Switzerland with Catherine. This fake peace is highlighted by several other references to fakeness: for instance, Henry is described as a "fake doctor". This fakeness shows that Henry cannot Œwill' peace. The reason he fails to achieve a real peace is because the language changes as well.

Language, and particularly the use of the word peace, is therefore inverted. Peace is a political term, a term that does not have a technical meaning. Henry realizes this when he overhears the carabinieri questioning the officers during the retreat. They use political language, "It is you and such as you that have let the barbarians onto the sacred soil of the fatherland". Henry cannot adopt that language, and thus he chooses "a separate peace", i.e. a peace that has nothing to do with politics. This peace can also be interpreted as his choice of language; he denounces the political rhetoric and instead uses the technical language that he can trust. In this sense technical language is equated with peace, political language with war.

The word "peace) is further given an entirely different meaning by the line that immediately follows it. "I felt damned lonely and was glad when the train got to Stresa". Stresa is where Catherine is located, and thus it seems that Henry is choosing love over war. In this case, "peace" merely means that he would rather be with Catherine than be in the war.

This is in fact the choice that he makes, both by returning to Catherine and then fleeing with her to Switzerland. However, like the symbols, the word "peace" is falsely interpreted. The flight to Switzerland placed Henry and Catherine in a world where everything seems "peaceful".

This false peace is two-fold: it is an escape from war, and it is an escape from sentimental language. Neither of them notice the falseness of the peace, nor realise the impending danger. Catherine comments, "Isn't it fine rain? They never had rain like this in Italy. It's cheerful rain". This is the first time that someone thinks of rain as a positive symbol and gives rain its more common definition. Unfortunately, this is a trick; the rain is related to death throughout the novel. Thus the rain, like the peace, is false in Switzerland. Catherine's complicated childbirth, which takes place during the rain, undermines her statement.

Henry's use of language crumbles around the same time; he becomes overly sentimental and "whiny" and explodes with numerous unanswerable questions. It is therefore the fact that language, in the form of symbols and words, cannot be trusted that causes him to give up on his technical language.

The combination of natural symbolism with death and language creates a powerful unity to the events of the novel. The deaths are foreshadowed by the rain, which is used as a substitute for emotion. Thus the rain represents not only death, but also the grief, pain, and despair that accompanies death.

It further represents a form of purging, a means of forgetting what has just happened. By having symbols stand for the emotional content of the plot, Hemingway cleverly removes the need to use extraneous language.

This allows him to write much of the novel in the dry, technical language that he is famous for while still retaining the emotional content. It is important to notice that the breakdown of language at the end of the novel is not permanent. After having nearly given up his technical language, Hemingway returns to it in the final passage. Hence the novel ends with the word "rain" rather than the expected emotional outpouring.

## WEATHER SYMBOLISM

In A Farewell to Arms, Ernest Hemingway attempts to tell the unvarnished truth about war—to present an honest, rather than a heroic, account of combat, retreat, and the ways in which soldiers fill their time when they are not fighting. Yet Hemingway's realistic approach to his subject does not rule out the use of many time-honored literary devices. For instance, weather is to this day a fundamental component of the war experience. Hemingway depicts weather realistically in A Farewell to Arms, but he uses it for symbolic purposes as well.

Rain, often equated with life and growth, stands for death in this novel, and snow symbolizes hope: an entirely original schema. In stories such as "To Build a Fire," by Jack London, snow and ice quite logically represent danger and death. After all, one can freeze to death, fall through thin ice and drown, or perish beneath an avalanche. In Chapter II of A Farewell Arms, on the other hand, it is snow that ends the fighting described in the book's first chapter. Thus snow stands for safety rather than its opposite. (Note, though, that although snow covers the bare ground and even the Italian army's artillery in Chapter II, stumps of oak trees torn up by the summer's fighting continue to protrude—a reminder that winter is of course not permanent but merely a reprieve from combat, a cease-fire.)

Shortly thereafter, Frederic Henry describes the priest's home region of Abruzzi as a "place where the roads were frozen and hard as iron, where it was clear and cold and dry and the snow was dry and powdery ...," and the context leaves no doubt that this characterization is a positive one. Late in the novel, the argument between the Swiss policemen over winter sports not only provides much-needed comic relief; it also marks the beginning of Henry and Catherine Barkley's second idyll. (The first takes place in summertime, in Milan.)

Immediately afterwards, Henry and Catherine find themselves in the Swiss Alps, with snow all around. Thus they have temporarily achieved a life of both purity (the mountains symbolize purity in this novel, versus the corruption of the lowlands) and safety. These chapters positively radiate contentment. Starting in the very first chapter of A Farewell to Arms, rain clearly symbolizes death: "In the fall when the rains came the leaves all fell from the chestnut trees and the branches were bare and the trunks black with rain," Henry tells us. "The vineyards were thin and bare-branched too and all the country wet and brown and dead with autumn."

The rain symbolism is not entirely a literary conceit, either, as rain actually precedes an outbreak of fatal illness, the cholera that kills seven thousand that fall. Later, during their Milan idyll, Catherine makes the symbolism of the rain explicit for Henry—and for the reader: "I'm afraid of the rain because sometimes I see myself dead in it," she says to him. "And sometimes I see you dead in it." Lo and behold, during Henry and Catherine's trip from the armorer's to the hotel near the train station on his last night with her, the fog that has covered the city from the start of the chapter turns to rain. It continues to rain as they bid one another farewell; in fact, Catherine's last act in this part of the novel is to signal to Henry that he should step in out of the rain. Back at the front, "the trees were all bare and the roads were muddy."

It rains almost continuously during the chapter when the tide of battle turns and the Italians begin their retreat from Caporetto and from the Germans who have joined the fighting. The rain turns to snow one evening, holding out hope that the offensive will cease, but the snow quickly melts and the rain resumes. During a discussion among the drivers about the wine they are drinking with dinner, the driver named Aymo says, "To-morrow maybe we drink rainwater." Hemingway by this time has developed the rain symbolism to such a degree that the reader experiences a genuine sense of foreboding—and indeed, the following day will bring death to Henry's disintegrating unit.

It is raining while the fugitive Henry rides the train to Stresa, raining when he arrives, and raining while Henry and Catherine spend the night together in his hotel room. The open-boat trip across Lake Maggiore takes place in the rain, with an umbrella used as a sail. (Ominously, the umbrella breaks.)

And in Chapter XL, as Henry and Catherine are bidding farewell to their wintertime mountain retreat for the city in which Catherine's baby is to be born, Henry tells us that "In the night it started raining."

Finally, when Henry leaves the hospital for lunch during Catherine's protracted, agonizing delivery, "The day was cloudy but the sun was trying to come through"—a literal ray of hope. During the operation, however, he looks out the window and sees that it is raining. Just after the nurse has told him that the baby is dead, Henry looks outside again and "could see nothing but the dark and the rain falling across the light from the window." At the novel's end, Henry leaves the hospital and walks back to his hotel in the rain. In fact, the final word in A Farewell to Arms is "rain," evidence of weather's important place in the story overall.

Hemingway doesn't quite trust us to detect the rain/snow pattern of symbolism and understand its meaning; therefore he underlines the significance of precipitation in his book by having Catherine tell Henry that she sees them dead in the rain. And so the weather symbolism in A Farewell to Arms is perhaps unnecessarily obvious. Yet Hemingway's use of this literary device is hardly rote symbolism for its own sake.

Rain and snow both drive his plot and maintain our interest, as we hold our breaths every time it rains in the novel, praying that Catherine will not perish during that scene. (We know that Henry will survive the rain, because he is the story's narrator.) Thus, while writing a brutally realistic saga of life during wartime, Ernest Hemingway also crafted a novel as literary as the great-war stories that preceded A Farewell to Arms. Arguably it is as powerful as any story ever told.

## SETTINGS

The setting of A Farewell to Arms is Italy, where they were fighting Austria, during World War I. The story is about Frederick Henry, an American, who served as a lieutenant in the Italian army to a group of ambulance drivers. At the start of the novel, Frederick was a drunk who traveled from one house of prostitution to the next. Yet he was discontent with his unsettled lifestyle. Frederick meets Catherine Barkley an English volunteer nurse, who serves in Italy, at a near by hospital. In the first few chapters, Frederick's life is seeing Miss Barkley, drinking with the others at his barracks, and driving the ambulance.

Frederick is in a bunker, preparing to drive the ambulance when, the bunker is shelled. One of his drivers is killed, two are wounded, and Frederick is hit in the knee. Frederick is forced to go to a hospital. Frederick transfers to the hospital where Catherine is stationed. Catherine was very experienced with love and loss. She lost a fiancé in the war. Frederick slowly fell in love with her and in his love for her he found commitment. Catherine volunteers to work nights so they can spend time together. Frederick recuperates and returns to the front line after spending a week traveling with Catherine. But Catherine tells him that she is pregnant. Frederick admits to feeling trapped.

At the front line Frederick again starts driving ambulance. The Italian army is forced to retreat, though. While retreating Frederick looses three of his ambulances and two of his men. He is almost killed by the Carabinieri or army police, when they are stopping officers at a bridge. Frederick escapes into the river and later finds Catherine. They run of to Switzerland when they are tipped of that the police are after Frederick. They spend the winter in Switzerland, taking walks, and enjoying the "winter sport". Spring rolls around, and one night Catherine is awakened in the night because she's having the baby. They go to the hospital and are put in a room.

The birth takes a very long time, and there are complications. The doctor suggests a caesarean section. The baby is brought to another room and the doctor holds it upside down and smacks it. The baby is dead; it was choked by its umbilical cord. Frederick seems unmoved. They sew up Catherine; she looks very gray. Frederick goes to eat dinner. When he comes back they tell him that Catherine has hemorrhaged. Frederick prays to God that He may spare Catherine, he pleads to not let her die. He goes in to see her; Catherine knows she is going to die. They make Frederick leave, Catherine hemorrhages again and she dies. Frederick cries, he won't talk to the doctor; he goes in by Catherine but says she feels like a statue. Frederick walks off into the rain.

When Frederick entered Catherine's hospital room, for the first time, he prayed and showed some emotion. He cried. In the end of the novel, Frederick is faced with a life-changing occurrence. He lost something of real value to him. It took the loss of something so important to make the real Frederick Henry surface. He asked God to save his greatest love after taking his child and did not really receive and answer. He concluded death is the end and when it comes, there is nowhere to go. Character Analysis: There were really only two main characters in this book, Frederick and Catherine. I will describe them, and how they changed through the book.

Frederick Henry was an American. He was often referred to as Tenete. Frederick and Ernest experience many of the same situations. Both were drinkers, and were involved in World War I in a medical capacity. They were both shot in the knee, and both met nurses whom they fell in love with while they were hospitalized. In the beginning of the novel he is a ladies man. But when he finds Catherine things change. He slowly fell in love with her, and he found commitment. For once he didn't feel lonely and insecure.

Catherine was sick and this was when you see who Henry really has become. "I sat outside the hall. Everything was gone inside of me. I did not think. I could not think. I knew she was going to die and prayed that she would not. Don't let her die. Oh, God, please don't let her die. I'll do anything for you if you won't let her die. Please, please, please, dear God, don't let her die. God please make her not die. I'll do anything you say if you don't let her die." Then Catherine died. Frederick had finally found someone to love, admire, and settle down with, and something terrible happened. It revealed how he has changed as a person.

He changed from an over-sensuous womanizer to a person who had settled down and sought everything he hoped in life, but lost. Catherine Barkley was an English volunteer nurse, stationed in Italy. She knew what love and loss where.

She had already lost a fiancé in the war. In the beginning of her relationship with Frederick she was not sure about him. But she fell in love with him. She always seemed very insecure. She always made Frederick tell her that he loved her. She was always afraid that he'd leave her. "'You do love me?'(Catherine)"I really love you. I'm crazy about you."(Frederick)"You really love me?" "Don't keep on saying that" ". Toward the end of the book Catherine realizes that Frederick is there to stay. She misses her family, and talks about visiting them. She's afraid that the baby will cause Frederick to feel trapped. But he says he'll be okay. Catherine is brave, according to Frederick.

Catherine isn't as well developed as Frederick. It goes deeper into Frederick's feelings. But both of the characters are well developed. The rest of the characters in the book are flat. It never goes into depth about them. Both of the characters are very believable. Catherine might be a little naive, but I believe I could see both of them walking down the street next to me. I sympathize with Frederick a lot. He lost his wife (practically) and his child. He couldn't understand why God took Catherine. Just like some people who can't understand why their husband or wife was killed. In the end everyone must die, and that is what Frederick believed.

This book was a typical love story: a Romeo and Juliet placed against the odds. In this novel, Romeo was Frederick and Juliet was Catherine. Their love had to survive the obstacles of World War I. The background of war-torn Italy added to the tragedy of the love story. The war affected the emotions and values of each character. The love between Catherine and Frederick had to withstand long separations, life-threatening situations, and the uncertainty of each other's condition. This novel was a beautiful love story of two people who needed each other in a period of complete upheaval.

Evaluation: I believe the theme of A Farewell to Arms is: Hopelessness-no matter how hard we fight to live, we end up defeated, but we are here and we must go on. An example is when Catherine is fighting to stay alive, she gives everything but she dies. Frederick wants to live with Catherine forever, but she's taken away from him, and in the end, Frederick will also end up defeated and dead. My evaluation of the theme as a Christian is that it is outrageous. The world is so hopeless because they don't have the truth. When they die, they expect hell or nothing. When we die we have the hope of eternal life. Frederick didn't look forward to anything; he just knew that in the end he would die. I look forward to heaven and meeting Jesus and all the other saints in heaven. The Bible disagrees with this totally as shown in Isaiah 40:31 "But those who hope in the Lord will renew their strength. They will soar on wings like eagles; they will run and not grow weary, they will walk and not be faint."

Symbolism is really used a lot in this book. I believe that rain is a symbol of disaster. When things went very badly in the war, the start of winter came with permanent rain. Miss Barkley is afraid of the rain, she often sees herself dead in it, or she sees Frederick dead in it. It is raining the entire time that Catherine is in childbirth and when both she and her baby die. A metaphor is used when Frederick jumps in the river to save himself. "Anger was washed away in the river along with any obligation."

There is foreshadowing when Catherine dies; she predicts that she will die. Its ironic that Catherine and the baby die, you think that everything will be all right. The book was hard to read. I often got lost while reading dialogue between two people because it doesn't say who's talking. The sentences are very short and he writes as if you were there next to him, and he was just telling you a story. It had a great plot and there was a big twist when Catherine and the baby die. A lot of other writers thought he used a lot more symbolism, making it even harder to read.

Ernest Hemingway was twisted; his view of the world was typical of the "lost generation". I would recommend the book because it has been called one of the greatest war novels ever. It was an excellent book even though it was hard to understand. I would also recommend doing a little research before you start reading so you know what to expect and how to understand it. There is great power in being an author; you can make things happen which do not necessarily occur in real life. Hemingway acted out his feeling of inadequacy and powerlessness by hunting, drinking, spending lots of money, and having many girlfriends. I believe Hemingway had Catherine Barkley and her child die because he believed that death comes to everyone; it was inevitable. Death ends life before you have a chance to learn and live. He writes, in A Farewell to Arms, "They threw you in and told you the rules and the first time they caught you off base they killed you... they killed you in the end. You could count on that. Stay around and they would kill you." This shows the hopelessness that enveloped him.

## ESCAPE FROM REALITY

In Ernest Hemingway's A Farewell to Arms, Fredric Henry gets involved with Catherine Barkley to escape the insanity of war. Frederic loves Catherine. Catherine loves Frederic. The extreme situation of war and fate allowed both of them to be thrown together and fall in love. This love for one another was an escape into another world for Frederic. It provided him emotionally with a private place, where he could go to separate and evade the horrible realities of war occurring in and around him. Under any other normal circumstances this love probably would have never happened, but the pitcher had the curve ball in for Frederic from the first throw. He wanted him out.

From the beginning, Frederic and Catherine's relationship started in a strange state. Frederic knew Catherine was a little cooky, but he still continued to pursue her. He did not even love her at first, but he still needed a way of escaping his present situation, so he decided what the hell, and went after her. Plus, he really didn't think he had anything to loose. There were no stakes named from the start. He didn't really care if he lost anyway.

"I did not love Catherine Barkley nor had any idea of loving her. This was a game, like bridge, in which you said things instead of playing cards. Like bridge you had to pretend you were playing for money or playing for some stakes.

Nobody had mentioned what the stakes were. It was all right with me. But this is where Frederic made his mistake. He kept his distance from right and wrong regarding war and love. He had separated himself from war and seemed to have no place in it at all, mentally or physically (for example when he is in the hospital in Book Two). But when Aymo is killed by his own army, Frederic discovers the reality that he is not really separated from this event at all. He is very much part of this war whether he likes it or not.

At this point, he seems to go a little crazy himself and gets scared. He needs a way to escape immediately and ends up separating himself again through love. Frederic had not been prepared for the stress and pressure of the reality he had faultily deluded himself from. So in order to escape, he resolves to desert the army completely and reunite with Catherine. At least when he is with Catherine he is in another place literally and symbolically (in Switzerland in her tent of hair). This is now an obsession with Frederic because he can totally separate himself from war through her love. He realizes he has got nothing but this love to hold on to. Whether it is delusional, symbolic, or literal-it is not war.

Even when she is about to give birth (the ultimate consummation of their love for one another), he become nervous. Not only is the baby a product of their love for one another, but it will forever connect him to the reality of his present situation even when war is over. Here neither of them can handle this. Catherine shows this physically through her death and the child's death. Frederic shows this through his odd behaviour, such as being afraid of numbers over two. That would leave him connected to something he wants to be totally separated from. He loves Catherine and his to be child, but he would rather sacrifice them to be totally separated from this war.

True, under any other normal circumstances this love probably would have never happened. But that is life, throwing everyone curve balls left and right. It started raining. The game got a little hectic. Confused, both Henry and Barkley walked up to the plate at the same time. It didn't matter who hit the ball, all they heard was the crack against the bat, and started running, ignoring the other players, as they sped from first to second to third. It was still raining.

Henry was relieved when he made it home, but Barkley twisted her ankle in a mud puddle. Her loyalties turned back and were tagged out between third and home. When he got back to the dug-out, it was still raining, and realized she wasn't there. He told the coach to mark down the run for Barkley. Give him credit, he just didn't know the stakes were going to be this high. He realized he would have to be the one counted out this time. He wanted to be counted out anyhow.

## TRUTH

If The Sun Also Rises was one of the best books I have ever read, then A Farewell to Arms is Truth. I simply cannot believe that these books existed so long without my knowledge of how grand they are. I consider myself to read constantly, more than almost anyone I know, and here in less than a month I read two books that are undoubtedly among the best I have encountered. When I finished FTA I was of course stunned by the death of Catherine and the baby and Henry's sudden solitude. "What happens now?" I felt, as I so often do when I finish a book that I want to go on forever. This is infinitely more difficult with a book that has no conclusion, and FTA leaves a reader not only emotionally exhausted but also just as alone as Henry and with nowhere to go.

The entire work was aware of where it was going and what was going to happen next, and then to stop the way it did was unfair. Now, I've read enough essays while deciding which would be the topic for my class presentation that I know many people see that the unfairness of life and the insignificance of our free will are apparently the most important themes in the book, but I don't agree. I also don't agree that it is a war story or a love story. Exactly what it is, though, is not clear to me. Can't art exist without being anything? "There isn't always an explanation for everything."

War and love are obviously important themes in the book, and the relationship between the two is explored by

Hemingway and, somewhat, by Henry. In the first two Books we are in the war and the war is overwhelming. In the last two Books we are in love. And, just as the first two Books are peppered with love in the time of war, the last two Books are tinged with war in the time of love. The third Book is the bridge between the two 'stories' and it is not surprising that it centers on the escape. It is during the escape that Henry resolves that he is through with the war (a war in which he really has no place) and decides that all he wants is to be with Catherine.

Until the third Book Henry doesn't seem to be agonizingly concerned with matters of right or wrong in the war and it seems, in fact, separate from him. Even when he is injured it doesn't appear that he is really a part of the war which surrounds him.

He maintains a distance from it and this distance isn't really closed until Aymo is killed by his own army, he discovers that Bonello is only staying with him out of respect, and he is almost killed as a spy. After this he resolves to desert the army and be reunited with his love, Catherine. Henry is no dummy and he could easily tell that everything was not all correct with Cat, which leads to the question of his love for her. You must admit that Cat is a bit well flaky when they first meet.

She loses that persona soon enough, although I couldn't help but distrust her integrity until somewhere in the middle of the fourth Book. It is also difficult to believe wholeheartedly in his love for her until much later in their relationship, and it leaves me wondering if he is leaving his involvement in the war because of his unfailing love for Cat or if Cat and any feelings he has for her are just excuses to escape the insanity of the war he experiences in the third Book.

When he is with Catherine, they are in another place, untouched by the war, both symbolically (in the tent of her hair) and literally (in Switzerland). It seems like I don't ever say anything earth-shattering, or even critical, in these response papers, and I'm not sure if I'm supposed to do that. The line, "The war seemed as far away as the football games of some one else's college," is beautiful.

## DYSFUNCTIONAL HENRY

In Ernest Hemmingway's A Farewell to Arms, the protagonist, Frederic Henry is both dysfunctional and tragic. Throughout the story Henry lives up to this description of shear tragedy and dysfunction. The main elements that aid in making him both tragic and dysfunctional are: the fact that the love he and Catherine shared at the end of the book was doomed, this love was only "role-playing" to him at first, and he went AWOL on the Italian army.

The first detail that contributes to making Henry a dysfunctional character is that he uses role-playing as a way of escaping the realization of the human mortality which is unveiled by the war. This role-playing begins on Henry and Catherine's third encounter. After this meeting the two become increasingly comfortable with their roles. It is as if their whole relationship is a "game". Neither one of them mistakes role-playing for a truly intimate relationship, but both recognize that it can be a useful device for satisfying certain emotional needs. This role-playing is a very dysfunctional characteristic of Frederic Henry.

The second point that makes Henry a dysfunctional character is that he deserted the Italian army. Not only was this illegal but it could have cost him his life. Henry, although an American, had made a commitment to the Italian army, to protect and serve Italy. This characteristic alone is enough to make one dysfunctional, as it does to Henry. In addition to being a dysfunctional character, Henry is also a tragic character. Catherine is pure tragedy. Although the relationship that the love that Henry gains for Frederic and Catherine had started out to be only role-playing it turned into something much more, it became true love. This love was more than could be explained in words.

Their love during an ugly war was not to be recreated or modeled even as much as through a baby conceived by their love. The baby could not be born alive because their love was beautiful yet doomed so that nothing could come out of it. "In a world where the abstracts of glory, honour, and sacrifice meant little to Frederic, his physical association with Catherine was the only thing he had and it was taken away from him long before she died." In conclusion, these three main items aid in making Henry a dysfunctional and tragic character. Henry had fled his duty as a soldier, giving up on the country he had confided in. Henry was engaged in a relationship which started as a mere game, grew into love and ultimately ended in the tragic death of his precious wife and child. Frederic Henry is a tragic and dysfunctional character in a tragic and dysfunctional story.

## SELF ACTUALIZATION

The Italian front of World War I, while remembered as less devastating than the blood bath in France, reflected every deplorable aspect of war. The effects were far reaching; nearly 600,000 Italian soldiers lost their lives, and more than a million were wounded. Among both the enlisted and civilians, no person escaped the poisonous touch of the war. Such was the case with Frederick Henry, an American architecture student in Rome at the time the war began. When he joined ranks as an Italian Lieutenant, Frederick never anticipated the misery that would accompany military life. However, save a few chapters mid-novel, Hemingway's A Farewell to Arms is by no means a painful account of the tribulations and tragedies of war.

In the midst of pervasive evil, Frederick finds salvation in the form of love. His relationship with Catherine Barkley is a respite from the savagery. Their "union" leads him to establish his own principles and is ultimately his refuge from the massive chaos of war. Hemingway gives several clues throughout the novel that foreshadow Catherine's role in Frederick's development as well as the impact that their relationship has on his life. The reader can trace a pattern of regression from the war, each time mirrored by a progression in his attachment to Catherine. Conversely, a period of deeper devotion to Catherine predicts a revolution in his regard to the war. By the novel's conclusion, a reformation has occurred in Frederick Henry. He is transformed from a disillusioned young man, into a weathered soul that has suffered life's greatest agonies: to lose in love and to lose in war. When Henry is first introduced, he is arrogant and dissolute and has yet to establish any parameters for his life. The reader is given no indication of why he abandoned architecture to join a foreign army. We are left to assume that it was an impulsive measure, probably an attempt to establish routine or order in a chaotic life. Immediately Henry exhibits dwindling enthusiasm for the war. When conversation at the dinner table turns to the topic of where Frederick ought to vacation on his leave, a critical example of his immaturity (thus far) surfaces.

The officers, who take joy in raucous chiding of the priest to the outfit, insist that Henry visit the whorehouses in each of their favourite cities. The priest however, extends a warm invitation for Frederick to visit his family's scenic, picturesque hometown. Frederick does not yet appreciate the value of the untainted and cleansing countryside, and opts for "nights in bed, drunk, when you knew that that was all there was not caring in the night, sure that this was all and all and all and not caring." When he has returned to the front, he experiences deep remorse for ignoring an opportunity to see a place where "it was clear cold and dry and the snow was dry and powdery and hare-tracks in the snow and peasants took off their hats and called to you." Even the language and voice which Hemingway uses to describe the contrasting locations highlights the fallacy in his choice.

Frederick is longing for something greater than can be satisfied by cheap alcohol and solicited sex, but he has not begun to understand his own neediness. Responding to Frederick's ambiguity in regard to "army life," Hemingway follows with a series of chapters introducing and developing the character of Catherine Barkley. Initially, it is clear that Catherine and her bizarre "games" puzzle Henry. His compliance stems, not from the love he feigns, but from purely physical desire.

The priest clarifies the difference between true love and Frederick's lust, "When you love you wish to do things for. You wish to sacrifice for. You wish to serve." And although he consents that he does not feel love for Catherine, he prefers her company to that found in the brothels. As though he has "learned his lesson" by forgoing the trip to the countryside, Frederick chooses to endure her eccentricities at the chance of establishing a relationship. At this point, the only type of relationship he desires with her is a sexual one, but by fostering the necessary trust to entice her to bed, he "accidentally" begins to fall in love.

As Hemingway began book two, he planned for dramatic changes in Frederick's life. During a portentously ironic stream of consciousness, Frederick divulges his brazen regard for the war. "I knew I would not be killed. Not in this war. It did not have anything to do with me." What Frederick chose to ignore is that the mortar shells and bullets are impartial. The enemy was the enemy, and the Austrians wanted Italian soldiers dead. As chance would have it, just such a trench mortar plowed through Frederick's dugout the next day while he was stationed near Plava, and although he withstood the pain stoically, it was immense and the damage to his body was extensive. This served only to further remove Frederick's commitment to the Italy's cause.

Not only does Frederick face the possibility of permanent maiming, but any fragment of a sense of duty has been injured, as well. His disconcerted opinion of the army gave way to resentment. Frederick finally established an exacting set of criterion by which he intended to live. He began to differentiate between hollow pleasure and philosophical fulfillment. This is demonstrated by his rejection of the attempts to decorate him for his "bravery," as he insisted that there was nothing brave about hiding in a dugout eating macaroni.

Conversely, in his conversation with the priest, Henry shows a fervent interest in understanding what it means to feel love. Frederick's transformation is on the brink of emergence, and in Hemingway's response to this fore shadowing, we again see how he uses the relationship with Catherine to actualize this growth. This twist of fate was Hemingway's tool for a transition into the most significant period of development in the couple's relationship.

The events of the second book serve primarily to solidify

their mutual trust, security, love and respect. Against the backdrop of pleasant summer weather, the two try futilely to erase the ravages of the ongoing combat. Though they are not untouched by the scarring effects of war, tender devotion abounds. He is undoubtedly captivated by her mere presence. "She came in the room she looked fresh and young and very beautiful. When I saw her I was in love with her," explained Frederick. He no longer is the "simple creature" that could feel fulfilled and contented by casual sex.

He has sampled the love of which the priest spoke so highly and concurs that its splendor is unsurpassed. Despite any previous reservations, Frederick willingly and completely commits to Catherine. In fact it is he who encourages a legal wedding between the two, but Catherine insists that a ceremony is unnecessary. "What good would it do to marry now? We're really married. I couldn't be any more married There isn't any me. I'm you. Don't make up a separate me." Her relatively liberal attitude has an important bearing on the events after their reunion in book four, and Hemingway seizes the opportunity to suggest that Catherine can and will support any decision of Frederick's both morally and spiritually. Her idea of their "oneness," paired with her open-minded tolerance, makes her the ideal partner to support Frederick in his upcoming trials.

In Book Three, Hemingway follows his well-established trend, and reverts the focus of the novel again to the war. Immediately, Frederick is ushered back to the front, where he finds himself entirely detached from army life. He no longer associates with an existence that represents hollow pleasures and is not attracted to the rigidity and order associated with the army. Nonetheless, in the midst of an enormous retreat, all he could find was confusion and disorder. Book Three serves three purposes. First, it responds to the joyous summer lived in Book Two, by following with great pain and sorrow. In the same manner, this portrait of despair serves as a test of endurance for Frederick.

His persistence during the grisly days of retreat is maintained by his focus on Catherine. Secondly, the atmosphere of life-less, defeated, and demoralized soldiers foreshadows the tragedy that is to follow in Book Five. Frederick is gaining respect for the finality of death as he is a first hand witness (and even perpetrator) of the deaths of colleagues. Finally, the desertion is his is ultimate act of self-actualization and commitment to Catherine. Henry makes a "farewell to arms" and washes himself of any responsibility to a war in which he has little interest. Book Four is a brief interlude of peace and normalcy for the couple.

Once they have escaped to Switzerland, Catherine and Frederick anticipate an idyllic existence. But Book Five is close at their heels, and unimaginable tragedy looms in Hemingway's foreboding words, "If people bring so much courage to this world the world has to kill them to break them, so of course it kills them." Of course, Hemingway has given away the ending, but only as Book Five ends, is the reader aware of the magnitude of Frederick's loss. Frederick is a transformed man, schooled by her love, forever changed by the war, and a completed person for their time together.

## ROLE PLAYING

In Hemingway's novel, A Farewell to Arms, the principle characters, Henry and Catherine, are forced by the war to face the fact of human mortality. As a defence mechanism, the two main characters, and several others, turn to "role-playing" as a way to escape reality. Hemingway utilized role-playing as a way to explore the strengths and weaknesses of the characters. By placing Henry's ordered life in opposition to Catherine's topsy-turvy one, and then letting each one assume a role which will bring them closer together, Hemingway shows the pair's inability to accept their own mortality.

John Stubbs' has written an essay that examines the "role-playing" that Henry and Catherine use to protect themselves from the discovery of their insignificance and "powerlessness in a world indifferent to their well being " Stubbs begins by showing other examples, notably in In Our Time and The Sun Also Rises, in which Hemingway's characters revert to role-playing in order to escape or retreat from their lives. The ability to create characters who play roles, he says, either to "maintain self-esteem" or to escape, is one Hemingway exploits extraordinarily well in A Farewell to Arms and therefore it "is his richest and most successful handling of human beings trying to come to terms with their vulnerability."

As far as Stubbs is concerned, Hemingway is quite blatant in letting us know that role-playing is what is occurring. He tells that the role-playing begins during Henry and Catherine's third encounter, when Catherine directly dictates what is spoken by Henry. After this meeting the two become increasingly comfortable with their roles and easily adopt them whenever the other is nearby. This is apparent also in that they can only successfully play their roles when they are in private and any disturbance causes the "game" to be disrupted.

The intrusion of the outside world in any form makes their role-playing impossible, as evidenced at the race track in Milan, where they must be alone. The people surrounding them make Catherine feel uncomfortable and Henry has to take her away from the crowd. He goes on to describe how it is impossible for them to play the roles when they are apart and how they therefore become more dependent upon each other's company.

Stubbs goes on to explain how, "neither mistakes role-playing for a truly intimate relationship, but both recognize that it can be a useful device for satisfying certain emotional needs." He says that originally Henry and Catherine are playing the "game" for different reasons but eventually move to play it as a team. Henry is role-playing to regain the sense of order he has lost when he realizes the futility of the war and his lack of place in it. Catherine is role-playing to deal with the loss of her fiance and to try to find order in the arena of the war. When they are able to role-play together, "the promise of mutual support" is what becomes so important to them as they try to cope with their individual human vulnerability.

He also analyzes the idyllic world introduced early in the story by the priest at the mess and later realized by Henry and Catherine in Switzerland. They fall fully into their roles when they row across the lake on their way to their idealized world. The fact that they actually are able to enter this make-believe world strengthens their "game" and allows it to continue longer than it would have otherwise. And once they are in this new world they adopt new roles which allow them to continue their ruse. They also need to work harder to maintain the "game" because far from the front they are both still aware the war is proceeding and they are no longer a part of it.

The world in which they exist in reality (!) is not conducive to role-playing because it tries repeatedly to end their "game". Stubbs manages to uncover numerous instances in which the two are role-playing and he makes a very interesting case that this is exactly what they are doing and not just his imagination reading into the story. He does make certain assumptions, that their love is not "real", that the characters are searching for order, which are not completely justified or even necessary to prove his point. He also forces an intentionality upon Hemingway which could have been avoided without harming his theory.

Towards the end of the essay Stubbs infers that their role-playing is "inferior to true intimacy," which is a point that, although he defends well, is not central to his theory and seems to detract from his objectivity. The essay is a valuable tool to help the reader understand this view of what is happening through Henry and Catherine's relationship and how they use each other to maintain their self-images, provide themselves with psychological support, and in a way escape the war. Hemingway may not have been trying to purposely create a role-playing scenario, but Stubbs' essay will benefit someone wishing to explore this aspect of the relationship of the two main characters in greater depth.

## Chapter 5

# Themes, Motifs and Symbols

### THEMES

Themes are the fundamental and often universal ideas explored in a literary work. "The Grim Reality of War" - as the title of the novel makes clear, A Farewell to Arms concerns itself primarily with war, namely the process by which Frederic Henry removes himself from it and leaves it behind. The few characters in the novel who actually support the effort—Ettore Moretti and Gino—come across as a dull braggart and a naïve youth, respectively. The majority of the characters remain ambivalent about the war, resentful of the terrible destruction it causes, doubtful of the glory it supposedly brings.

The novel offers masterful descriptions of the conflict's senseless brutality and violent chaos: the scene of the Italian army's retreat remains one of the most profound evocations of war in American literature. As the neat columns of men begin to crumble, so too do the soldiers' nerves, minds, and capacity for rational thought and moral judgment. Henry's shooting of the engineer for refusing to help free the car from the mud shocks the reader for two reasons: first, the violent outburst seems at odds with Henry's coolly detached character; second, the incident occurs in a setting that robs it of its moral import—the complicity of Henry's fellow soldiers legitimizes the killing. The murder of the engineer seems justifiable because it is an inevitable by-product of the spiraling violence and disorder of the war.

Nevertheless, the novel cannot be said to condemn the war; A Farewell to Arms is hardly the work of a pacifist.

Instead, just as the innocent engineer's death is an inevitability of war, so is war the inevitable outcome of a cruel, senseless world. Hemingway suggests that war is nothing more than the dark, murderous extension of a world that refuses to acknowledge, protect, or preserve true love.

## THE RELATIONSHIP BETWEEN LOVE AND PAIN

Against the backdrop of war, Hemingway offers a deep, mournful meditation on the nature of love. No sooner does Catherine announce to Henry that she is in mourning for her dead fiancé than she begins a game meant to seduce Henry. Her reasons for doing so are clear: she wants to distance herself from the pain of her loss. Likewise, Henry intends to get as far away from talk of the war as possible. In each other, Henry and Catherine find temporary solace from the things that plague them. The couple's feelings for each other quickly pass from an amusement that distracts them to the very fuel that sustains them.

Henry's understanding of how meaningful his love for Catherine is outweighs any consideration for the emptiness of abstract ideals such as honour, enabling him to flee the war and seek her out. Reunited, they plan an idyllic life together that promises to act as a salve for the damage that the war has inflicted. Far away from the decimated Italian countryside, each intends to be the other's refuge. If they are to achieve physical, emotional, and psychological healing, they have found the perfect place in the safe remove of the Swiss mountains. The tragedy of the novel rests in the fact that their love, even when genuine, can never be more than temporary in this world.

## MOTIFS

Motifs are recurring structures, contrasts, or literary devices that can help to develop and inform the text's major themes. Readers of Hemingway's fiction will quickly notice a consistent thread in the portrayal and celebration of a certain kind of man: domineering, supremely competent, and swaggeringly virile. A Farewell to Arms holds up several of its minor male characters as examples of fine manhood. Rinaldi is a faithful friend and an oversexed womanizer; Dr. Valentini exhibits a virility to rival Rinaldi's as well as a bold competence that makes him the best surgeon.

Similarly, during the scene in which Henry fires his pistol at the fleeing engineering sergeants, Bonello takes charge of the situation by brutally shooting the fallen engineer in the head. The respect with which Hemingway sketches these men, even at their lowest points, is highlighted by the humour, if not contempt, with which he depicts their opposites. The success of each of these men depends, in part, on the failure of another: Rinaldi secures his sexual prowess by attacking the priest's lack of lust; Dr. Valentini's reputation as a surgeon is thrown into relief by the three mousy, overly cautious, and physically unimpressive doctors who precede him; and Bonello's ruthlessness is prompted by the disloyal behaviour of the soldier whom he kills.

Henry and Catherine begin flirting with each other in order to forget personal troubles. Flirting, which Henry compares to bridge, allows Henry to "drop the war" and diverts Catherine's thoughts from the death of her fiancé. Likewise, the horse races that Catherine and Henry attend enable them to block out thinking of Henry's return to the front and of their imminent separation. Ironically, Henry and Catherine's relationship becomes the source of suffering from which Henry needs diversion. Henry cannot stand to be away from Catherine, and while playing pool with Count Greffi takes his mind off of her, the best divertissement turns out to be the war itself. When Catherine instructs him not to think about her when they are apart, Henry replies, "That's how I worked it at the front.

But there was something to do then." The transformations of the war from fatal threat into divertissement and love from distraction into pain signal not only Henry's attachment to Catherine but also the transitory nature of happiness. Pathos radiates from this fleeting happiness because, even though happiness is temporary, the pursuit of it remains necessary. Perhaps an understanding of the limits of happiness explains the count's comment that though he values love most in life, he is not wise for doing so.

The count is wiser than he claims, however. He hedges against the transitory nature of love by finding pleasure and amusement in games, birthday parties, and the taking of "a little stimulant." That one can depend on their simple pleasures lends games and divertissement a certain dignity; while they may not match up to the nobility of pursuits such as love, they prove quietly constant. The notions of loyalty and abandonment apply equally well to love and war. The novel, however, suggests that loyalty is more a requirement of love and friendship than of the grand political causes and abstract philosophies of battling nations.

While Henry takes seriously his duty as a lieutenant, he does not subscribe to the ideals that one typically imagines fuel soldiers in combat. Unlike Ettore Moretti or Gino, the promise of honour and the duties of patriotism mean little to Henry. Although he shoots an uncooperative engineering sergeant for failing to comply with his orders, Henry's violence should be read as an inevitable outcome of a destructive war rather than as a conscious decision to enforce a code of moral conduct. Indeed, Henry eventually follows in the engineering sergeants' footsteps by abandoning the army and his responsibilities.

While he does, at times, feel guilt over this course of action, he takes comfort in the knowledge that he is most loyal where loyalty counts most: in his relationship with Catherine. That these conflicting allegiances cannot be reconciled does not suggest, however, that loyalty and abandonment lie at opposite ends of a moral spectrum. Rather, they reflect the priorities of a specific individual's life.

Upon meeting, Catherine and Henry rely upon a grand illusion of love and seduction for comfort. Catherine seeks solace for the death of her fiancé, while Henry will do anything to distance himself from the war. At first, their declarations of love are transparent: Catherine reminds Henry several times that their courtship is a game, sending him away when she has played her fill. After Henry is wounded, however, his desire for Catherine and the comfort and support that she offers becomes more than a distraction from the world's unpleasantness; his love begins to sustain him and blossoms into something undeniably real. Catherine's feelings for Henry follow a similar course.

While the couple acts in ways that confirm the genuine nature of their passion, however, they never escape the temptation of dreaming of a better world. In other words, the boundary between reality and illusion proves difficult to identify. After Henry and Catherine have spent months of isolation in Switzerland, Hemingway depicts their relationship as a mixture of reality and illusion.

Boredom has begun to set in, and the couple effects small daily changes to reinvigorate their lives and their passion: Catherine gets a new haircut, while Henry grows a beard. Still, or perhaps because of, the comparative dullness of real life (not to mention the ongoing war), the couple turns to fantasies of a more perfect existence. They dream of life on a Swiss mountain, where they will make their own clothes and need nothing but each other, suggesting that fantasizing is part of coping with the banal, sometimes damaging effects of reality.

## SYMBOLS

Symbols are objects, characters, figures, or colors used to represent abstract ideas or concepts. Rain serves in the novel as a potent symbol of the inevitable disintegration of happiness in life. Catherine infuses the weather with meaning as she and Henry lie in bed listening to the storm outside. As the rain falls on the roof, Catherine admits that the rain scares her and says that it has a tendency to ruin things for lovers.

Of course, no meteorological phenomenon has such power; symbolically, however, Catherine's fear proves to be prophetic, for doom does eventually come to the lovers. After Catherine's death, Henry leaves the hospital and walks home in the rain. Here, the falling rain validates Catherine's anxiety and confirms one of the novel's main contentions: great love, like anything else in the world good or bad, innocent or deserving—cannot last.

## CATHERINE'S HAIR

Although it is not a recurring symbol, Catherine's hair is an important one. In the early, easy days of their relationship, as Henry and Catherine lie in bed, Catherine takes down her hair and lets it cascade around Henry's head. The tumble of hair reminds Henry of being enclosed inside a tent or behind a waterfall. This lovely description stands as a symbol of the couple's isolation from the world.

With a war raging around them, they manage to secure a blissful seclusion, believing themselves protected by something as delicate as hair. Later, however, when they are truly isolated from the ravages of war and living in peaceful Switzerland, they learn the harsh lesson that love, in the face of life's cruel reality, is as fragile and ephemeral as hair.

## Chapter 6

# Hemingway and Brecht

For several decades modern realistic literature has been dominated by two names: Ernest Hemingway and Bertolt Brecht. They were born at almost the same time Brecht in 1898 and Hemingway in 1899 and died not long apart Brecht in 1956, Hemingway in 1961. Thus they were respectively 59 and 62 years old; both died at an age when one could still have expected new and great works from them. A strange common trait was that, despite an almost classical realistic form of expression, they were avant-garde artists, and that both had clarity and objectivity as an aesthetic ideal. The truly modern thing in their style is the markedly anti-sentimental, anti emotional attitude. Both were politically leftist.

Each within his field the novel for Hemingway and the drama for Brecht exercised enormous influence on the writing of his time. Strangely enough, both on various occasions named the Bible as their most important literary model. Both helped to create the same stylistic sensibility out of an inborn aversion to, and distrust of, big words and expressions of pathos. It is not possible to imagine modern world literature without them.

In general the points of similarity are so strong and so numerous that it is astonishing that you don't see their names mentioned together more often. Both began writing early, and had things published before they were twenty. Both were in the medical corps toward the end of the First World War. Both achieved world renown at thirty Brecht with the Threepenny Opera and Hemingway with A Farewell to Arms and The Sun also Rises in 1927-28. It goes without saying that both were also active anti fascists. One could continue to find parallels almost indefinitely, but the differences were great as well. The novelist, whose art was a quiet communication to the individual reader, was an adventurer and soldier; he had been in the line of fire in a number of wars, he loved ocean fishing and big-game hunting, boxing, fights, liquor and good food. The dramatist and director Brecht, the activist revolutionary communist, whose art lives primarily on the stage in physical action was himself a purely intellectual desk-person, both to adopt any but a sitting position. His dislike of physical movement was legendary; if he had a car handy, he wouldn't go a hundred yards on foot. Hemingway sought the most violent death he could find; he blew out his brains with a shotgun. Brecht died of thrombosis.

Literary folk unfortunately seem to be occupied either with Brecht or with Hemingway. This is too bad, because the two of them belong together, and because the work of one can in many ways shed light on that of the other: Hemingway's theme was the individual in relation only to himself, Brecht's theme was the person in relation to society. It is remarkable how few there are who have dealt with both aspects of being human. There is a certain class of writers distinguished by the fact that the times they lived in seem to a special degree to have taken up residence in them; contemporary history has become flesh and blood in their personalities, so that the problems and conflicts of their age ooze out of their work, as it were whether voluntarily or no.

The first part of our century has incorporated itself in the figures of Hemingway and Brecht perhaps more strongly than in any other writers living and working at the same time. Each in his way stands as a monument over the first fifty or sixty years of this strange century. It began as a century with problems, and developed into an epoch where the "problems" gradually proved to be dilemmas—problems, that is, which can no longer be solved by any known or inherited means. In sixty years, or less, the very atmosphere of the time has been transformed from an insouciant optimism to a blank despair. We can illustrate it with a couple of well-known quotes from

Bert Brecht: "A peaceful face is a sign of insensitivity" or "A conversation about trees is almost a crime". This dreadful turnaround in the feeling about life occurred in the course of the 1920s and 1930s. Today it has broadened into practically the only attitude which can be taken with complete seriousness. To continue quoting from the same poem ("To those born after us"): "Those who laugh have simply not yet received the dreadful news."

Today the situation is such that practically all responsible people see the world like that, albeit there appear to be those walking among us who have not yet received "the dreadful news", even after the year 1945. In Hemingway and Brecht, knowledge of the "news" is obviously inborn, and forms the very point of departure for the work of both as writers; their common problem is thereby set from the first syllable: How can one manage to live in this world at all? For others the question ripened later, but since the mid-century this despair has become symptomatic of humanity in general. It's a matter of living at times in the word's most literal sense of surviving.

Insofar as one assumes that it is good or desirable to go on living, that there is a kind of duty to live which replaces earlier generations' desire to live, the elementary problem of existence is itself transformed into a moral question. Even the word "moral" loses its original meaning of an ethical code, and acquires the almost military sense of morale. "The troops' morale is unshakable" means not that the soldiers and officers abstain from drinking liquor or lying with girls, but that they continue to hold out, that they don't give up the fight. To conquer the urge not to go on living becomes our first and most important moral commandment.

This one central theme became for both Hemingway and Brecht the problem they tried to solve each in his own way, but with the same spirit and intent. Writing is primarily a moral problem for both, and for both the struggle for truth lies in finding a tenable basis for the commandment "Thou shalt go on living!" The hand-me-down ecclesiastical and bourgeois moral code of negations "thou shalt nots" are replaced by a "thou shalt." The word moral today has an exclusively active meaning. This means in practice that nearly all traditional middle-class morality is forced into a more or less museum existence, a kind of luxury for those who still have peace of soul, those who haven't yet received the dreadful news. In the same way traditional esthetics are likewise relegated to the museums; instead of the inherited duty to serve "the beautiful," it has become the artist's and in particular the writer's task to serve the true: his ethic and his esthetic both lie in the key phrase "intellectual honesty." We can survive only if we understand more of the world than before, and we can come to understand more of the world only to the degree we pursue the truth with precision and without compromise. It is our sole possibility, even if it begins by leading us into a steadily deeper despair and isolation. The illusions we have built on have shown themselves to be deadly.

The task must be to find something different and surer, something which in its truth-content is just as tenable in the moral sphere. It follows as a given that artistically and philosophically we are living in a time of iconoclasm, of idol-smashing and continual destruction of old values and moral norms which to the "peaceful," those who have not yet received the dreadful news, must look like an age of pure and sheer destructiveness. The values which must be destroyed likewise include traditional esthetic norms to the degree that they build on illusion in art.

An up-to-date art in our epoch both must and should be "destructive" in the sense that, both in form and thought-content, it is anti illusionary. Its task on every plane is to destroy illusions not for destruction's sake, but so as to find, if possible, what true and clear reality may lie behind an outer image: the truth which perhaps still lurks behind the illusion.

I recall Arne Næss saying in a conversation a few years ago: "We are forced to keep going over thin ice, with deep, black water under us." The utterance is characteristic for the only viable and hence the only worthwhile attitude in modern philosophy, but it is just as relevant for what is vital in modern art and literature. It is in this sense of the word moral that the enormous influence which Brecht and Hemingway have had on the century's literature must be regarded as a healthy and stimulating inspiration. It should be obvious that a lifelong wandering over thin ice, with full consciousness of the black water underneath, eventually comes to mark its man.

The trek becomes not only strenuous, but also very bad for the nerves. We have to the degree that we have awareness full clarity over the fact that death is right under the soles of our feet. Our ignorance is boundless. We don't know who we are, we know nothing about the dark, we know that we live in a time which to an unheard-of degree has given human brutality and bestiality free rein, we don't know why, we know only that we are. Conventions, traditions and our penchant for overlooking the truth have been among the circumstances which have brought us to the brink of catastrophe. If we don't tear the veil aside ourselves, other forces will, and will do so in an even more disagreeable manner.

It begins to be urgent. It begins to be life-threatening to waste a minute. It begins to be a moral crime to sustain an illusion. Yes, it begins to be morally criminal just to let a traditional illusion stand without tearing it down. For the artist the criminal state sets in the minute one fails to use one's tools and talents to strengthen our critical attitude of hostility to illusion. Today even the most refined and sublime l'art pour l'art means selling out to the entertainment industry.

By God we don't need unwinding or relaxation: we need more then ever before in world history an awakening. But we also have more need than in earlier times of strength to tolerate what we see once we are awake. For Brecht and Hemingway the awakening is no longer a problem: the real question is one of strengthening the troops' morale, of finding a valid and tenable basis for at least the tiny hint of optimism necessary to sustain life. Practically every word they wrote relates to this; the smiling Brecht and the deadly serious Hemingway are out on the same errand.

## Chapter 7

# Hemingway and the Beasts

In Hemingway's writings certain themes recur with such frequency and such power that is natural to look at them more closely. The hero is wounded. He bears outward, or in some cases inward, traces of violence and abuse. His battle consists of conquering dread, a dread which is connected with earlier experiences, and which appears as fear of death or fear of life two apparently polar forms of dread, which in reality are the same. Since life ends with death since death, in other words, is a constituent part of life it is unthinkable to accept life without simultaneously recognizing death as life. Life includes death.

The same applies to pain. It is a pitiful zest for life which does not at the same time rejoice in death. Hemingway's hero is placed in naked circumstances, where the human lot has cast off its veil: life, pain, death. You can't have the one without the others. If you keep accounts, pain and death become such dominant entries that they must be regarded as assets if life is to go on. In Hemingway's world, death begins in childhood, as described with unsurpassed mastery in the short story "Indian Camp" in which the boy Nick is present while his father, the doctor, performs a Caesarean section on an Indian woman, without anesthesia, equipped only with a jackknife and fishing leaders to sew the wound up with.

The Indian woman's husband lies in the upper bunk during the operation, with the woollen blanket drawn up over his head. When they lift up the blanket, he has cut his throat. The razor lies open on the blanket.

*"Take Nick out," says the father.*

Here Nick meets life. Afterwards he asks his father three questions:

*Does it always hurt so much to have a baby?*

*Do many people kill themselves?*

*Does it hurt to die?*

It is here that Hemingway's long autobiography begins; this is how it feels to be human. Nick, the hero, has received his wound. He is scared to death, and all his later experiences are more or less repetitions and variations of the same theme. Nick has learned what it means to be a human being on earth; it was a boy invalid who left the Indians' hut with his father afterwards.

*Do many people kill themselves?*

*Does it hurt to die?*

Among certain literary critics there is a sort of tradition which assumes that the Hemingway hero, and hence Hemingway himself, is a kind of half-imbecile subhuman, incapable of thinking, interested in nothing but drink, whores and blood—a thoroughly stupid hero. Nothing can be more stupid than this judgment itself; and it is most clearly disproved by certain of Hemingway's writings on literature. They are some of the most intelligent things ever written about literature.

Does it hurt to die? Of course it hurts to die. Do many people kill themselves? Yes, many do. Then it must hurt to live as well? Yes, it hurts to live. Hemingway has come into the world, and at first cruelty, violence and pain fill his whole field of vision. It bids fair to become his only theme; but soon another one is added: What does one do to survive? Hemingway's father shot himself when the boy was fourteen or fifteen. But he had learned two things from him: to hunt and to fish. In Green Hills of Africa he asks himself why he has always hunted so much, why he has killed so much. It was probably not right for him always to be killing animals. But, he says, if I hadn't killed so many animals I might have killed myself.

In the same book he approaches the matter from another side. After an open break of his upper arm, with inflammation and gangrene, he once lay sleepless for five weeks in a hospital. "Alone with the pain" at night he comes to understand how an animal with a gunshot wound feels if it gets away from the hunter. All night he lay and felt through how everything must develop, from the bullet which enters and crushes the shoulder blade until all is finished. And because he was "a little out of his head", he thought that what he was going through was perhaps a punishment for everything that all hunters had done.

When he was well again, he decided that if it really was a penalty he had paid, then at least in the future he would know what he was doing when he hunted. And he resolved to quit the day he could no longer shoot well enough to kill cleanly. At bottom this is Hemingway's worst complaint against life—that we aren't killed "cleanly." All his war experiences are collected in A Natural History of the Dead, one of the most chilling of all the contributions to the 20th century's apocalypse, an implicit repetition and intensification of Nick's experience at the Indian camp.

The war, for Hemingway, is merely a summation of our true human circumstances and limits. Here life is more honest, because it has shed its mask. Besides hunting and war, there is bullfighting. Hemingway is himself a passionate observer, and he has also tried his luck as an amateur bullfighter. His account of his own efforts in the arena belongs to the few humorous lines in his writings. He has written a whole book about bullfighting, Death in the Afternoon. It is one of the oddest documents any writer has left, and I must confess that it was heavy going, despite the fact that photographs and bullfighters' biographies take up a great deal of the book. It must be the most thorough work of nonfiction ever written about bullfighting, and has found particular appreciation, and buyers, in Spain.

Here as always Hemingway is a specialist in the subject he writes about, a fanatical specialist, whose highest goal is to write so "precisely" and "purely" that what he has written will perhaps be relevant and true after his death. One of his main points is that bullfighting is not a sport. It is a tragedy, in three acts, where every slightest detail is determined in advance.

Accidents, deaths, exaggerated foolhardiness or visible fear and cowardice have no place in the arena, and destroy the esthetic effect of the drama. It is wrong for the bullfighter to die in the arena; it is the bull who must die. Along with the bull and the matador there is a third person on the stage: death enters with them, and the amphitheater is one of the few places where one can study Death up close. Not a visible masquerade-death, not a theater-death, but the living, invisible Death, the majesty itself. But he is to take the animal, not the matador.

Hemingway adds that bullfighting is a good thing to write about, precisely because one meets death here, "and death is a good thing to write about. " The same book contains the famous lines about how love can't end well, because even if all other dangers are surmounted one of the parties will outlive the other. And a man who has outlived a good wife is the loneliest of all human beings. The end is always very sad. He cloaks it in a conversation with "Old Lady".

*"It must be hard to be a man," she says.*

*"Yes," replies Hemingway; "very few survive it."*

We must return for a moment to Hemingway's claim that a bullfight is not a sport but a tragedy in three acts, where every detail is determined in advance. There is also an entirely different word for such a play, such a tragedy, in which all is predetermined and proceeds according to a fixed ritual, but we shall come back to that later. Both in the hunting stories and in the bullfighting book it is evident that as a rule Hemingway's sympathy is partly, and sometimes completely, on the side of the game or the bull; he identifies sometimes with the man, sometimes with the beast, but most often with both.

This gives the whole an inner and distinctive ambiguity, which I've found in no other descriptions of beast and man; they have life and death in common, and they meet there. Hemingway's books teem with fishermen, and naturally these descriptions of nature are of a quite different, more ethereal character than the others; for good reasons they aren't so bloody as war, big-game hunting and bullfighting. Fish and fishing have an entirely different function in his writings than game, beast of prey or bull. The lonely man with the rod fishing endlessly up and down a river seeks what all fishermen with a spiritual life get out of fishing: peace of soul. In its universality it quite simply belongs with being outside, with being alone in the woods and camping out, sleeping deeply, and looking at the river when you wake the great, slow river. Fishing is to a much greater degree a convalescence than hunting can be.

Only against the background of the strangely dark pathos in Hemingway's work as a whole does it acquire its full meaning. If you follow the main lines through Hemingway's writings, you will very easily discover that everything deals with a sick, mortally wounded man's fight to overcome the dread arising from his meeting with life. And in his later books, both in the vilified Across the River and Into the Trees and in The Old Man and the Sea, a figure emerges who is as liberated as a conscious human being can be.

In any case the aging Hemingway hero is a wholly different person, and much more healthy, than the young one. It is also natural that in Across the River and Into the Trees we are transported, along with the old officer ready to die, back to the places where other Hemingway heroes many years earlier, during the First World War had their first and worst war experiences.

*Let us sum up some of the chief themes in Hemingway:*
*Dread of life and death; overcoming that dread.*
*Big-game hunting. (War.)*
*Bullfighting.*
*Fishing.*
*A fixation on the Mediterranean region.*

The last point, the fixation on the Mediterranean basin, also embraces as a kind of substitute Cuba and parts of Latin America. Most of Hemingway's books take place in Italian or Spanish-speaking countries, and he has an unusual command of both languages (as well as German and French). Regarding the first point I shall merely note that Hemingway has never made a cult of his dread, on the contrary he has tried to hide it so far as possible; and this may well be the main reason for the snarling and almost inarticulate contempt he shows for T. S. Eliot and the modernism linked with Eliot's name. (Ezra Pound, on the other hand, he befriended and admired.) Hemingway believes with all his might in a kind of "will to health"—and if this belief at times takes the form of a cult of the macho with clearly infantile features, it's worth bearing in mind the fifteen-year-old who found his father after a suicide by shotgun.

In For Whom the Bell Tolls he touches on this indirectly by letting the hero think about his father, who also shot himself, and reminisce about how he had felt when he understood for the first time that his father was "yellow. " It is undeniably strange to hear a grown man label a suicide as "yellow," but a person must have some way to keep going. It is necessary to state that Hemingway wants to be healthy; and this will to health despite everything must be regarded as the truly moral element in Hemingway's writings. It is in the deepest sense battle literature, where the battle in reality takes place within the hero, and only apparently outside him.

*This "apparently" is significant, for it reveals Hemingway's use of symbols.* We are used to a "modern(ist)" symbolism (e. g. Tarje Vesaas in this country) in which the "symbols" are not an organic part of the action, but are artificial contrivances labeled in big red letters:

Note: Symbol! In Hemingway the symbols are implicit; they follow the laws of reality to such a degree that in themselves they form a whole, full-blooded story, completely "right" and "exciting" on the external plane as well. The reader is at liberty to discover that he is dealing with very profound and true, really durable symbols. Most readers don't discover it at all, and read Hemingway approximately the way they read ordinary adventure yarns.

Consciously and unconsciously Hemingway trusts that reality itself is built up of symbols which possess sustaining power; and this gives his writing the ambiguity which makes it true myth, and hence alive and lasting literature. On the writer's part it's a matter of treating reality with respect, and then using his eyes to see with. Just as you do in Rilke you will find in Hemingway that the words "precision," "exactitude," etc. continually recur when he writes about writing. Without this trust in reality a writer might as well let his pen be. The world will get along splendidly without him.

This use of real symbols is what makes literature both an exact science and an art. Without it no truth can take up residence in a book, and what you write will never serve on several planes. It will never become truth in the full meaning of the word. Every book must be built on one of the primal mythic themes which we know from fairy tales, myths, legends etc. In literature there is no other possibility than the retelling of myths; the old motifs must be rediscovered, the world deciphered.

In The Hunt lies one of the great motifs, in the primitive hunt, the fight between human and beast. Ancient heathen and Christian pictorial art contains one of the most powerful and richest motifs in existence. The true fight between man and beast takes place within the person in the inner forest, jungle or what you will. That is the locus of the fight. Within the individual the feral forces and the human forces meet. The animal is dread, savagery, rapaciousness, often of majestic size and beauty. The hunter follows the spoor, fights, kills or tames the beast. It is strength, speed, nature meeting thought, cunning, perseverance. It is a game, but a great and serious game. A drama. The next stage of the relation between man and beast is that of the shepherd, who doesn't kill but protects. Only then is the human master of the beast.

Hemingway says of bullfighting that it is not a sport; it is a tragedy with a precisely predetermined plot. We have another word for the content of such an expression, namely: cultus. The Spanish bullfight descends from three sources: the ancient Roman arena, the circus which was spread all over the Mediterranean basin; from the bullfights in Crete; but above all from the Mithraic mysteries, which were widespread around the Mediterranean and had their origin in Asia Minor.

The cult of Mithra went through a great expansion within the Roman army in the period before the birth of Christianity. Mithra was the god who was born on earth in a cave, and became the master and conqueror of the "bull" which represents the human instinct and passion. He was the victor over the bestial nature. That bullfighting has remained alive in a particular corner of Europe, in Spain, Portugal and Southern France—and in parts of Spanish-speaking America—must be bound up with deep-seated traits and needs in the psyche of the people itself.

In any case one is dealing with a passionate and violent national character, stamped by the Inquisition, wars, vendettas and violence, strangely combined with a high and unique, complex culture. The church knew what it was doing when it allowed bullfighting to live on. It is obvious that in bullfighting Hemingway has met a symbolic world which reaches very deeply into whole subconscious which drives him on so violently—and which is clearly divided from his conscious being by a very thin layer, precisely because of his liability, all the terrified sensitivity which has been his inborn torment.

The book about bullfighting, Death in the Afternoon, is—to a stronger degree than any of his other books—written by a sick and despairing man. Death is present on practically every page, and Hemingway's need to see it whole both from the bull's and from the matador's side is never denied. He feels himself one with them both.

I know no other writer who evokes the mood of the decadent world of antiquity so strongly as Hemingway does; an infinity of darkness, passion and suffering forms a sounding board behind practically everything he has written. All of The Sun Also Rises could have taken place during the last days of Pompeii. And no one else shows a stronger need to escape from it. The road from the Michigan woods where Hemingway grew up to the amphitheaters of the Roman Empire is not so long as one would think. But the bloody sand from the arena, and the cold clear water in the trout streams and in the Black River, are very different things.

It looks as if what for Hemingway unites modern America with the decadent Roman empire is first and foremost cruelty—a total absence of everything which one in the deeper sense can call Christianity. Lynching of Negroes, violence and murder—that is Hemingway's picture of America. He hates his homeland more ardently than any other American writer. Only the woods and the Black River are different. Through all the dark and heavy, bloody production which Hemingway now has behind him, there runs the story of the fisherman; the boy with the fishing pole, the war veteran by the trout stream, and the last, great image: the old man and the sea.

What is the fish?

What happens to a person when he has taken a fish up out of the clear deep cold down there? The fish stands as one of the most meaningful symbols from Christian antiquity. It was the chief sign, the secret mark by which the Christians recognized each other. The symbol built on the letters in the Greek word for fish: ichthos. I and Ch which stand for the initials of Jesus Christ, and the three next letters for the initials in the Greek words for God's son, the savior.

The fish itself, drawn or carved on stone and brick, is one of the most common relics we have from the life of primitive Christianity. Yet the image "fish" is by no means exhausted by a mere explanation of the literal meaning. Too much lies behind and beneath. The Fisher King in the Grail legend. The apostles were fishermen. Somewhere deep down in the unconscious we know what "fish" means. Franz Werfel says in a poem about a healing spring that this radioactive, healing water comes from a source lying so deep under the earth that the Fall didn't reach it. Something similar applies to the fish. All who have really fished know that when the line sinks in the water, then one is in another world.

So deep, so primal is the very activity of fishing, that it still has complete mastery over the soul. It is an image of the sort which C. G. Jung calls an archetype; it has endlessly deep tracks in the psyche, and the action reaches down into our most archaic layer. The fly, the hook, or the spoon bait which enters the water sinks in reality down into the mind. Everyone who has fished knows that fishing yields some of the loveliest material for our dreams. Only in dreams is one a true Fisher. A dream about fish and fishing is the highest blessedness; the great, dark, arrow-swift shadow down in the air-clear water is life itself. It is just because fishing is such a strong and symbolic activity that it is such a thoroughly therapeutic part of life. The fish is from before the Fall, and everything around it is purity, health, life and blessedness. And it lives in the pond, in the river, the lake, in the ocean. The fish has purity as a life element. Watch a trout moving between the stones at the bottom of the river! The ocean and the lake and the river are not merely purity; they are also life's first dwelling-place; they are nature's mother-world, all things' origin, ground and source. The great healing doctor. The point and the surface, the star and the ocean all meet here.

The Old Man and the Sea is the modern book which in my perception comes closest to Greek tragedy. Not in exposition, peripeteia, catastrophe, etc., but in its purely inner attitude. Here the man and his fate are all alone. Man. Sky. Sea. Boat. If these four words don't mean more than man, sky, sea, and boat, then there isn't a word in the world which means anything whatsoever. All external circumstances are taken away, only the human and the battle remain.

Deep, deep under him, down in the darkness, blue, there moves a being, wet, shiny, big and strange. What kind of thing is it?

It is the Fish.

Who knows it? Who has seen it? Who knows where it comes from? It is life's mystery incarnate which he has beneath him. The mystery itself, everything strange on earth the only, only thing which counts. Everything else is babble, gibberish, dust and ashes. He is on the ocean with life. He has contact, connection with it; through the thick wet line he feels the vibration of its secrets. Who has understood the expression in a fish's eye?

Who is the swordfish? It is the ocean's proudest, most dignified, bravest, noblest possession. It is strong enough to swim more than 60 miles an hour, strong enough to drive its sword through oak planks two feet thick. The man pursues it from the jolly boat. Alone. Alone. For three days it drags him out to sea, farther out than any fisher before him. This is a fairy tale, a fable, just as deep and true as "The Fisherman and his Wife" in Grimm. He talks to the fish, and he understands it. He is close to the very inmost, ultimate thing in life. And he takes the fish.

Then he sails back to land with the fish lashed to the side of the boat. It is bigger and more beautiful than any fish he has ever seen before. And there is no doubt about it: This is the fish; the last proud beautiful secret of life. Then come the sharks. He defends the fish, but they take it, piece by piece. They come, bite, go. They "come like pigs to the trough" and the ones he kills with knife, harpoon and club use their last death throes to swallow the mouthful they have taken. When he sails into Cuba's harbor at night, nothing but the skeleton remains of the fish. But it is the skeleton of the biggest swordfish seen in Cuba in human memory.

The story of The Old Man and the Sea is the truest and deepest portrayal ever achieved of Hemingway and his writings. It is the first victory signal he has sent, and it tells us everything we can know about Hemingway: No one has been further out to sea. No one has caught a bigger fish. And no one has brought less home with him.

## Chapter 8

# Winter in Bellapalma: Harbinger of Works to Come

Italy and Germany are the two cultures which most strongly impart a cosmopolitan flavour to Jens Bjørneboe's writing. Both crop up in his poetry, novels, essays and plays. For Bjørneboe they have a polarity which finds its strongest expression in his two pivotal works from 1966, Moment of Freedom and The Bird-Lovers. Bjørneboe's knowledge and love of German culture was deep but because learning about Nazi atrocities at a vulnerable age had shocked him into his first awareness of human evil intensely ambivalent.

On the other hand, Italy stood for healing, in myriad ways which are detailed in his most complex work, Moment of Freedom. Leif Longum comments that, while Italy and its culture likewise play an important part in Bjørneboe's writings, this relationship is a happy one, free of the ambivalence he felt towards everything German. He hardly ever mentions Fascism, for instance, a surprising fact in view of his preoccupation with German Nazism and all it stands for. It is as if Fascism was just an unfortunate accident, unrelated to its Italian background.

Among Bjørneboe's first published writings were a series of travel essays written in 1950 for the Oslo newspaper Aftenposten—which often included drawings by the author, such as a trattoria in Florence. Since Bjørneboe at that time had recently made the transition from painting to writing, it is no surprise that Italy and its art loom large in his early poetry, with poems on Cimabue, Donatello, Michelangelo,

Lorenzo the Magnificent, the San Callisto catacomb, and more. When a multi-pronged crisis plunged him into a severe depression in 1957 it was to Italy he fled, remaining for a year and a half. The comic novel Winter in Bellapalma, published in 1958, dates from this period. It is a tongue-in-cheek tribute to Hemingway (Bjørneboe had published the essay Hemingway and the Beasts three years earlier), and uncharacteristically lighthearted for Bjørneboe. So different was it from the novels of social criticism for which he had become known that it was all but ignored in Norway at the time, and still tends to get short shrift in discussions of his work.

And yet it prefigures his later writings in important ways. The middle section of Moment of Freedom, "The Praiano Papers", is based on material written at around the same time nearly a decade earlier than the rest of the novel. In the interim between Winter in Bellapalma and the two works from 1966 Bjørneboe discovered Brecht. In a 1964 essay, "Ernest Hemingway and Bertolt Brecht" (a juxtaposition, perhaps, that only Bjørneboe would make), he quotes Brecht's line, "Those who laugh have simply not yet gotten the dreadful news."

He continues:

In Hemingway and Brecht, this knowledge of the "news" is obviously inborn, and forms the point of departure for the work of both as writers; their common problem is thereby given from the first syllable: How shall one manage to live in this world at all?

It appears that Winter in Bellapalma was a spinoff of the battle with depression recorded in "The Praiano Papers."

Bjørneboe was discovering "Florentine laughter" as a tool for his own his survival:

This laughter is the reason why the Tuscans invented science and the clear Tuscan drawing in their cool paintings; laughter means distance. Conversely: where laughter is absent, madness begins the moment one takes the world with complete seriousness one is potentially insane. The whole art of learning to live means holding fast to laughter; without laughter the world is a torture chamber, a dark place where dark things will happen to us, a horror show filled with bloody deeds of violence. While Bjørneboe's early novels are not devoid of surrealistic humour, he had not yet learned to integrate "Florentine laughter" with other elements in the way that is characteristic of his later work. The comedy of Winter in Bellapalma and the despair of "The Praiano Papers" were kept in separate compartments, as it were. Bellapalma bears a strong resemblance to the pretty whitewashed tourist and fishing town toward the end of "The Praiano Papers." The cosmopolitan, alcoholic narrator first appears here, but in comic mode.

The novel's affectionate lampooning of the Italian style of invective could be seen as a preliminary exercise for his tongue-in-cheek use of invective in his later books. The climactic showdown between the macho fisherman Tomaso and the gay ballet dancer Martin brings to mind the description of the bullfight in Moment of Freedom, in which "the bullfighter has danced the bull into impotence." But it is The Bird-Lovers which Winter in Bellapalma prefigures most strongly. Central to both is the theme of the impact of tourism and easy money on the fabric of the community.

The plot of Winter in Bellapalma revolves around the fishermen's demand that the town resources be diverted from building more tourist amenities to constructing a breakwater—which would improve the fishing but destroy the beach, and hence the tourist trade. Since the area has been fished out and the nearest fishing grounds destroyed with dynamite, this plan is unrealistic. Here again we see an inversion of Hemingway: The fishermen's revolution loses momentum when they realise that they would have given up their present easy life to go far out to sea in all kinds of weather. By contrast, Bjørneboe's essay on Hemingway concludes a discussion of The Old Man and the Sea with this comment on its author: No one has been further out to sea. No one has caught a bigger fish. And no one has brought less home with him. The burlesque of Winter in Bellapalma is replaced by savage satire in The Bird Lovers. Bellapalma has already become a tourist town, and it is made clear that there is no way back to the status quo ante. In The

Bird-Lovers the question is whether the tourist entrepreneurs can be prevented from taking over in the first place. The deal depends on the natives' willingness to sacrifice a favourite traditional pastime hunting and cooking songbirds in favor of creating a bird sanctuary.

Of Hemingway's hunting, Bjørneboe writes:

It is evident that as a rule Hemingway's sympathy is partly, and sometimes completely, on the side of the game or the bull; he identifies sometimes with the man, sometimes with the beast, but most often with both. This gives the whole an inner and distinctive ambiguity, which I've found in no other descriptions of beast and man; they have life and death in common, and they meet there.

In The Bird Lovers the Italians' identification with the songbirds is brought out in a surrealistic scene in which three of the characters are discussing methods of capital punishment and three others are discussing methods of cooking songbirds:

*Caruso*: We will have a real dinner today!

*Cavalli*: The electric chair is the worst in America

*Rosa*: So delicious.

*Cavalli*: In America they also use the gas chamber.

*Rosa*: with white beans.

*Marco*: The electric chair isn't so bad. You pass out at once and

*Piccolino*: Smothered in oil and lemon and garlic. Delicious small birds.

*Fidele*: They jump and squirm in the chair for quite a while and it smells like burnt flesh in the room

*Picclino*: Do you roast them on a spit, Rosa?

The tourist entrepreneurs, meanwhile, turn out to be former Nazis who once occupied the village. For all their sentimental talk about "our feathered friends," the birds they identify with as shown on their posters, and in the Song of the Bird Lovers are predators:

*Birds are sweet and kind, but man is mean and full of hate.*
*Anyone who kills a bird will earn a tragic fate!*
*Buzzard, kite and vulture's kin,*
*Eagle, hawk, and peregrine!*

The natives' desire for revenge on their former oppressors further complicates the plot, but it does not follow the expected trajectory. The excerpt from Winter in Bellapalma, The Town Fathers Quell a Revolution, invites comparison with The Bird-Lovers' final scene. The role played by the town priest, Father Leone, in resolving the conflict in favor of "progress" is a clear prototype of Father Piccolino's role as defence advocate for the Nazi war criminals in The Bird-Lovers.

*Bjørneboe wrote in his 1971 essay "Literature and reality":*

We live in a world which is characterized not by problems, but by dilemmas—problems which can't be solved. If literature brings solutions, if it brings answers, then it lies. With its reality-content it can only contribute to posing the questions more sharply and clearly and drastically than before.

The question posed in Winter in Bellapalma—and still more sharply, clearly and drastically in The Bird-Lovers—is whether any other values, idealistic or otherwise, can stand up against economic greed. The biting pessimism and the mock-exultation with which The Bird-Lovers ends should not obscure the empirical spirit in which Bjørneboe continually struggled to write.

## Chapter 9

# A Clean, Well-lighted Place

Nineteen-fifty four Nobel Prize winner Earnest Hemingway's short story A Clean, Well-Lighted Place written in 1933 is a story of despair and loneliness. Unlike so many of his other stories when his characters are reflected as heroes, this story is perhaps written on a more personal level that might give us some insight to the man that Hemingway really ways.

Born in Illinois in 1899, Hemingway's life was influenced early on with literature as he became a reporter directly after high-school. He served in WWI, in which he became seriously injured and then lived in Paris for a time. His passions were writing and hunting. In many of his other works, his characters typically displayed courage and integrity. Suffering from a mental condition that caused memory loss, Hemingway took his life with his favourite shotgun in 1961, an act very much unlike most of his literary characters, but surprisingly foretelling. In A Clean Well-Lighted Place Hemingway unwittingly relates the main character to himself.

A Clean, Well-Lighted Place is a story about a lonely, but dignified older gentleman who basically has insomnia and can't sleep. He is not like other men who go to bodegas and bars. He does not go to party or to meet women. He goes to escape the darkness, and to have a drink. It is also mentioned in the story that he tried to kill himself, but was saved by his niece.

There are three main characters in this story, the two waiters and the deaf old men. Also mentioned are the old man's niece and the barman at the end of the story, but these are not fully developed characters. The waiters have two different views towards the old man. The younger waiter assumes that since the old man is financially stable then he has nothing to despair. He views him as a vagrant type because he only can see him as a drunk who holds him up, and on occasion who gets so drunk he leaves without paying his bill.

*"Last week he tried to commit suicide." one waiter said.*

*"Why?"*

*"He was in despair."*

*"What about?"*

*"Nothing."*

*"How do you know it was nothing?"*

*"He has plenty of money."*

The younger waiter has resentment towards the older man because he has a lot waiting for him at home, and he is eager to get home. He says,

*"I wish he would go home. I never get to bed before three o'clock. What kind of hour is that to go to bed?"*

*"He stays up because he likes it."*

*"He's lonely. I'm not lonely. I have a wife waiting in bed for me."*

*The younger waiter gets more and more impatient, he says, "I wouldn't want to be that old. An old man is a nasty thing."*

But the older waiter defends him because he understands, being older himself, and similar in nature to the old man, he says, "Not always. This old man is clean. He drinks without spilling. Even now, drunk. Look at him." Shortly after this the younger waiter kicks the old man out.

The dialog between the two waiters establishes a difference between the two that is very distinct. The younger waiter is eager to get home, he has a wife that he loves, a warm bed to go to, and he has time on his side. He has the ignorance that only a younger man who has not yet experienced the world has about him. He cannot see past the liquor that the old deaf man drinks to see that he is good and different from the other patrons that come to visit their cafe. And he cannot distinguish between the clean, well lit cafe and the dark bodegas that stay open all night with vagrants.

The older waiter is very similar to the old man. He understands the loneliness that the old man feels. He says "We are two different kinds." "It is not only a question of youth and confidence although those things are very beautiful. Each night, I am reluctant to close up because there may be some one who needs the cafe." The younger man still not quite understanding replies, "Hombre, there are bodegas open all night long." "You do not understand. This is a clean and pleasant cafe. It is well lighted. The light is very good and also now there are shadows of the leaves." The older waiter sees the cafe for what it is. They say goodnight at this point.

The older waiter and the old man both have a fear of nothingness, going home to nothing. The nothingness that the dark night brings. It was a fear of being nothing, it was something that went away when it could be seen in a clean and well lighted place or in the light of day. In the end, the older waiter is forced to go out into the night also. He goes to a bodega, so that he does not have to go right home. Before he goes, he does some self-examinations. He asks himself what it is that he fears, and his answer was "nada y pues nada y pues nada" which essentially means, "Nothing, and then nothing, and then nothing."

To all of those whose waking hours are spent in the still of the night, this story speaks to you. For everyone who has ever been alone in the still of the night, when it was dark, and all you ever wanted was a clean, well-lighted place to go to, this story is about you. Old or young, rich or poor, there are people out there every where that fear "nada".

## Chapter 10

# The Sun Also Rises

The book the sun also rises by Ernest Hemingway contains 251 pages filled with sadness, devastation and lost love. The plot is based on real people the Hemingway knew and that angered a lot of his friends, if any. Robert Cohn, the main character, is feeling inferior because he is jewish and starts a boxing career to feel better about himself. He married the first girl he meets out of college. Then, he meets a new woman in ca and then takes her to Europe with him while he is working on his novel.

He returns to the US To get it published. His friend, Jake Barnes, who lives in Paris, is asked by Cohn to travel to South America with him to watch bull fights and meet women to "fall in love with". Jake, not interested, stays close to home. "Listen Robert, going to another country doesn't make any difference. I've tried all that. You can't get away from yourself by moving from one place to another. There's nothing to that." However, by staying home, Jake finds trouble.

Jake goes to a cafe and meets Georgette, a beautiful woman with an awful smile whom Jake finds boring. Jake takes Georgette to BAL, a dance club and while there, he meets Lady Brett Ashley, the "love of his life" and she is also an alcoholic nymphomaniac. Cohn shows up and also gets infatuated with Brett. However, Brett leave with Jake and Cohn is now extremely jealous, while Georgette is left alone but later leaves with someone. Jake and Brett ride around Paris talking about how they want to be together but can not. Jake goes home later that night, thinks about Brett and ends up crying himself to sleep. "This was Brett that I had felt like crying about. Then I thought of her walking up the street and stepping into the car, as I had last seen her, and of course in a little while I felt like hell again." He wakes up at 4 am to the sound of a drunken Brett arguing with the landlord of Jake's building. She gets up to his apartment but soon leaves and instead, asks Jake to meet her the next day.

Brett, either confused or playing with Jake's mind, also has a Count meeting her. Cohn stops by the next day and takes Jake to lunch. Cohn keeps bugging Jake about Brett until Jake tells him that Brett is engaged at the moment. Cohn "confesses his love" for Brett. Then, Jake annoyed by Cohn's questions tells him to "Go to hell I misjudged you You're not a moron. You're only a case of arrested development." Brett unfortunately never shows up to meet Jake. Though Jake runs into his old friend Harvey Stone who is a unlucky and at the time poor gambler.

Cohn shows once again that he is a fighter, not a lover. He and Stone nearly fight and Frances embarrasses Cohn in public and he took it in silence. Brett and the Count show up later that night at Jake's house for drinks and Brett and Jake talk more about how they "love" each other. After they dance together, Brett tells Jake that she is leaving to San Sebastian for a while. Jake later that week spots Brett at a cafe with Mike Campbell, her fiancée.

Mike succeeds at inviting himself and Brett on Jake's trip to Spain. When they arrived in Spain, it was a week full of partying and drinking. They party all night and Brett meets Pedro Romero, a Spanish Bull fighter. Brett falls in "love" which only causes more trouble for her and Jake. On one day of the "fiesta" it rains and there are no bull fights. Jake and friends have a drink with Romero and while Brett talks to Romero, Mike is very rude. Once again, Cohn almost starts a fight. After Jake helps arrange a meeting between Brett and Romero, Cohn demands to know where Brett is and when Jake does not tell him, Cohn calls Jake a pimp and beats him up. Jake then returns to the hotel only to find Cohn crying and begging for forgiveness. Jake is reluctant but finally forgives him. Cohn then plans to leave Spain in the morning. The next morning, Jake finds out that Cohn also beat up Romero and Romero asked him to leave in the morning. Brett still spends most of he time with Romero. Romero does very well in the last bull fight.

Brett leaves with Romero and does not say good-bye to Jake. After, the festival is done Jake heads north to San Sebastian where he swims and relaxes after being in Spain. Only there a few days, Jake receives a telegram from Brett who is in Madrid and needs help. Jake cuts his trip short and heads to Madrid. Jake locates Brett in a poor motel. Brett tells Jake that she asked Romero to go because she did not want to hurt his feelings. Jake comforts her and they leave the hotel together and again, talk about their lost romance.

## JEALOUSY IN "THE SUN ALSO RISES"

In the novel The Sun Also Rises, by Ernest Hemingway, a reader is forced to decide weather the spite that the Jake has for Chon originates from Jake's racist background, or his deeply seeded jealousy of Chon for having a brief affair with Brett. Even though it is clear that Jake has racist views, the hatred he has for his former friend Chon is strictly based on the jealousy he feels towards Chon for the weekend he spent with Brett.

Jake goes in to great detail about Chon's early life. He speaks highly and admiringly of Chon, but in a condescending way. A reader get her first hint on page one that Jake has some racist feelings toward Chon. He speaks of how Chon's nose was flattened in a boxing match and concluded the sentence with " and it certainly improved his nose". This can be taken as a reference to the stereotypical "Jew" nose that is often associated with Jewish people. Jake and Chon are close friends, and Jake likes him up to the point where he becomes involved with Brett. Jake goes on and on about all of the relationship mistakes in Chon[1]s life.

There is an hint of jealousy that appears in Jake's tone. He states that women began to become attracted to Chon as he got older, and that it changed him so that he was not so pleasant to have around. There is racism in Jake[1]s tone, but

Jake[1]s problem with Chon is strictly one of jealousy. By this time Jake has already developed an extreme distaste for Chon's endeavors with women, but these feelings their peak when Chon and Lady Brett have a brief affair. Jake, having unconditional love for Brett, blames the entire incident on Chon. In turn, Chon makes as point to rub it in Jake's face. Jake says " it was giving him pleasure to be able to talk with the understanding that I knew there was something between them" Jake has a great deal of trouble dealing with this. It has nothing to do with the fact that Chon is Jewish, Jake is merely jealous of him.

It would not be manly for Jake to openly admit his jealousy, and blame the jealousy on his harsh feelings toward Chon. As a result Jake falls back on the fact that Chon is Jewish, and uses that as an excuse for his anger. One of the reasons that Jake was so hurt by Chon[1]s affair with Brett was that Jake knows that Brett will always love him, and has no feelings for Chon other than a temporary lust. Chon is unable to accept the fact that Brett does not care at all for him, and he makes it very difficult to for people to enjoy his company. "Bill says he makes me sick and he can go to hell, and I am damn glad he is staying here ").

These is not a racial based opinion, Chon just has an unpleasant personality. Everyone in the group agrees that Chon's presence is not enjoyable, but nobody feels it the way Jake does. In this story Jake allows the woman that he to loves run his life and occupy his thoughts. Jake is a bitter person, and he is living in a time of unhappiness and depression that resulted from the war. The hate he feels for his former friend Chon is not one of racism; before the incident with Brett they were close friends. This is just another case of a woman coming in between two male friends. The affair might not have even affected that relationship; it is Chon's reaction to the affair that spoils the friendship. Jake is jealous of Chon because he knows that Brett loves only him.

## THE LOST CHARACTERS

In the novel The Sun Also Rises, by Ernest Hemingway,

the lost generation is discussed. After the WWI, many were affected in different ways. This post-war generation is described by discrimination, lack of religion, escapism and inability to act. The First character that is introduced into the novel is Cohn. He, as an outsider, is Jewish.

Throughout the novel he is looked down upon in one way or another, but already he is separated from the rest which is shown when he is being described: "He had a hard, Jewish, stubborn streak". This quote already shows that he is Jewish, and therefore different from the rest. Also, the fact that his streak is `hard [and] stubborn" shows that he is hard to deal with or be around. Even thought he is discriminated against, he is one of the very few that inform these people of the `lost generation' exactly how worthless they are when he says to Jake "You know what's the trouble with you? You're an expatriate. One of the worst type Nobody that ever left their own country ever wrote anything worth printing.

Not even in the newspapers") and "Hello, you bums" He literally rubs into Jake's face what kind of a waste he has become once he left his country. It is rather surprising that the one who is much disliked and discriminated against sees the worthless characteristics of the others. The significance of the word `bums' used must be noticed since a bum is an idle worthless person by definition. This very well describes the `lost generation.'

Nevertheless, racism isn't the only separation that the people make. Even the concierge, who one would think would not be too proud, "[takes] great pride in telling me which of my guests were well brought up, which were of good family, who were sportsmen, a French word pronounced with the accent on the men. The only trouble was that people who did not fall into any of those three categories were very liable to be told there was no one home, chez Barnes). This shows how important wealth and back ground is, but the ones who are part of the `lost generation' are not included into any of those simply because their background is forgotten, and they are all worthless people. Though this might not be seen as racism, it sure can be seen as discrimination.

Also, the people from the 'lost generation' weren't intact with any religion in specific. Even Jake "was a little ashamed, and regretted that [he] was such a rotten Catholic, but realized there was nothing [he] could do about it, at least for a while, and maybe never). This shows how these bums literally lack religion as a whole, they know the concept but have no hope. In this 'lost generations,' everyone is constantly trying to escape. However, Jake understands that there is no better place then any other when he says "'Listen, Robert, going to another country doesn't make any difference. I've tried all that.

You can't get away from yourself by moving from one place to another. There's nothing to that). This really shows how lost this generation is, and even though traveling might be used, it is not helpful in the long run. Also, it shows that Jake has already tried to escape by traveling to different parts of the world, yet he is left to be the same part of the 'lost generation.' Meanwhile, while Cohn, the scapegoat, tries to escape this reality, he "takes a bath, has a shave and a haircut and a shampoo, and something put on his hair afterward to make it stay down. It can be seen that though he is in a way an outsider, he still finds it necessary to, in some way, to escape this reality and the worthlessness.

Meanwhile, Jake remembers from the war that "There was much wine, an ignored tension, and a feeling of things coming that you could not prevent happening. Under the wine I lost the disgusted feeling and was happy. It seemed they were all such nice people). This shows how alcohol helped the now veterans escape reality, which is a habit that follows them even after the war. It lets them, for a little while, forget who they really are and all their troubles. The fiesta was also a get away where "The things that happened could only have happened [there] Everything became quite unreal finally and it seemed as though nothing could have any consequences. It seemed out of place to think of consequences during the fiesta). This shows how this other way of escapism provided the same for the worthless, and the amount of alcohol beverages was unlimited, to fuel the escape.

Also, this 'lost generation' is shown by Jake's inability to do what he should towards Brett. He admits it when he says "That seemed to handle it. That was it. Send a girl off with one man. Introduce her to another to go off with him. Now go and bring her back. And sign the wire with love. That was it all righ). This shows how he is unable to act the way that he should, especially if he is supposedly in love with Brett.

The way that he contradicts his desires with his actions and the worthlessness of his actions show the instability of the 'lost generation.' The book ends with the quote "Yes Isn't it pretty to think so". It is significant because it shows that even thought everything is gone, escapism remain. Jake says so after hearing Brett out while she questions what might have happened between the two of them. He admits that it would be nice to think so, but reality is harsh and not every wish comes true if one is a part of the lost generation.

In conclusion, the 'lost generation' was literally lost. Their actions did not lead to anything positive in their lives and their discrimination was pointless. Most importantly, instead of doing something about their problems, these bums used escapism which also didn't get them far. Without hope, these worthless people weren't worth much and did not live their lives as good as they could have. That is the story of the 'lost generation.'

## LOST GENERATION

Ernest Hemingway's The Sun Also Rises (1926) has been considered the essential prose of the Lost Generation. Its theme of alienation and detachment reflected the attitudes of its time. In fact, the term "Lost Generation" was originally coined in a conversation by Gertrude Stein, a member of the expatriate circle in 1920's Paris. While spontaneous and meaningless when first spoken, the expression would unwittingly go on to become the label for the expatriates from the United States and England who had rejected traditional American and British conventions for the more appealing lifestyle of Left Bank, Paris.

Congregating in cafés located along the Boulevard Montparnasse to drink, talk and watch the crowds pass by, the Lost Generation was comprised of exiles who had spurned the pre-war values of love, romanticism, optimism, prosperity and hope that they had grown up believing in, all shattered by the war. As well as the glitter and potential of the Great Boom of the 1920's, which they now saw as American and money-based, and therefore corrupt and insincere. Unable to reconcile themselves with their past beliefs, and unwilling to accept those of their present mainstream society, the Lost Generation was left morally bankrupt and spiritually sterile, with only the fleeting pleasures of alcohol and sexual promiscuity as comfort.

Many Americans in Paris became bohemian writers and artists as a reactionary protest to the business- and consumer-based culture in the United States, their days spent lounging in cafés and their nights hopping from one meaningless relationship to the next. For the Lost Generation, love, hope and religion were foreign concepts after WWI, replaced by a world of sexual liberty and moral indifference. The lounging in the cafes and the promiscuity of the generation is very much connected with their traumas from the War. They are suffering from post-traumatic stress and are trying to deal with it.

In 1926, Ernest Hemingway wrote The Sun Also Rises, a semi-autobiography based on his adventures in France and Spain in 1924-25. Despite having already received moderate critical acclaim for his prior works, it would be this novel that would gain him international success and make him the leader of the so-called Lost Generation. Focusing on the events that took place between a group of American and English expatriates traveling from Paris to Pamplona, The Sun Also Rises was an immediate success and almost instantly became a bible for many disillusioned individuals after it was published because it was the first piece of fictional literature that had fully captured the feelings of moral decay and social alienation shared by the Lost Generation:

"You're an expatriate. You've lost touch with the soil. Fake European standards have ruined you. You drink yourself to death. You become obsessed with sex. You spend all your time talking, not working. You're an expatriate, see? You hang around cafés."

The satirical portrayal of the Robert Cohn, the last chivalric hero and defender of an outworn faith, and his absurd willingness to endure public humiliation for Lady Brett Ashley's unforthcoming affection, served only to reinforce the Lost Generation's belief that love had died in WWI, as did all the other pre-war values that Cohn unwaveringly stood for. While tragic in that the source of Cohn's persecution came exclusively from those who simply could not understand his obstinately idealistic outlook, the fact that his mere existence was nonetheless a painful reminder to the expatriates of America's betrayal was enough to justify their racist and spiteful actions.

It was also the universal quality of Hemingway's other characters, which reflected every type of individual in the Lost Generation from the defeated exiles who had accepted their empty, meaningless lives to the expatriates who had acknowledged the moral and spiritual decline of society but were unwilling to surrender themselves to the hollow existence that it offered, and the actions of these individuals that made The Sun Also Rises so appealing to its audience. While some readers found themselves in the characters of Bill Gorton, Mike Campbell and Count Mippipopolous, who had resigned their lives to ethical stagnancy and the superficial pleasures of cynical humour, casual indifference and expensive wine, many others associated with the characters of Lady Brett Ashley and Jake Barnes, the American expatriate whom Hemingway had originally based on himself.

Jake's quest to rediscover his moral bearings through his pilgrimage to Burguete and Pamplona, he tries to built up a new set of values during the novel and more or less establishes a new elite of people who are "in" or "out", as well as Brett's moral redemption in the final act at Madrid, were echoed by the thousands of expatriates in Europe who were desperate to find their lost hope and values. Furthermore, unlike his passive companions, Jake's unwillingness to accept his disconnection from God ("I was a little ashamed, and regretted that I was such a rotten Catholic, but realized there was nothing I could do about it, at least for a while. I only wished

I felt religious and maybe I would the next time.") and his inability to love ("Oh, Jake, we could have had such a damned good time together." "Yes, isn't it pretty to think so?"), was a source of inspiration for Hemingway's generation, a sign that there was a possibility of salvation for a group that seemed destined to be lost forever.

## UNCONDITIONAL LOVE

In the novel The Sun Also Rises, written by Ernest Hemingway the main character makes a decision to introduce the woman he loves to a young bull fighter. Jake makes this decision very much against the will of his friends, but in doing so he pleases.

*Brett*: Jake does this because he is unconditionally committed to Brett, and is willing to do whatever necessary to bring her happiness, even if it is only temporary.

Jake's first reaction to the news that Brett is interested in meeting and spending time with Romero is one of negativity. He learns of this from he friend Montoya and tells him "Don't give him the Message". He did not think that it would be a good idea for Brett to have anything to do Romero, and did not want him to receive the message that invited him to have coffee with their group. At this point it is clear that Jake does not approve of this proposed encounter. His later decision to introduce them supports the idea that Jake is unconditionally devoted to Brett, and her happiness.

The introduction was a very strange one. It was not as if Jake went out of his way for it to happen. It was much more the will of Brett. She raved on and on about Romero and insisted to Jake that they go and find him. Jake did not fight her on this issue, but he certainly did not provoke it. Jake was more of a stooge for Brett. She would have had her way even if Jake had not helped her. She uses her feminine charm, and there is, little that Jake can say. At one point she says "Oh, darling, please stay by me. Please stay by me and see me through this.

Jake is to wrapped around her finger to refuse. There is no question in Jake[1]s mind that he will be losing Montoya as a friend and also the respect that others had once held for him, yet he choose Brett over these losses. Jake even goes as far as to make an agreement with Montoya that he breaks upon the introduction of Brett to Romero. It says when Romero walked into the room he started to smile, but then say the group with Romero then at that point "he did not even nod" This was at the first introduction.

The real damage had nod even been done yet, but Jake proceeded because he wanted to make her happy. In this story Jake is forced with a decision that will change a great deal of his life. He decision ultimately costs him a good friendship, and takes away the respect that his other friends had once had for him. He does this consciously and unselfishly without hesitation. This does not mean that he has lost his moral creditability as a character, but rather the opposite. Jake becomes a stronger character after this because is shows his unconditional devotion and love for Brett.

## THE LOST GENERATION

The book The Sun Also Rises, by Ernest Hemingway is a perfect example of what life was like after the war. It was about unrealistic love of a young Lady Brett Ashley, and the post war adventures of Jake Barnes and his friends. "In an age of moral bankruptcy, spiritual dissolution, unrealized love, and vanishing illusion, this is the lost generation," and that is exactly what Hemmingway writes about in The Sun Also Rises.

Jake Barnes lived a real casual life style. He is a writer that goes out with his buddies almost every night, and drinks. "Oh Jake", Brett said," we could have had such a damned good time together." His only true desire is a Lady Brett Ashley, he is madly in love with her but all he can do is sit back and watch her toy with the other men. Many times he has purposed his love to Brett, she loves him as well, but will not have a romantic relationship with him because her sexual desire is too great and Jake cannot have a sexual relationship because he has no penis, it was castrated during the war.

Jake was also an "aficionado" of bull fighting during one of his fiascos he and his friends and Lady Brett Ashley went to Pamplona. First Brett introduced her new fiancé named Mike, a war veteran and a bankrupt drunk. Mike would later get on Robert Cohn's case for bugging Brett and acting like a stalker. Cohn and Brett had a brief fling in San Sebastian, but Cohn could not accept that Brett had no emotional feelings for him and that love affair meant anything. Cohn doesn't realise that Brett is a permiscius lady. During that week, Jake, Mike, and Bill (Jake's Friend) relize how much they hate Cohn and they all start to antagonize him.

While at the bullfights, Brett falls in love with a young "matador" named Pedro Romero, Jake helps her get involved with Romero, Cohn finds out and beats up Jake, and Romero, and then Cohn leave Spain and goes back. Brett realizes that she will only do Romero harm and asks Jake to take her away from him. It seems every time Brett would get in trouble Jake would always come to the rescue, because he is hopelessly in love with her. But Jake doesn't realise he is her scapegoat, and so he keeps running to her every time she is in need of help, hoping that someday she will return the favor with accepting his love for her.

Jake goes through so many conflicts, and the primary reason is the aftershock of the war. In The Sun Also Rises, Hemmingway portrays a life style of dissolution due to the effects of the war. Jake Barnes, Robert Cohn, Mike, Bill, and Lady Brett Ashley are all part of a generation of lost morals and vanishing illusions; they are all part of the lost generation. In this paper, I will describe what critics have to say about Ernest Hemingway's novel The Sun Also Rises and his short story A clean well-Light Place. First I will describe the basic plot of the story, then go one to describe each of the characters by what the critics have to say about them. I will start off with the main character and narrator Jake Barnes. Then go to Lady Brett Ashley, Robert Cohn, Pedro Romero, and finally I will fish off that section with a little about Bill Gordon. Then I will describe a little of how Ernest Hemingway's characters fit into what critics have to say about the story.

After that, I will then go into describing how the four American Themes were used in the novel. After that, I will evaluate the criticism of the book using one or two quotes from the book. From there, I go into my next literary work. I describe the basic plot of A Clean Well-Light place. Then I describe the themes of the story. I then go on to describing the criticism, or at least what I could find on the short story. I continue with my evaluation of the criticism of the book. Also using one or two quotes.

I conclude my paper by giving my evaluation of each of the works, and evaluating the author's style, content, and themes. In The Sun Also Rises, meet Jake Barnes, the main character and narrator of the novel. He and his friend Robert Cohn meet a lady named Lady Brett. Here is the story of their adventure. In The Sun Also Rises, a group of young Americans move to Paris after World War I. Jake Barnes, a newspaperman who is in love with Lady Brett Ashley, Robert Cohn, a Jewish former Princeton student who was outcast, Lady Brett Ashley, an older Englishwoman who also love Jake Barnes, but can't consummate their love because he was wounded in his genitals.

As they travel through Paris drinking and sitting at cafes, they met up with Brett's fiancé Mike Campbell and his friend Bill Gorton. Jake plans a trip to Pamplona, Spain for a festival full of bullfighting and the running of the bulls. Before everyone got to Spain, Mike, Brett and Robert already being there, Mike and Brett decided to take a side trip to San Sebastian. Robert followed them like a lovesick puppy. While in Spain they met up with a bullfighter named Pedro Romero, who Brett falls madly in love with. After the festival is over, Brett leaves with Pedro and goes to Madrid, Mikes goes to a town on the French border, Bill goes back to Paris, and Jake leaves for San Sebastian to relax.

When Jack arrives, he finds out that Pedro wants to marry Brett, but she turned him down. She tells Jake about how happy they might have been together. The conflict of this novel is that one loves another and that person loves someone different. No one can truly get what he or she wants. Jake tells this story in first person. Psychology of the individual was definitely present in this novel. You could always tell what

Jake was thinking. American Dream is also present because everyone wanted to have the perfect life. 'The difficulties of interpreting The Sun Also Rises in a clear and relatively certain manner stem in the main from two factors: the use of a particularly opaque first-person narrator; and the fact of Jake's wound which has rendered him impotent, while leaving him normally responsive to sexual desire. The first factor results in the bewilderment a reader will have in trying to locate the norms of 'truth' in the novel; that is, since the entire novel related directly by Jake Barnes, the reader can never be sure how reliable Jake's observations and judgments are.

In the novel, Jake goes from being at a stage of anguish and at times, a state of self-pity at the beginning to accepting himself as he is at the end. He also discovered the appreciation of nature, companionship, and bravery. Jake emerges as the Hemingway Hero, a cynical realistic individual who will hide his feelings in himself and who will await the inevitable reckoning which life presents itself, of the novel. In book one, we start to see the outlines of the Hemingway Hero in Jake. He is capable of showing sorrowful, deep emotions. He is also tender, compassionate and thoughtful. You see this in Jake when Brett and Jake have their initial meeting together. Until meeting Brett, Jake was more interested in Robert Cohn.

Readers may think that Cohn is Jake's best friend because in the first chapters, most of the information is about Cohn. As the story continues, the narrator unmasks Cohn. We discover Cohn not being the pleasant companion, but the ant! i-hero to Jake.

Jake becomes more aware of Cohn's boy-man personality in Chapter IV when two lovers argue. So in the end of Book one, Jake goes from being a friend to being suspicious and increasingly belligerent acquaintance of his fellow American. Early on readers usually make the conclusion that something is wrong with Jake. It is implied that that he can not have sex. When Spain comes into to play with the story, Jake changes in a very distinct way. He loves Paris, but he loves Spain in a very different way. His French capital provides him with a refuge from the States, the chance to live individually and freely. Jake feels an intimate contact with the nature and existence when he's in Spain. Because of her four lovers and the attendant fact that the plot, such as it is, revolves about the ensuing complications, Brett stands out as the most fascinating protagonist of the total group of actors in the novel. Without a doubt, Brett is very colorful and adds an exotic approach to his characters. Although Brett appears rather late in the novel, she begins to dominate the action in Book one. Just like Jake and Robert, Brett wears a mask.

They also identify Brett as an extreme example of the 'lost Generation. Robert Cohn is labeled one of the most bitter verbal depictions of a character in the novel. He is the exact opposite of the Hemingway Hero. Hemingway probably described Cohn as a Jew, not for any overt demonstration of anti-Semitism but to explain part of the young man's problem. Some critics have read into this character a Hemingway attack on the defects of the American character. If this is true, and there seems to be more than a modicum of accuracy in the criticism, then the unfavorable attributes of American youth are: a basic immaturity, reliance upon physical strength, a thin veneer of romanticism, the lack of appreciation for the simple virtues of companionship, good food and drink, and the inability to adjust to the demands of an older civilization.

Robert Cohn is an example of the boy-man, the adolescent playing the role of a mature individual. Without Cohn's presence in the novel, the positive morality would not have been so fully illustrated; one arrives at a clearer understanding of Jake Barnes and Pedro Romero's dedication to life and death. Cohn is basically bewildered by the world of his contemporaries and he does not understand the members of his own generation. He doesn't belong to the group he associates with. Hemingway is implying that Cohn does not belong in Europe. In Book two, Cohn is more sentimental and requires more recognition and appreciation.

Cohn is also bored at the festival in Spain and is critical and cynical the whole time. Pedro Romero is the young Spanish matador who enters the story late, and is not involved in much of the action in general. In a lot of ways, Pedro is an idealization of the Spaniard: concise pride, honour, and bravery. 'Romero is untamed and uncorrupted by the decadence of the modern world so that he is fundamentally a symbol and a stereotype rather than a living complex to fathom. Some say that Romero is the answer to the rush of American civilians and youth in the rise of the death in Europe after World War I. Bill Gordon, is probably one of the most successful characters. He also belongs to the 'lost generation in spirit and sympathy, but learned how to work hard, and he adjusted well to the 1920s.

'For many people in America, the years immediately following World War I and World War II were characterized by anger, discontent and disillusionment.' (Kwan, The Sun Also') This simple quote describes the main characters in this book. Jake is angry because of his wound, and that he can't consummate his love with Brett. Cohn is angry and discontent because he, same as Jake, can not consummate his love with Brett, but for different reasons. Cohn is the Hemingway anti-hero so he is very critical of everything and is not open for change. Brett is the disillusioned one. After losing the love of her life, she just gone from man to man, disillusioned that she'll find someone to make her whole, but she never does. The major themes of American literature in this work are psychology of the individual, American Dream, Individual in Society and Nature and the Land.

Psychology of the individual is shown through Jake Barnes. He tells the story through first person and you always know how he's feeling, and how he feels about the other characters. Although his feeling about the other character may be different from what the characters are really like, but that still shows what he is thinking. The war also plays a role in the Psychology. The war has implict the character's approach to daily life. American Dream is in this novel, but it's killed. Post-World War I attitudes of the characters disapprove of the war and the US getting into the war, so they've moved to France.

The war has left them with a cynical view of the United States, and therefore isn't as much American Dream as it is achieving their personal dreams. Individual in society is shown through each of the characters and how! they react to their surroundings and situations that occur. Brett being the very man-friendly woman that she is, has been known to have many relationships that mean nothing to her, and don't last her very long. Robert Cohn shows his views when he follows Mike Campbell and Brett around Sebastian the whole time like a lovesick puppy. Also when he is very critical of everything at the festival in Spain. Jake shows it through being the Hemingway Hero, how he over comes tragedy, first with Lady Brett, then finally with the acceptance his wound, and his impotency.

And finally the Nature and the Land, you have the background of the land, the rivers, the mountains and the plains. But unlike some of his other novels, this nature shows the aftermath of wrath and destruction after World War I, not during it. 'At five o'clock I was in the Hotel Crillion waiting for Brett. She was not there, so I sat down and wrote letters. They were not very good letters but I hoped their being on Crillion stationery would help them. Brett did not turn up so about quarter to six I went down to the bar" (Hemingway, The Sun Also Rises, 41) This quote show the emerging of the Hemingway Hero. He's beginning to get over his bitterness and starting to feel those deep sorrowful emotions that the stereotypical hero does. 'We often talked about bulls and bull-fighters. I had stopped at the Montoya for several years. We never talked for very long at a time. It was simply the pleasure of discovering what we each felt.'

This passage also agrees with the critics when they said that Paris has a special place in Jake's heart, but Spain meant something totally different to him. He loves Spain in a different way. He loved to learn about Spain and talk to people about the culture. In Paris, he liked to drink and sit at cafes. In A Clean Well-Lighted Place, two waiters are sitting at their cafe talking and waiting to close up. While they are waiting they are discussing the old man sitting out on the terrace, and why he would have wanted to commit suicide. As old deaf man is sitting out on the terrace drinking brandies, he flashes to the waiters for another. When the young waiter goes over to the table to tell him he's had enough and must go home because the waiter wants to close up and go home himself to his wife waiting in bed for him. When the waiters close up the cafe, the young waiter goes home, and the old waiter goes to find another cafe/bar that's open. He goes to another bar, and he discusses the nadas with another bartender. There isn't much American Dream, Individual in society, or Nature and the land. The only theme in this short story is Psychology of the Individual.

This comes at the end of the story when they discuss the nadas. The nadas, pertaining to nothing, and nothingness, these people discuss their fear of nothing, the clean well-lighted caf that the waiter works in is like a refuge for those that have no where to go, and need some, not nothing. The Hemingway hero doesn't make its appearance quite as obvious as it did in the novel. The older waiter would be the stereotypical hero in this short story because of wanted to help people escape from nada, just like he wants to.

He's trying to help others as he helps himself. This portrays the deep and sorrowful emotions by having a place for the lonely people to go to. 'Our nada who art in nada, nada be thy name, thy Kingdom nada, thy will be nada, in nada as it is in nada. Give us this nada our daily nada and nada us our nada as we nada our nadas and nada us not into nada but deliver us from nada y pues nada' This passage states that if you believe in nothing, you are nothing, and in a way you have noting to live for. You just wander around. In the story the darkness is the nothing and the nothing is death. The clean well-light place was a place where people could go to escape the nothing, to believe in something, and be something.

AS the two waiters sit in the bar they discuss why the man might have wanted to commit suicide. The young waiter can not understand the one man's despair. He doesn't understand how he can have all that money, and yet want to kill himself. The Sun Also Rises is a very good piece of literature. It has a very intreqit, well developed, easy to follow plot, and a very good portrayal of the four American themes. Ernest

Hemingway also has very developed, constant characters. Jake did change in the novel, but that was a physical, believable change.

Their attitudes are also very developed and intriqit with their surrounds after the war. The Clean Well-Lighted Place is also a very good piece of literature. Although in this short story, Hemingway sows his pessimistic side. He discusses even the riches people may be happy, but if they don't believe in something then they are nothing, and the poorest people who believe in something are the happiest. The darkness in this story is death and death is nothing, the light is life, and happiness. The old deaf man was happy sitting in the caf drinking his brandies in the well-lighted caf.

The older waiter wasn't very happy sitting the dark bar talking to the bartender and drinking. Their conversation describes the nothing that is surrounding them. They are all scared of the nothing, which is death, but the old man. He was the one with the courage to stand up and be he. He believed in himself, and believing in something is having something to believe in, not believing in nothing. Therefore the old deaf man was the happiest out of all the characters. Even the! young waiter who had his wife waiting for him at home.

Being a woman, I don't necessarily agree with Hemingway's style of disgracing the woman, and making all the men seem macho. But then again, if I were a guy, I'm sure I would be agreeing with his style of writing. Among the sexist characteristics that Hemingway has he is a very talented writer, and has written some very meaningful novels, that involve themes that still stand true today. His content is varies from book to book. The Sun Also Rises and A Farewell to Arms are during and post war activities. A Clean Well-Lighted Place having to do with death, and nothingness. By doing this Hemingway doesn't get boring by writing about the same topic every time he writes. Hemingway writes about all four themes. In The Sun Also Rises, all four themes come into play with the characters. A Clean Well-Lighted Place mostly has the psychology of the individual because of what the story pertains to.

## JAKE BARNS AS A CODE HERO

Ernest Hemingway is a renowned American author of the Twentieth century who centers his novels on personal experiences and affections. He is one of the authors named "The Lost Generation." He could not cope with post-war America, and therefore he introduced a new type of character in writing called the "code hero". Hemingway is known to focus his novels around code heroes who struggle with the mixture of their tragic faults and the surrounding environment. Traits of a typical Hemingway Code Hero are a love of good times, stimulating surroundings, and strict moral rules, including honesty. The Code Hero always exhibits some form of a physical wound that serves as his tragic flaw and the weakness of his character. In Ernest Hemingway's The Sun Also Rises Jake Barnes is the character who maintains the typical Code Hero qualities; while Robert Cohn provides the antithesis of a Code Hero.

Jake Barnes, the narrator and main character of The Sun Also Rises, is left impotent by an ambiguous accident during World War I. Jake's wound is the first of many code hero traits that he features. This physical wound, however, transcends into an emotional one by preventing Jake from ever consummating his love with Lady Brett Ashley. Emotional suffering can take its toll on the Code Hero as it did with Jake Barnes. Despite the deep love between Jake and Lady Brett, Jake is forced to keep the relationship strictly platonic and stand watch as different men float in and out of Lady Ashley's life and bed.

No one other than Jake and Brett ever learn the complexity of their relationship because Jake's hopeless love for Brett and the agony it entails are restricted to scenes known to themselves alone. Therefore, Jake suffers in silence because he has learned to trust and rely only upon himself, which is conducive to the Hemingway Code as well. Jake is an American who travels to Europe to satiate his appetite for exotic landscapes and to escape his pain. Jake tries to live his life to the fullest with drinking, partying, and sporting with friends.

With these pastimes, Jake hopes to hide from his fault and get on with the life he has been made to suffer. Watching and participating in sports help accentuate the Code Hero's masculinity and provide the sense of pride Jake has lost. This gain of pride is essential in the Hemingway Code. Jake attends fishing trips with friends, he visits Pamplona, Spain to witness the running of the bulls, and he acts as a mediator between arguing friends. These characteristics reveal his strong character built of courage and grace. Jake, as with any Code Hero, is a man of action who spends more time achieving goals than talking about them.

Jake's friend, Robert Cohn violates everything a Hemingway Code Hero represents. He is rich, gifted, and skillful and is ready to discuss his emotions in detail. Robert refuses to admit defeat when Brett rejects him repeatedly. Unlike Jake, when Cohn is hurt, he insists on complaining to everyone instead of suffering in silence. Cohn does nothing to assert his masculinity, either. He allows people, especially women to ridicule him and knock down his self esteem. Cohn obviously can not stand up for himself and does not take action when he should. Consequently, Robert has no self control. When a matador sleeps with Brett, whom Cohn is in love with, he takes out his jealousy by beating him repeatedly. Although a man of action, Jake, the quintessential Hemingway Hero, knows when to control himself, Robert Cohn does not.

On the whole, Jake Barnes strictly adheres to the qualities of the typical Hemingway Code Hero. He relies solely on himself, utilizes his assets, enjoys bullfights and other honorable activities. He is an individual of action and speaks not of what he believes; rather he just does what he believes to be right subtlety without any fanfare. Jake has lived with disappointment and frustration all his life, yet he overcomes it and uses the lesson to his advantage. On the other hand, Robert Cohn, who has had the easy life is the perpetual loser. He allows people to walk all over him and continually feels sorry for himself.

Robert Cohn is the false knight, who, in theory should be the victorious protagonist but will always turn out to be a shallow person who lives on the fringes of life. In the end, the person who does not possess the Code Hero qualities can never discover himself, and therefore never truly be happy young man by the name of Ernest Hemingway was born in 1898 and grew up in a suburb of Chicago Illinois. His father was a doctor. As a boy, he and his father spent time together hunting and fishing in Michigan. Hemingway wrote for his school newspaper. During his youth Hemingway also played football and swam.

After graduating from high school, Hemingway was hired with the Kansas City Star newspaper. While writing for the Kansas City Star, Hemingway began to develop his own unique style of writing. Later, Hemingway worked for the Red Cross as an ambulance driver during World War I. Only a few days before he would turn twenty years old, Hemingway was wounded in the leg and sent back to the United States. In 1921, the Toronto Star sent Hemingway to Europe as a journalist writer.

While in Paris he published two books. The Sun Also Rises was published in 1926 and was his first novel that made him a well-known writer. Hemingway loved to write about his adventurous activities. During the Spanish Civil War in the 1930's, Hemingway wrote For Whom the Bell Tolls. Many people thought this was one of his best novels. Hemingway later wrote a novel about showing the need to accept life with honour. In 1952 he published this novel entitled The Old Man in the Sea.

Hemingway won the Pulitzer Prize in 1953 for this novel. Hemingway loved to experience nature. He loved adventure; and enjoyed hunting, fishing, and watching bullfights. These adventurous experiences helped shape his style of writing. Young writers later copied this style. They also copied his style of writing in short and direct sentences. Hemingway looked at life as a game. He shaped literature into writing about how mankind is eventually totally defeated. He has been put down for writing about how men are always tough and not be afraid of danger. Hemingway became depressed during the last years of his life, and shot and killed himself in 1961.

## ALLEGORICAL FIGURES

The Sun Also Rises is a novel by Ernest Hemingway (1926). Hemingway deliberately shaped the protagonists in The Sun Also Rises as allegorical figures (Bloom, 1985, pp. 107). The novel symbolizes the impotence felt by the main characters after World War I. Jake Barnes, the narrator, had a wound from an "accident" that happened during the war. The injury damaged his genitalia.

As a result, Barnes could no longer make love, but could still feel the desire. Barnes felt physically less than a man. Barnes made a comment about hating "homos".

This shows that Barnes was insecure about his masculinity. For this reason, he later found himself strongly attracted to the young bullfighter, Pedro Romero, whose manhood stood without women. The wound is a symbol of life in the years following World War I. It was used as a metaphor of the impotence felt after the war. The wound can also be seen as a parable that reminded Barnes constantly that accidents could always happen and could not be prevented. This can be seen in a passage from the novel. "It was like certain dinners I remember from the war. There was much wine and ignored tension, and a feeling of things coming that you could not prevent happening."

Lady Brett Ashley was also an allegory of the impotence after the war. She first appeared with a group of homosexuals, she wore a man's hat over her short hair, which gave her a masculine appearance, and she spoke of men as her fellow "chaps". All completed the distortion of sexual roles and released her from her womanly nature. This is similar to Barnes' condition. Brett stepped off of the romantic pedestal to stand beside her equals. Robert Cohn was an old fashioned romantic. He lived by what he read and neglected reality. Women dominated Cohn. To make him feel like a man, Cohn became a boxer. Boxing turned him into an "armed romantic" Cohn became an editor and a novelist.

He liked the authority of editing and the honour of writing, but was a bad editor and a poor novelist. He looked for internal strength in outward signs. Cohn always found himself ready to fight for a woman and when he did, he knocked down his opponent like a knight. However, when Cohn went against Pedro for Brett, Brett told him off, Pedro wouldn't fall, Brett stayed with Pedro, and Cohn went home alone. This shows the difference between physical and moral victory. Pedro fought with dignity and his spirit remained untouched by Cohn; Cohn's spirit was crushed. Cohn based his manhood on skill at boxing or on a woman's love, not on internal strength. Cohn found that romantic love was dead.

Pedro Romero's manhood stood without women. This was the reason that Barnes was so attracted to him. "Cohn and Pedro are seen as extremes and Barnes remains the unhappy medium" Romero provides an image of integrity against which Barnes and his generation are weighed. From this point, Pedro can be seen as the real hero, man whose code gives meaning to a world where love and religion are defunct, where the proofs of manhood are difficult and scarce, and where every man must learn to define his own moral condition and then live up to them.

Hemingway purposely shaped the main characters in The Sun Also Rises as allegorical figures. Jake Barnes and Brett Ashley were two lovers desexed by the war. Robert Cohn was the false knight who challenged their despair. Pedro Romero personified the good life which will survive their failure.

## "THE SUN ALSO RISES" ALIENATION

What I would like to show you by writing this essay is that for many individuals in many different generations, for some less for others more explicit, the time they live in does not fit their outlook on life. Because of this they live different lives than their generation and the cultural setting and standards of their era would expect them to live. They feel alienated and left out, or they are strange in the eyes of others, eccentric even, they do not fit in their time and the set of moral and aesthetic standards they live in.

These are the individuals, of whom I could give you many examples. However, what is more interesting to me, sometimes an entire generation in a certain cultural setting, environment and time, can experience a feeling of alienation, estrangement, of having no ties with the past and no ties with the present or the future too. Not an individual who feels stranded in the wrong time, in the wrong place and perhaps even on the wrong planet. No, an entire generation living in a vacuum, feeling completely alienated of their time, waiting for the future, waiting for their lives to start.

The cultural settings of an era are due to many factors. The period I would like to describe is called the roaring twenties, its generation The Lost Generation. The early years of the Twentieth century were dominated by the First World War which dragged the United States in a war it did not want. The Communist uprising in Russia that had as a consequence a completely new map of the world and which wiped out the last of the autocratic nobility. The new inventions like cars, airplanes, radio, electric light, which in the twenties resorted into house-hold appliances like washing-machines and vacuum-cleaners.

There was hope but it was false hope. The hope was based on old values and thoughts and on unstable economical and political forces. The years immediately following World War I were besides hope also characterized by anger, discontent, and disillusionment. Society had been devastated by a global conflict that resulted in unprecedented death, destruction and resentment. The survivors who came of age during this era just after WW I, were termed the Lost Generation, they were left disjointed and alienated from both the world before and the new world that emerged after.

Many of the generation left their homes to roam the world, to look for better morals and better lives unable to identify with either pre- or post war values, both of which, after the war, seemed deceptive and perverted. They became social exiles and were abandoned by their country and left to rediscover and redefine themselves in a world that had stifled their hopes, dreams and beliefs, in a world that after the war looked superficial and was based on economical values.

It was during this time that literature in an attempt to capture the attitudes, emotions and opinions of the generation took a different tone and view. Because of the stream of consciousness, started by James Joyce and further developed by other authors like Virginia Woolf, literature had the tools and could therefore describe the feelings and outlooks of an entire generation. The works of the most successful writers of this generation literally became bibles to those who thought they had lost their identity but had rediscovered themselves in these books.

To such people, these novels became their defining elements, and by resurrecting their individualism, they had found a point of departure from which they could finally rebuild their lives. In the period following the First World War, one novel emerged as the dominant literary work that best captured the disorder felt by the common man. It is semi-autobiographical, written by an individual who felt as disillusioned and abandoned by society as the rest of the generation did.

## THE SIGNIFICANCE OF THE TITLE OF "THE SUN ALSO RISES"

A good title is one of the most important elements of a book. A good title can hint at the theme and is something to keep in mind while reading a book itself. A very effective title is one that teases the reader, makes him ponder over its meaning and relationship to the book. One such book/title is The Sun Also Rises by Ernest Hemingway. The title suggests an importance of time and a cyclical motif. Yet it also has a hopeful tone, focusing more on beginnings than on endings.

There are many cycles in the book and one of the most evident is that of Lady Brett Ashley and men. Brett has affairs with Cohn and Romero in the course of the book. In both cases there is a process of wooing, acceptance, and eventual rejection that takes place. It is also suggested that having affairs is a common practice for her, making that a cycle in and of itself.

The idea of cycles is also evident in a more ritualized form through the bull fighting and the Catholicism. Bull fighting is a very stylized affair that is mentioned throughout the whole book. Catholicism is also very ritualistic and is concerned with a religious cycle of life, death, and resurrection. Both add to the cycle motif Hemingway creates. One of the best examples of cycles and the passage of time is the contrast of Romero and Belmonte. Belmonte is an old bull- fighter who has passed his prime; his sun is setting. Romero is a young bull- fighter who is just coming into his own; his sun is rising. Belmonte, "no longer had his greatest moments in the bull- ring.

He was not sure that there were any great moments". This contrast suggests the cycle of life and death. Good bull- fighters come and go. Just as Romero is in his prime, someday he too will be an older bullfighter, unable to move with the same grace he had in his youth. This cycle of life and death can be seen on a much larger scale by looking at the ex-patriots. The ex-patriots are members of the post- World War I generation that is sometimes referred to as the Lost Generation.

They went through the horrors of War and depression in their young lives and found themselves living in Europe and seemingly devoid of morals, spirituality, and purpose. This might lead one to think that their best days are passed, but I do not think that is what Hemingway believed. The title "The Sun Also Rises" suggests that while things might be bad for them now, there is always a tomorrow. Hemingway is hopeful for the future and dismisses the past and present by showing it as part of a greater cycle. There is another possible interpretation of the title and that is as a sexual metaphor. The sun may be rising but Jake's winky sure ain't. With this interpretation there seems to be a theme of unrequited love. Jake loves Brett and she feels the same about him. Yet he is an incomplete man.

He lost a part of himself in the war. To a certain degree his whole generation lost something in the war. And that is why they struggle on trying to find satisfaction and fulfillment in life, yet never able to fully achieve it. The sun is setting on the lost generation; their best days have passed them by. And that is why the thirty-four year old Brett cannot be with the nineteen year old Romero. They are on different sides of the cycle. It is also possible that Hemingway is saying that the sexual nature of relationships is not important. This is a bit of a stretch but if one looks at the title as in contrast to Jake's impotence, then it basically means: so what if your winky doesn't rise, the sun does.

The title "The Sun Also Rises" is great in that it makes the reader ponder its meaning and relevance to the story. Why did Hemingway not call the book "The Sun Is Setting"? He shows enough images of loss and heartbreak to give this book a possible depressing tone. Yet that is not the ultimate message. He is not trying to dwell on the fact that the fiesta is over. That is because there will be other fiestas. The Sun Also Rises is about cycles. One can never be saddened by an ending, a new beginning is always just around the corner. And so although the sun may set on good times, it always rises again.

## THE MALE CHARACTERS

Before World War I, the world had a set of expectations for what a man should be. After the war, the brave soldier returned, but only after being stripped of these qualities. The war involved a lot of time huddling hopelessly in trenches and dugouts that were under enemy bombardment. Furthermore, many of the soldiers developed close relationships with one another. These friendships became quite intimate, and with a need for sufficient food and clothing, they began to rely on each other for emotional and domestic support. World War I thus feminized the male soldier, revealing a much more sensitive person beneath the uniform.

With a newfound closeness between males, the army had to establish a difference between what was an acceptable form of male relationship, and a deviant one. In spite of homosexuality being considered deviant, males could still have equally intense emotional bonds, as long as they remained nonsexual. An anxiety towards homosexuality and a feeling of inadequacy towards his own male character followed the soldier through peacetime. In a world changed forever, the male characters in Ernest Hemingway's, The Sun Also Rises, struggle to face their new role as a male, and prove to themselves and others that they are still masculine.

The character Jake serves the symbol for the man who has

been feminized by the war. His wound has rendered him impotent. He is no longer a man since he cannot perform the male sexual function. But Jake is not the only one, every man who came out of the war was changed, not in the same way necessarily, but in an equally demeaning manner. Their wound would be considered mental. The experiences of the war left them unable to fit the previous definition of "male." The horrific conditions of World War I warfare shattered the prewar notion of the brave soldier.

The men became helpless and weak, and this did not conform the ideal of a tough and stoic soldier, who fights with courage to perform his duty for his country. Humility and fear forced them to re-evaluate themselves. Unfortunately, after the war, the world still expected the same from them, and this is where a struggle started. Jake's struggle is physical; he is expected to be able to provide sexual love for a woman. This disability challenges his relationships, particularly with the character Lady Brett.

Brett refuses to establish a commitment to him because he cannot make love to her. Brett's definition of romance requires the act of penetration, and she is unwilling to settle for alternate forms of sexual pleasure. For Jake, it is impossible for him to be the same man he was before the war, and Brett's presence constantly reminds him of his impotence. Other characters also reinforce his anxiety. One scene sets them in a night club, where Brett confronts Jake, and mentions she can get "safely drunk" with the crowd she is with. "'It's a fine crowd you're with, Brett,' I said." "'Yes. Aren't I? And when one's with the crowd I'm with, one can drink in such safety, too.'"

From the reading, one can deduce that the crowd Brett is with is homosexual. Jake shows an intolerance, "I was very angry. Somehow they always made me angry." His anger is irrational, and thus demonstrates the stress over his masculinity; these men still have the sexual ability Jake hasn't, but they do not take advantage of it. Jake's anxiety shows that he has been unsuccessful in regards to redefining himself as a male. Although his struggle is the result of a physical wound, it is symbolic for all men who made a similar struggle mentally, with the loss of masculinity. Hemingway refers to an anxiety over homosexuality, and masculinity in general, later in the book as well. This is when Jake and his friend Bill take a fishing trip together. Although Bill was not physically altered by the war like Jake, he retains the mental affects the war had on him. Bill constantly feels he must prove his masculinity to Jake. Although he loves Jake very much, he practically underlines the fact that he does not love him sexually. "Listen. You're a hell of a good guy, and I'm fonder of you than anybody on earth.

I couldn't tell you that in New York. It'd mean I was a faggot." Bill's trouble over close male relationships probably stems from his war experiences; the feminizing influence on male bonds. The war defined homosexual relationships as devious, and even though two soldiers could share an intense emotional relationship, this could never extend to sex. Even after the war, Bill finds it important to affirm the nonsexual nature of his relationships. Bill's joke about being called a faggot can be read as one such affirmation. Although he considers Jake his best friend, he finds it necessary to make it clear he does not love him sexually.

To Jake, this is probably obvious, and Bill's joke seems unnecessary. He even extends the joke to say that the Civil War was all about homosexuality. "That was what the Civil War was all about. Abraham Lincoln was a faggot. He was in love with General Grant. So was Jefferson Davis. Lincoln just freed the slaves on a bet." Bill jokingly explains that the Civil War was a result of repressed homosexual tension, and reveals his own hidden anxiety towards it. Perhaps Bill unconsciously meant to refer to World War I, replacing it with the Civil War. Regardless, this brief conversation manifests the notion that World War I created; that homosexuality is deviant.

This belief created an anxiety in it's soldiers that resulted in a false need to prove their heterosexuality. While Bill feels like he must prove himself, Jake must try even harder. These are just two men who's masculinity was affected by World War I. In some ways, these men feel like they must try very hard to live up to the image that has been sprung against them. In other ways, they feel like they have been changed forever, and it is now impossible to live up to this image. The result was a redefinition of manhood.

A coming to terms with certain unchanging aspects of oneself, such as Jake's impotence (the symbol of feminineness) had to be made. However, certain notions, such as the deviant nature of homosexuality, still made the men question themselves. The culture around them reinforced these sensitivities, and however far the men had come, still made them feel abandoned and inadequate. After these men had faced themselves, they still had to face society at large. A damaged masculinity was just one of the characteristics of the Lost Generation that caused a separation between them, and the rest of the world.

# Chapter 11

# The Life and Death of Hemingway

In novels or other literary works many authors write about things they dream about. Many write about what stories they have heard from fellow companions. None have written about such vivid, yet traumatic experiences as the twentieth century writer, Ernest Hemingway. That is why Hemingway's tend to concur to his real life experiences. To start, consider that he was raised in an extremely strict household. He was born and raised in Oak Park, Illinois. He had an equitably happy, upper middle class childhood. As he grew older he started having feelings of bitterness towards his parents, mainly his mother who was seen as selfish and magisterial by Hemingway.

When he was in his teens he became interested in literature. He wrote stories for his high school newspaper and subscribed poems and stories to the school magazine. When he graduated in 1917 he took a junior reporter position on the "Kansas City Star", writing feature stories. In his journalism he began to show interest in powerful yet objective writings of violence, despair, and emotional disturbance, which dominated his writings. He also participated in World War I, which greatly impacted his writing, as a Red Cross ambulance driver in Italy. He was wounded in both legs by a shrapnel explosion. He fell in love with the nurse that was caring for him, who left him not long after for an older man.

He returned to Oak Park, and also upper Michigan to write about his childhood, teenage, and wartime years. In 1921 he married Hadley Richardson, divorced March 10, 1927, he moved to Paris to further his writing career. Here he quit journalism as a result of his maturing as a distinguished writer.

From the maturity he had accomplished he was able to write over twenty-five books. He eventually returned to journalism to support himself. He was recognized as a major force in literature when he wrote A Farewell to Arms, One of the first novels in Hemingway's literary career. His first publication was Three Stories and Ten Poems, which didn't turn out to be a big success. But his most acclaimed novella, The Old Man and the Sea, which won him the Pulitzer Prize, tends to stand out overall.

This novel also is the one that mostly compares, in short, to his life. In the novella the main character is named Santiago, who is an elderly man but very strong willed and who also loved to deep-sea fish, as did Hemingway. Representing Hemingway's strong will, in that Hemingway survived three marriages and World War I along with several other wars. Santiago was also a drinker, that of which Mr. Hemingway was also a drinker, quite a heavy one at that. In the novella there was also a young Cuban boy by the name of Manolin. He was a courageous boy that loved the sea.

Many people believe this boy represented his son John Hadley Nicanor. Manolin loved the old man, like a son should love a father. The oldest of Hemingway's children loved his father very much, just like the boy in the story. Santiago was relatively poor; he lived in a small shack on the shore with hardly anything to eat or much money, which is how Hemingway felt, even though he was quite wealthy for his time. Hemingway was known for his drunken quarrels, he was very skilled in fist fighting.

Santiago was skilled in fighting the great fish that he caught as well as for his stubbornness well associated with fist fighting. The fish represented Hemingway's love life. The multiple divorces, wives, and death of one former wife, was like the sharks slowly eating away at the Marlin, that Santiago had worked so hard to catch. Santiago's travels to many different places on the ocean represents Hemingway's passion for travel, he traveled all over the world, from Spain and Italy to Cuba and Africa. He settled in Cuba, which is where The Old Man and the Sea takes place. In the fiction Santiago feels he is beaten by the elements of nature, the fish and the sharks. Hemingway was conquered by his own elements. Hemingway committed suicide, July 2, 1961, at about 5:00 a.m. in Ketchum, Idaho. He used a double barrel shotgun fired at the head; his father used a pistol. The many things that had recently happened overwhelmed him.

He had just undergone shock therapy for saying that the FBI was following him, but he couldn't convince any one that they actually were. The FBI was keeping tabs because he had lived in Cuba until Fidel Castro took over. From the shock treatments, he became very weak mentally. Disabling his writing ability, also believed to have collaborated to his suicide. In 1951 Hemingway's mother, Grace, died. All of these, plus many more could have contributed to his suicide and his being "beaten" by his own life.

## SOLDIERS HOME

Many of the titles of Ernest Hemingway's stories are ironic, and can be read on a number of levels; Soldier's Home is no exception. Our first impression, having read the title only, is that this story will be about a old soldier living out the remainder of his life in an institution where veterans go to die. We soon find out that the story has nothing to do with the elderly, or institutions; rather, it tells the story of a young man, Harold Krebs, only recently returned from World War I, who has moved back into his parents' house while he figures out what he wants to do with the rest of his life.

And yet our first impression lingers, and with good reason; despite the fact that his parents' comfortable, middle-class lifestyle used to feel like home to Harold Krebs, it no longer does. Harold is not home; he has no home at all. This is actually not an uncommon scenario among young people (such as college students) returning into the womb of their childhood again.

But with Harold, the situation is more dramatic because he has not only lived on his own, but has dealt with — and been traumatized by — life-and-death situations his parents could not possibly understand. Hemingway does not divulge why Krebs was the last person in his home town to return home from the war; according to the Kansas City Star, Hemingway himself "left Kansas City in the spring of 1918 and did not return for 10 years, [becoming] 'the first of 132 former Star employees to be wounded in World War I,' according to a Star article at the time of his death".

Wherever he was in the intervening time, by the time Harold gets home, the novelty of the returning soldier has long since worn off. All the other former soldiers have found a niche for themselves in the community, but Harold needs a while longer to get his bearings; he plays pool, "practiced on his clarinet, strolled down town, read, and went to bed". What he is doing, of course, is killing time. The problem, of course, has to do with Harold's definition of who he has become.

He recognizes he has changed, and this change is played out dramatically against the backdrop of a town where nothing else has changed since he was in high school. His father parks his car in the same place; it's still the same car; the girls walking down the street look like the same girls, except more of them have short hair now. Imamura comments, "Krebs admires them, yet he protects himself from the danger of sexual involvement as if he were still suffering from a previous affair".

And Daniel Slaughter observes that "One gets the sense while reading 'A Soldier's Home' that watching the girls was a healing process". What has happened here, really? Why is Krebs unable to adjust to life back in Oklahoma? Why can't he talk to girls, or manage to do anything productive with his time? These answers can be found in a careful examination of what Krebs was doing before the war and what happened while he was in Europe. Prior to the war, Hemingway tells us in the very first paragraph, Krebs attended a Methodist school in Kansas.

He was not out of place then; Hemingway says "There is a picture which shows him among his fraternity brothers, all of them wearing exactly the same height and style collar". There is a tremendous poignancy in this detail; at least one of these young men, so concerned about his appearance, would soon be shipped overseas to the most horrific war the world had ever known. The fact that his college was a religious institution is also significant, for it shows that he was, at that time, in synch with his mother's religious values.

At least, he did not have any reason to doubt them, or not enough strength to resist them (or her). Hemingway tells us before the first paragraph is over that Krebs "enlisted in the Marines in 1917". The Marines are an elite fighting force who today advertises they are looking for "a few good men" indicating that if the prospective soldier is not out of the ordinary, he need not apply.

However, was Krebs a good Marine? J.F. Kobler observes that there is at least some indication in "Soldier's Home" "that Krebs did not fight bravely in the war. Krebs admits to himself that he has lied in public about his military experiences, but he cannot stop lying to himself about the real extent and the psychological effect of his lying". We know for sure that he was "badly, sickeningly frightened all the time". Certainly his war experiences were not glamorous, and he brings home quite a collection of battle-scarred baggage, not the least of which is his guilt over having to live a lie.

Krebs even connects the politics of courting with "lying", which he has already told us makes him feel "nauseated". As Lamb points out, "The shadow that renders Krebs incapable of action and that lies at the crux of the story is stated in three sentences that follow immediately after his first statement that young women are not worth it: 'He did not want! any consequences. He did not want any consequences ever again. He wanted to live along without consequences.'

His desire to avoid consequences is his single overriding motivation. He fondly recalls the French and German women because relationships with them were uncomplicated and without consequence; there was no need even to talk. He wants the hometown women but does not act on these desires because they are too complicated and not worth the consequences. He is attracted to his little sister because he can shrug off her demands and she will still love him. But his mother repels him because her demands are complex and unavoidable" But it is not until his mother confronts him over breakfast about his future that he realizes that he cannot continue to live at home any more.

Robert Paul Lamb observes that before Harold's mother begins her lecture, she takes off her glasses; "this gesture seems to imply that she either can not, or does not want to 'see' him". His mother, in other words, does not want to be distracted by Harold's point of view while she is expounding on hers. This somewhat echoes his earlier observation that "Later he felt the need to talk but no one wanted to hear about it". Essentially, no one wants to recognize Harold's unique identity. His mother pressures him to get a job by arguing that "There are no idle hands in [God's] Kingdom," to which Harold significantly observes, "I'm not in His Kingdom" And he's not.

The world he discovered during World War I had no hand of God in it. His mother then observes that all the other boys "just your age" are settling down and becoming "really a credit to the community".

This hearkens back to the first paragraph of the story, in which Harold observes a picture of himself with his fraternity brothers, all sporting identical haircuts and collars. Harold is no longer like everybody else; he's not sure who he is, but he's sure of that. Finally, his mother asks whether he loves her. He replies quite truthfully that he does not. We know that this is because his entire worldview has been turned upside down by his traumatic experiences in the war, and the ability to genuinely love requires an emotional balance he does not have right now. But his mother does not understand this, because she cannot identify with his experiences; as Tateo Imamura observes, "Krebs' small-town mother cannot comprehend her son's struggles and sufferings caused by the war. She devotes herself to her religion and never questions her own values" (Imamura, 102).

So he lies to please her, and kneels down as she prays to please her and then he knows he has to go away. Harold lies out of an inability to force a painful issue and take a stand. He may feel that he acquiesces out of compassion, but in fact he is not secure enough in his own self to risk! a confrontation that could be painful or guilt-inducing. Harold veers onto the edge of self-revelation with his straight-forward answers about the Kingdom of God and his lack of ability to love, but when his mother begins to cry he waffles; she will never see that he isn't the boy he was in high school or perhaps, the boy she thought he was.

"I'm afraid of the rain because sometimes I picture myself dead in it" This is a short quotation from, A Farewell to Arms, (1929), by Ernest Hemingway. A Farewell to Arms has a very unexpected death in the end. The reader sympathizes with the main character as he matures from the beginning to the conclusion of the novel. A Farewell to Arms is a love story during World War I. The novel is centered on Lieutenant Fredric Henry, an American who has volunteered for the Italian army driving ambulances in Europe because the United States has not yet entered the war.

Fredric is known as being a lost man searching for order and value in his life. He is very subdued and does not care about himself or about the war. In the first book of the novel, Fredric is characterized, along with the other characters. Throughout the first book, Fredric takes a leave of absence from the war and travels the country looking for his purpose in life. During the second book, Fredric returns to the warfront town and meets with his closest friend, Rinaldi, who introduces Fredric to Catherine Barkely. Catherine is a French nurse with whom Fredric falls in love immediately.

Fredric finds commitment with her, and they start to spend time together. Their relationship brings order and value to his life. He starts to care more about himself and Catherine. Being away from the war, Fredric feels safe with Catherine. When they are together, the war seems to not exist. "The war seemed as far away as the football games of someone else's college," says Fredric Catherine is experienced when it comes to love and loss since she lost her fiancé in an earlier war. She cannot depend on another person so she tries not to depend on Fredric to bring order to her life and less chaos. This then allows her to be emotionally stronger when Fredric has to go off to war again.

While off at war, Fredric and his other driver friends are

sitting in a cave, when the Austrians attack. Fredric is hit in the knee while trying to help his friend, who dies. Fredric is taken to the hospital in Milan. When he arrives at the hospital, Rinaldi and Catherine come to visit him. During his recuperation from having knee surgery, Catherine becomes one of his nurses. Fredric and Catherine's love affair starts again. They now get to spend more time together and isolate themselves from everything and everyone else.

Book three is when Fredric realizes he doesn't want to be part of the war, but only with Catherine. Fredric convinces himself that he has a "fine life". Catherine then finds out that she is pregnant with Fredric's baby. After a few months, Fredric is sent back to the warfront and has to leave Catherine. While at war, Fredric leaves his troops because they did not follow his orders. German troops are looking for Fredric for leaving his troops. "Along the top of the stone bridge, I could see German helmets moving". Floating down the Taglimento River, Fredric goes through the Venetian fields and then rides a train to safety.

Returning to Milan, in the fifth book, Catherine is not at the hospital and has gone to Stresa for time off. They stay in a motel and find out that Fredric will be arrested if they stay there. Leaving during the middle of the night, they travel to Switzerland to find safety. There they live in the mountains above Montreaux until Catherine gets closer to having the child, and then they move into a hotel in Lausanne. Until the end of the novel, Henry relies on Catherine for order in his life. Catherine's and Fredric's love ends when Catherine dies of hemorrhages while giving birth to their stillborn baby. When Fredric sees his baby boy, he feels no sense of fatherhood and only wants to be with Catherine.

During the last paragraph, Hemingway characterizes Fredric, when he sees Catherine's dead body lying on the hospital bed for the first and last time. Henry's response was, "it was like saying good-bye to a statue". Fredric then realizes that Catherine was the only symbol of the order and strength in his life. "If people bring so much courage to this world the world has to kill them to break them, so of course it kills them.

The world breaks every one and afterward many are strong at the broken places. But those that will not break it kills. It kills the very good and the very gentle and the very brace impartially. If you are none of these you can be sure it will kill you too but there will be no special hurry." Hemingway describes the separation between Catherine and Fredric, in this quotation.

People deal with death in very different ways. In this novel, Fredric has to learn how to live without Catherine in his life. Finding strength from within will allow Fredric to go on with his life. "After a while I went out and left the hospital and walked back to the hotel in the rain".

## Chapter 12

# The Perspective of Ernest Hemingway and Bryce Courtenay

The cultural heritage of the writer affects the perspective in which they write from or about. The cultural heritage affects the writers perspective in many different ways, among them are stereotypes and the setting of the story and the everyday activities that the character go through. Two prime examples of how an author cultural heritage affects the perspective that they write from is the South African author Bryce Courtenay and the American author Ernest Hemingway.

Bryce Courtenay was born and raised in South Africa and received his early education there. He spends the majority of his adolescent life in South Africa and in his final year in Africa he spent it in the copper mines of Central Africa, before he moved to England to complete his education. Courtenay spent his early life in Africa, and the African culture had a profound affect him. His time in the copper mines also had a penetrating effect on him and it is visible in his writing, when he wrote about the mines in Africa. In the book The Power of One, Courtenay writes form the perspective of a young British boy in South Africa which shows how cultural heritages affect the writer's perspective.

It is apparent that the prejudices had a astonishing affect on Courtenay, especially with the hatred between the Boers, Blacks and the British. Because of the hatred going on in South Africa at the time of his growing up and even today, you can sense a tone of racism in his writing. "Please, Meneer, he hates kaffirs (blacks) just like you." Frequently in the book the black are referred to kaffirs and other derogatory terms. Through the years, because of wars and other disagreements the Boers have come to hate the British, and vice versa and the Blacks in southern Africa have always been hated ever since the white Europeans arrived.

This hatred started between the British and the Boers when the British first came to Africa during the slave trade. The Boers from Europe, had migrated to Africa for freedom, freedom of religion and of the prejudices that they faced in Europe. There was peace between the British and the Boers until the Boer republics were found to be rich in diamonds and gold. Fortune hunters, mostly British, poured in to stake claims, which belonged to the Boers. That is when the tension increased. Soon after was the Boer War, and since then there has been a great amount of tension and hatred between the British and the Boers. " he stopped halfway down the alley and shouted in Afrikaans, 'I'll get you back for this, you rooinek (redneck, a derogatory term for the English) bastard.'"

Time and time again in the book you can feel the tension and hatred between each of the groups in South Africa. Another area of his culture that is present in the book "The Power Of One" is that of sports. There all sports all over this book and in his writings. In the African culture sports are very big. The sports which are the biggest in Africa are rugby and boxing. Both rugby and boxing are key parts of the African culture in the book. Boxing is the central focus of this book as it is huge throughout all of southern Africa and especially in South Africa where the story takes place. It is Courtenay's growing up in Africa where boxing is a huge sport that affected his writing.

In many cultures sports is a key part of their everyday life. This is also true in South Africa. It's the sports that give them a source of entertainment. In South Africa at the time of this story, which is during and after World War II, sports were one of the biggest forms of entertainment, the whole society was shaped around the days sporting events. For many of the poorer people, like the blacks who were suffering from apartheid, sports were one of the only sources of entertainment. As it is mentioned in the story, some blacks traveled many of miles just to see Peekay, the main character of the story, fight.

You also see the cultural differences in the book. There seems to be different sports for different cultures. One of the sports that is perceived more civilized in the book is rugby. It is played by both the British and the Boers, but not the blacks. It is evident at the time that the British thought that they were better than the Boers and the blacks. The Boers thought that they were better than the blacks, and equal to the British. And the blacks seemed to know their place as the low man on the totem pole. So when it came to certain sports, not all of those groups were allowed to participate or would participate.

When it came to boxing in South Africa, it was reserved to the Boers and the Blacks. And was said that it wasn't proper for the British to box, but many still did. And when it came to boxing the British and the Boers didn't even what to fight the blacks. Courtenay's experience in South Africa and their culture is shown in great detail in the story. It is evident, through this story and that of Courtenay's experience growing up in South Africa and being exposed to their cultural, and everything that comes along it, has affected his writing.

So in fact his cultural heritage affected his writing perspective. His cultural heritage being that of South Africa's. Ernest Hemingway was born in the United States in Illinois, his lifetime spanned 63 years, and among those years he experienced a couple of wars and a great depression. Hemingway started writing at an early age, after he finished high school Hemingway got a job as a reporter on the Kansas City Star. During World War I Hemingway tried to enlist in the armed forces but was rejected because of an old eye injury. So he then volunteered as an ambulance driver on the Italian front, and in 1918 he was badly wounded.

After the war he settled in Paris, France, where he began to write fiction. Later in life Hemingway was a war correspondent in Spain, China, and Europe during World War II. It was during those years in the United States and the other countries where Hemingway developed his writing style. In his travel to those foreign countries Hemingway picked up pieces of their culture and their heritage with him. He took their culture and heritage added to what he had from home. Even thought he traveled a great extent of his life, he still kept his culture from home with him. It was these cultural experiences that he wrote the most about.

Almost his entire different cultural heritage's affected his writing perspective. They appeared in virtually everything that he wrote. Being in these cultures many times Hemingway had a first hand experience in their practices. In Hemingway's case the aspect of a culture that stuck with him the most was sports. Hemingway wrote the most about many sports including, hunting, fishing, bullfighting and boxing. All of these sports were brought to him by the cultures that he was visiting, and by witnessing these events his writing perspective was molded.

The short story by Hemingway entitled "Fifty Grand", is about boxing and the practices that go on in the American culture. In the story the over-aged welterweight boxing champion is set to fight a bout in which he knows he is going to lose to the young challenger. So the champ bets fifty thousand dollars against himself, and in the final round of the match, he has the opportunity to win, but opts to lose and take the fifty grand. As the Brennan the former champ said at the end of the story, "It's funny how fast you can think when it means that much money."

As in the South African culture boxing was very big in the United States, and it is still big today. That story reflected the American culture that was brought up Hemingway. The factor of the American culture that affected his writing is the idea of doing everything you can for a buck, no matter what it takes. As it is shown here, the cultural heritages in the United States affected Hemingway immensely. No matter where a writer is from or where they go to, it seems that they pick up a piece of a culture.

This piece of culture that they pick up also seems to work its way into their writing, sometimes it just bits and pieces of the culture, other times it is on a much larger magnitude. But this piece of cultural heritage ends up affecting the perspective of the writer. Many times it just a small thing that the writer picks up, and sometimes it is more, but no matter how great or how minute it is, it affects the author and their writing. Although the book, A Farewell To Arms by Ernest Hemingway was not the type of book that had an exciting page-turning story, it can nevertheless be called a classic.

A classic has been defined as "a book that lasts through generations because of its universality of theme, ageless symbolism, word choice and the ordering of detail." This book has a universal theme, several ageless symbols, and a classic style that is as easily read today as it was 50 years ago. Although there were several themes in this book, a major theme seemed to dominate the story. This theme is the importance of love and loss in a male-female relationship. These two lovers were so absorbed in each other that they needed no one else in their life. "'Wouldn't you like to go on a trip somewhere by yourself, darling, and be with men and ski?' 'No. Why should I?' 'I should think sometimes you would want to see other people besides me.' 'Do you want to see other people?' 'No.' 'Neither do I.'"

This conversation shows that Catherine loves him so much that she is willing to be alone just so he can be happy. At the same time, Mr. Henry would probably like to go skiing but would never dream of leaving Catherine alone. Death wins out over love. "'It is very dangerous.' The nurse went into the room and shut the door. I sat outside in the hall. Everything was gone inside of me. I did not think. I could no think. I knew she was going to die and I prayed that she would not. Don't let her die. Oh, God, please don't let her die. I'll do anything for you if you won't let her die ". Hemingway went on for an entire paragraph of him pleading with God.

This is how he is able to show that Mr. Henry loves her more than anything, more than life its self. In a way, I think that they loved each other too much. They did not go out often or do anything that was with other people. They were always together. This is an unhealthy life style. They were creating their own fortress and isolating themselves from the world.

'"My life used to be full of everything,' I said. 'Now if you aren't with me I haven't a thing in the world.'" This quote further supports the idea that they are isolating themselves from the world. Since they were so cut off from the outside world, Mr. Henry has even a more difficult time going back into the reality of life after her death. This theme of man and woman isolated in love and finally their loss to dark death is universal.

The most profound aspect of this book would be its ageless symbolism. The free-living, heavy-drinking life that Catherine and Mr. Henry shared could be compared to the heavy investing, speculating and consequence-free life of the 20's. The product that came from Catherine and Mr. Henry's lifestyle was a dead child. The result of the over- investing of the 20's was the great depression. So the baby symbolizes the depression. Another point to consider was that Mr. Henry was a deserter. He left the army to be with Catherine.

Desertion was illegal and he paid for it by loosing that which he loved the most, Catherine. Rain was connected with pain or grief. He drank to dull this grief or pain. Rain is wet and "wet" is connected with alcohol. "We had each been drinking out of one of the bottles and I took my bottle with me and went over and lay flat on the hay and looked out the narrow window at the wet country." In this scene, he has been thinking of Cat and he decided that it would be best to drink his troubles away. When Hemingway said that the land was "wet", it usually meant that Mr. Henry was drunk. After Catherine and the baby died at the hospital, Mr. Henry walked home in the rain.

"After a while I went out and left the hospital and walked back to the hotel in the rain." He had just suffered a major loss and dealt with it in the only way that he knew; through alcohol. Although drinking at this point was not actually mentioned directly, we can nevertheless assume that he was going to make this connection just because of the setting in the rain. This book had many examples of symbolism and they all point to the fact that there is always a terrible price to pay for weak actions or for blind love.

The word choice and ordering of detail of this book also leads one to believe that they are reading a classic. Hemingway's style is one of simple, straightforward dialogue with the absence of slang. Many generations of readers can read and understand the story. An example of this simplicity of dialogue is as follows: "'Where do you want to go, Cat?' 'Montreux.' 'It is a very nice place,' the official said. 'I think you will like that place.' 'Here at Locarno is a very nice place,' another official said." Although this simple dialogue is very easy to read, it is also very powerful in its directness and simplicity. On the other hand, his use of language when describing scenery is very elaborate.

"The next year there were many victories. The mountain that was beyond the valley and the hillside where the chestnut forest grew was captured and there were victories beyond the plain on the plateau to the south and we crossed the river in August and lived in a house in Gorizia that had a fountain and many thick shady trees in a walled garden and a wisteria vine purple on the side of the house".

When describing these scenes, not only does he do it in an elaborate and detailed way, but he also runs his thoughts and sentences together as if it were all being spoken in one long drawn-out breath. The ordering of detail of this book was in a straight-forward, well-organized way. It was very linear and the story did not jump around between the present and flash-backs to the protagonist's past. This kept the story from becoming confusing. Hemingway's style is that of a classic author. Because of the universal themes, ageless symbolism, and style of word choice and story detail, A Farewell to Arms, by Ernest Hemingway can indeed be considered a classic literary work. The theme of love between a man and woman so self-absorbed that all else is ignored and the theme of life bringing them to a breaking point is a human story that all can sympathize with. The ageless symbolism that compares the loss of a baby, or hope, with the beginning of the American economic depression is profound.

The alcoholism in the story reflects the careless attitudes toward life by the people living at this time. The irresponsible attitudes, such as the decision to desert the army, only lead to heartache. Life is nothing but a game to these characters, until the reality finally smacks them in the face. Hemingway's simple and straight-forward dialogue and story line makes this an easy to read and understandable ageless story.

"Şidelights". The writer's job is to tell the truth," Ernest Hemingway once said. When he was having difficulty writing he reminded himself of this, as he explained in his memoirs, A Moveable Feast. "I would stand and look out over the roofs of Paris and think, 'Do not worry. You have always written before and you will write now. All you have to do is write one true sentence. Write the truest sentence that you know.' So finally I would write one true sentence, and then go on from there. It was easy then because there was always one true sentence that I knew or had seen or had heard someone say."

Hemingway's personal and artistic quests for truth were directly related. As Earl Rovit noted: "More often than not, Hemingway's fictions seem rooted in his journeys into himself much more clearly and obsessively than is usually the case with major fiction writers. His writing was his way of approaching his identity of discovering himself in the projected metaphors of his experience. He believed that if he could see himself clear and whole, his vision might be useful to others who also lived in this world."

The public's acquaintance with the personal life of Hemingway was perhaps greater than with any other modern novelist. He was well known as a sportsman and bon vivant and his escapades were covered in such popular magazines as Life and Esquire. Hemingway became a legendary figure, wrote John W. Aldridge, "a kind of twentieth-century Lord Byron; and like Byron, he had learned to play himself, his own best hero, with superb conviction.

He was Hemingway of the rugged outdoor grin and the hairy chest posing beside a marlin he had just landed or a lion he had just shot; he was Tarzan Hemingway, crouching in the African bush with elephant gun at ready, Bwana Hemingway commanding his native bearers in terse Swahili; he was War Correspondent Hemingway writing a play in the Hotel Florida in Madrid while thirty Fascist shells crashed through the roof; later on he was Task Force Hemingway swathed in ammunition belts and defending his post singlehanded against fierce German attacks."

Anthony Burgess declared: "Reconciling literature and action, he fulfilled for all writers, the sickroom dream of leaving the desk for the arena, and then returning to the desk. He wrote good and lived good, and both activities were the same. The pen handled with the accuracy of the rifle; sweat and dignity; bags of cojones." Hemingway's search for truth and accuracy of expression is reflected in his terse, economical prose style, which is widely acknowledged to be his greatest contribution to literature.

What Frederick J. Hoffman called Hemingway's "esthetic of simplicity" involves a "basic struggle for absolute accuracy in making words correspond to experience." For Hemingway, William Barrett commented, "style was a moral act, a desperate struggle for moral probity amid the confusions of the world and the slippery complexities of one's own nature. To set things down simple and right is to hold a standard of rightness against a deceiving world."

In a discussion of Hemingway's style, Sheldon Norman Grebstein listed these characteristics: "first, short and simple sentence constructions, with heavy use of parallelism, which convey the effect of control, terseness, and blunt honesty; second, purged diction which above all eschews the use of bookish, latinate, or abstract words and thus achieves the effect of being heard or spoken or transcribed from reality rather than appearing as a construct of the imagination (in brief, verisimilitude); and third, skillful use of repetition and a kind of verbal counterpoint, which operate either by pairing or juxtaposing opposites, or else by running the same word or phrase through a series of shifting meanings and inflections."

One of Hemingway's greatest virtues as a writer was his self-discipline. He described how he accomplished this in A Moveable Feast. "If I started to write elaborately, or like someone introducing or presenting something, I found that I could cut that scrollwork or ornament out and throw it away and start with the first true simple declarative sentence I had written. I decided that I would write one story about each thing that I knew about. I was trying to do this all the time I was writing, and it was good and severe discipline." His early training in journalism as a reporter for the Kansas City Star and the Toronto Star is often mentioned as a factor in the development of his lean style.

Later, as a foreign correspondent he learned the even more rigorously economic language of "cablese," in which each word must convey the meaning of several others. While Hemingway acknowledged his debt to journalism in Death in the Afternoon by commenting that "in writing for a newspaper you told what happened and with one trick and another, you communicated the emotion to any account of something that has happened on that day," he admitted that the hardest part of fiction writing, "the real thing," was contriving "the sequence of motion and fact which made the emotion and which would be valid in a year or ten years or, with luck and if you stated it purely enough, always."

Although Hemingway has named numerous writers as his literary influences, his contemporaries mentioned most often in this regard are Ring Lardner, Sherwood Anderson, Ezra Pound, and Gertrude Stein. Malcolm Cowley assessed the importance of Stein and Pound (who were both friends of Hemingway) to his literary development, while stressing that the educational relationship was mutual. "One thing he took partly from her [Stein] was a colloquial in appearance American style, full of repeated words, prepositional phrases, and present participles, the style in which he wrote his early published stories.

One thing he took from Pound in return for trying vainly to teach him to box was the doctrine of the accurate image, which he applied in the 'chapters' printed between the stories that went into In Our Time; but Hemingway also learned from him to blue pencil most of his adjectives." Hemingway has commented that he learned how to write as much from painters as from other writers. Cezanne was one of his favourite painters and Wright Morris has compared

Hemingway's stylistic method to that of Cezanne. "A Cezanne-like simplicity of scene is built up with the touches of a master, and the great effects are achieved with a sublime economy.

At these moments style and substance are of one piece, each growing from the other, and one cannot imagine that life could exist except as described. We think only of what is there, and not, as in the less successful moments, of all of the elements of experience that are not." While most critics have found Hemingway's prose exemplary (Jackson J. Benson claimed that he had "perhaps the best ear that has ever been brought to the creation of English prose"), Leslie A. Fiedler complained that Hemingway learned to write "through the eye rather than the ear. If his language is colloquial, it is written colloquial, for he was constitutionally incapable of hearing English as it was spoken around him. To a critic who once asked him why his characters all spoke alike, Hemingway answered, 'Because I never listen to anybody.'"

Hemingway's earlier novels and short stories were largely praised for their unique style. Paul Goodman, for example, was pleased with the "sweetness" of the writing in A Farewell to Arms. "When it [sweetness] appears, the short sentences coalesce and flow, and sing sometimes melancholy, sometimes pastoral, sometimes personally embarrassed in an adult, not adolescent, way. In the dialogues, he pays loving attention to the spoken word. And the writing is meticulous; he is sweetly devoted to writing well. Most everything else is resigned, but here he makes an effort, and the effort produces lovely moments."

But in his later works, particularly Across the River and Into the Trees and the posthumously published Islands in the Stream, the Hemingway style degenerated into near self-parody. "In the best of early Hemingway it always seemed that if exactly the right words in exactly the right order were not chosen, something monstrous would occur, an unimaginably delicate internal warning system would be thrown out of adjustment, and some principle of personal and artistic integrity would be fatally compromised," John Aldridge wrote. "But by the time he came to write The Old

Man and the Sea there seems to have been nothing at stake except the professional obligation to sound as much like Hemingway as possible.

The man had disappeared behind the mannerism, the artist behind the artifice, and all that was left was a coldly flawless facade of words." Foster Hirsch found that Hemingway's "mawkish self-consciousness is especially evident in Islands in the Stream." Across the River and Into the Trees, according to Philip Rahv, "reads like a parody by the author of his own manner—a parody so biting that it virtually destroys the mixed social and literary legend of Hemingway." And Carlos Baker wrote: "In the lesser works of his final years nostalgia drove him to the point of exploiting his personal idiosyncrasies, as if he hoped to persuade readers to accept these in lieu of that powerful union of objective discernment and subjective response which he had once been able to achieve."

But Hemingway was never his own worst imitator. He was perhaps the most influential writer of his generation and scores of writers, particularly the hard-boiled writers of the thirties, attempted to adapt his tough, understated prose to their own works, usually without success. As Clinton S. Burhans, Jr., noted: "The famous and extraordinarily eloquent concreteness of Hemingway's style is inimitable precisely because it is not primarily stylistic: the how of Hemingway's style is the what of his characteristic vision." It is this organicism, the skillful blend of style and substance that made Hemingway's works so successful, despite the fact that many critics have complained that he lacked vision.

Hemingway avoided intellectualism because he thought it shallow and pretentious. His unique vision demanded the expression of emotion through the description of action rather than of passive thought. In Death in the Afternoon, Hemingway explained, "I was trying to write then and I found the greatest difficulty, aside from knowing truly what you really felt, rather than what you were supposed to feel, was to put down what really happened in action; what the actual things were which produced the emotion you experienced."

Even morality, for Hemingway, was a consequence of action and emotion. He stated his moral code in Death in the Afternoon: "What is moral is what you feel good after and what is immoral is what you feel bad after." Lady Brett Ashley, in The Sun Also Rises, voices this pragmatic morality after she has decided to leave a young bullfighter, believing the break to be in his best interests. She says: "You know it makes one feel rather good deciding not to be a bitch. It's sort of what we have instead of God." Hemingway's perception of the world as devoid of traditional values and truths and instead marked by disillusionment and moribund idealism, is a characteristically twentieth-century vision. World War I was a watershed for Hemingway and his generation.

As an ambulance driver in the Italian infantry, Hemingway had been severely wounded. The war experience affected him profoundly, as he told Malcolm Cowley. "In the first war I was hurt very badly; in the body, mind, and spirit, and also morally." The heroes of his novels were similarly wounded. According to Max Westbrook they "awake to a world gone to hell. World War I has destroyed belief in the goodness of national governments. The depression has isolated man from his natural brotherhood. Institutions, concepts, and insidious groups of friends and ways of life are, when accurately seen, a tyranny, a sentimental or propagandistic rationalization."

Both of Hemingway's first two major novels, The Sun Also Rises and A Farewell to Arms, were "primarily descriptions of a society that had lost the possibility of belief. They were dominated by an atmosphere of Gothic ruin, boredom, sterility and decay," John Aldridge wrote. "Yet if they had been nothing more than descriptions, they would inevitably have been as empty of meaning as the thing they were describing."

While Alan Lebowitz contended that because the theme of despair "is always an end in itself, the fiction merely its transcription, it is a dead end," Aldridge believed that Hemingway managed to save the novels by salvaging the characters' values and transcribing them "into a kind of moral network that linked them together in a unified pattern of meaning." In the search for meaning Hemingway's characters necessarily confront violence. Omnipresent violence is a fact of existence, according to Hemingway.

Even in works such as The Sun Also Rises in which violence plays a minimal role, it is always present subliminally "woven into the structure of life itself," William Barrett remarked. In other works violence is more obtrusive: the wars in A Farewell to Arms and For Whom the Bell Tolls, the hostility of nature which is particularly evident in the short stories and the violent sports such as bullfighting and big game hunting that are portrayed in numerous works. "Hemingway is the dramatist of the extreme situation.

His overriding theme is honour, personal honour: by what shall a man live, by what shall a man die, in a world the essential condition of whose being is violence?" Walter Allen wrote. "These problems are posed rather than answered in his first book In Our Time, a collection of short stories in which almost all of Hemingway's later work is contained by implication." The code by which Hemingway's heroes must live (Philip Young has termed them "code heroes") is contingent on the qualities of courage, self-control, and "grace under pressure." Irving Howe has described the typical Hemingway hero as a man "who is wounded but bears his wounds in silence, who is defeated but finds a remnant of dignity in an honest confrontation of defeat."

Furthermore, the hero's great desire must be to "salvage from the collapse of social life a version of stoicism that can make suffering bearable; the hope that in direct physical sensation, the cold water of the creek in which one fishes or the purity of the wine made by Spanish peasants, there can be found an experience that can resist corruption." Hemingway has been accused of exploiting and sensationalizing violence. However, Leo Gurko remarked that "the motive behind Hemingway's heroic figures is not glory, or fortune, or the righting of injustice, or the thirst for experience. They are inspired neither by vanity nor ambition nor a desire to better the world. They have no thoughts of reaching a state of higher grace or virtue. Instead, their behaviour is a reaction to the moral emptiness of the universe, an emptiness that they feel compelled to fill by their own special efforts." If life is an endurance contest and the hero's response to it is prescribed and codified, the violence itself is stylized. As William Barrett asserted: "It is always played, even in nature, perhaps above all in nature, according to some form.

The violence erupts within the patterns of war or the patterns of the bullring." Clinton S. Burhans, Jr., is convinced that Hemingway's "fascination with bullfighting stems from his view of it as an art form, a ritual tragedy in which man confronts the creatural realities of violence, pain, suffering, and death by imposing on them an esthetic form which gives them order, significance, and beauty." It is not necessary (or even possible) to understand the complex universe it is enough for Hemingway's heroes to find solace in beauty and order. Santiago in The Old Man and the Sea cannot understand why he must kill the great fish he has come to love, Burhans noted. Hemingway described Santiago's confusion: "I do not understand these things, he thought. But it is good we do not try to kill the sun or the moon or the stars.

It is enough to live on the sea and kill our brothers." Despite Hemingway's pessimism, Ihab Hassan declared that it is "perverse to see only the emptiness of Hemingway's world. In its lucid spaces, a vision of archetypal unity reigns. Opposite forces obey a common destiny; enemies discover their deeper identity; the hunter and the hunted merge. The matador plunges his sword, and for an instant in eternity, man and beast are the same. This is the moment of truth, and it serves Hemingway as symbol of the unity which underlies both love and death. His fatalism, his tolerance of bloodshed, his stoical reserve before the malice of creation, betrays a sacramental attitude that transcends any personal fate." Death is not the ultimate fear: the Hemingway hero knows how to confront death. What he truly fears is nada (the Spanish word for nothing)-existence in a state of nonbeing.

Hemingway's characters are alone. He is not concerned with human relationships as much as with portraying man's individual struggle against an alien, chaotic universe. His characters exist in the "island condition," Stephen L. Tanner has noted. He compared them to the islands of an archipelago "consistently isolated [and] alone in the stream of society." Several critics have noted that Hemingway's novels suffer because of his overriding concern with the individual.

For Whom the Bell Tolls, a novel about the Spanish Civil War, has engendered controversy on this matter. While it is ostensibly a political novel about a cause that Hemingway believed in fervently, critics such as Alvah C. Bessie were disappointed that Hemingway was still concerned exclusively with the personal. "The cause of Spain does not, in any essential way, figure as a motivating power, a driving, emotional, passional force in this story."

Bessie wrote. "In the widest sense, that cause is actually irrelevant to the narrative. For the author is less concerned with the fate of the Spanish people, whom I am certain he loves, than he is with the fate of his hero and heroine, who are himself. For all his groping the author of the Bell has yet to integrate his individual sensitivity to life with the sensitivity of every living human being (read the Spanish people); he has yet to expand his personality as a novelist to embrace the truths of other people, everywhere; he has yet to dive deep into the lives of others, and there to find his own."

But Mark Schorer contended that in For Whom the Bell Tolls Hemingway's motive is to portray "a tremendous sense of man's dignity and worth, an urgent awareness of the necessity of man's freedom, a nearly poetic realization of man's collective virtues. Indeed, the individual vanishes in the political whole, but vanishes precisely to defend his dignity, his freedom, his virtue. In spite of the ominous premium which the title seems to place on individuality, the real theme of the book is the relative unimportance of individuality and the superb importance of the political whole." Hemingway's depiction of relationships between men and women is generally considered to be his weakest area as a writer.

Leslie A. Fiedler has noted that he is only really comfortable dealing with men without women. His women characters often seem to be abstractions rather than portraits of real women. Often reviewers have divided them into two types: the bitches such as Brett and Margot Macomber who emasculate the men in their lives, and the wish-projections, the sweet, submissive women such as Catherine and Maria (in For Whom the Bell Tolls). All of the characterizations lack subtlety and shading.

The love affair between Catherine and Frederic in A Farewell to Arms is only an "abstraction of lyric emotion," Edmund Wilson commented. Fiedler complained that "in his earlier fiction, Hemingway's descriptions of the sexual encounter are intentionally brutal, in his later ones, unintentionally comic; for in no case, can he quite succeed in making his females human. If in For Whom the Bell Tolls Hemingway has written the most absurd love scene in the history of the American novel, this is not because he lost momentarily his skill and authority; it is a give-away—a moment which illuminates the whole erotic content of his fiction."

In 1921, when Hemingway and his family moved to the Left Bank of Paris (then the literature, art, and music capital of the world), he became associated with other American expatriates, including F. Scott Fitzgerald, Archibald MacLeish, E. E. Cummings, and John Dos Passos. These expatriates and the whole generation which came of age in the period between the two world wars came to be known as the "lost generation." For Hemingway the term had more universal meaning. In A Moveable Feast he wrote that being lost is part of the human condition—that all generations are lost generations.

Hemingway also believed in the cyclicality of the world. As inscriptions to his novel The Sun Also Rises, he used two quotations: first, Gertrude Stein's comment, "You are all a lost generation"; then a verse from Ecclesiastes which begins, "One generation passeth away, and another generation cometh; but the earth abideth forever." The paradox of regeneration evolving from death is central to Hemingway's vision.

The belief in immortality is comforting, of course, and Hemingway evidently found comfort in permanence and endurance. According to Steven R. Phillips, Hemingway discovered permanence in "the sense of immortality that he gains from the otherwise impermanent art of the bullfight, in the fact that the 'earth abideth forever,' in the eternal flow of the gulf stream and in the permanence of his own works of art." Hemingway's greatest depiction of endurance is in The Old Man and the Sea in which "he succeeds in a manner which almost defeats critical description," Phillips claimed.

"The old man becomes the sea and like the sea he endures. He is dying as the year is dying. He is fishing in September, the fall of the year, the time that corresponds in the natural cycle to the phase of sunset and sudden death. Yet the death of the old man will not bring an end to the cycle; as part of the sea he will continue to exist."

Hemingway was inordinately proud of his own powers of rejuvenation, and in a letter to his friend Archibald MacLeish, he explained that his maxim was: "Dans la vie, il faut (d'abord) durer." ("In life, one must [first of all] endure.") He had survived physical disasters (including two near-fatal plane crashes in Africa in 1954) and disasters of critical reception to his work (Across the River and Into the Trees was almost universally panned). But due to his great recuperative powers he was able to rebound from these hardships.

He made a literary comeback with the publication of The Old Man and the Sea, which is considered to be among his finest works. In 1954 he was awarded the Nobel Prize for Literature. But the last few years of his life were marked by great physical and emotional suffering. He was no longer able to write to do the thing he loved the most. Finally Hemingway could endure no longer and, in 1961, he took his own life. In the 1980s Scribner published two additional posthumous works. The Dangerous Summer and The Garden of Eden. Written in 1959 while Hemingway was in Spain on commission for Life magazine, The Dangerous Summer describes the intense and bloody competition between two prominent bullfighters.

The Garden of Eden, a novel about newlyweds who experience marital conflict while traveling through Spain on their honeymoon, was begun by Hemingway in the 1940s and finished fifteen years later. While interest in these works was high, critics judged neither book to rival the thematic and stylistic achievements of his earlier works, which have made Hemingway a major figure in modern American literature. The fifth of Hemingway's posthumous publications, a self-termed fictional memoir titled True at First Light, was released on July 21, 1999 to coincide with the 100th anniversary of his birth.

The book, edited by Hemingway's middle son, Patrick, and paired down to half the length of the original manuscript, recounts a Kenyan safari excursion that Hemingway took with his fourth wife, Mary, in 1953. The story centers around Mary's preoccupation with killing a lion who is threatening the villagers' safety, and the narrator's involvement with a woman from the Wakamba tribe, whom he calles his "fiancee."

Many critics expressed disappointment over True at First Light for its peripatetic lack of vision, its abdication of intellectual intent (what New York Times critic James Wood termed "a nullification of thought") and its tepid prose. Kenneth S. Lynn, writing for the National Review, pointed out that "Ernest Hemingway's name is on the cover, but the publication of True at First Light is an important event in celebrity culture, not in literary culture. For the grim fact is that this 'fictional memoir' reflects a marvelous writer's disastrous loss of talent."

Many of the critics pointed to Hemingway's increasing preoccupation with the myth of his own machismo as a catalyst for the devolution of his writing. New York Times critic Michiko Kakutani commented, "As in so much of Hemingway's later work, all this spinning of his own legend is reflected in the deterioration of his prose. What was special—and at the time, galvanic—about his early writing was its precision and concision: Hemingway not only knew what to leave out, but he also succeeded in turning that austerity into a moral outlook, a way of looking at a world shattered and remade by World War I. His early work had a clean, hard objectivity: it did not engage in meaningless abstractions; it tried to show, not tell."

True at First Light also inflamed classic critical debate over the true ownership of authorial intention. While Hemingway's physical and mental deterioration, toward the end of his life, rendered his final wishes for unpublished works unclear, many critics have objected to the posthumous "franchise" of his deepest failures, novels that he, himself, abandoned. James Wood offered the observation that True at First Light's lack of substance may serve "as a warning to let Hemingway be, both as a literary estate and as a literary influence." There is evidence, however, that the literary storm the book stirred would not have bothered Hemingway much.

As Tom Jenks pointed out in a review for Harper's, "Hemingway's own belief was that in a writer's lifetime his reputation depended on the quantity and median of his work, but that after his death he would be remembered only for "Sidelights" his best." If this is true, then, as one Publishers Weekly reviewer opined, perhaps True at First Light will "inspire new readers to delve into Hemingway's true legacy."

## Chapter 13

# Old Man and The Sea

In the novel The Old Man and the Sea, Ernest Hemingway uses the literary device of metaphors. Hemingway uses the metaphor of the ocean to symbolize life and to depict the role that individuals play in life. Hemingway uses the metaphor of the lions to signify people who live their lives as active participants. The tourists in the novel represent the individuals, who in observe their lives and are not active participants. In the novels that Ernest Hemingway writes, he uses metaphors to reflect his life experiences and opinions. The ocean in "The Old Man and the Sea" is a metaphor, which represents Hemingway's personal view of life.

Hemingway believes that in life everyone must find their own niche and uses the metaphor of the ocean and the boats on it to demonstrate this.most of the boats were silent except for the dip of the oars. They spread apart after they were out of the mouth of the harbour and each one headed for the part of the ocean where he hoped to find fish. The old man knew he was going far out. Hemingway feels that in life there are people who participate in life and people who observe life as it passes just like on the ocean where there are boats that do not test their boundaries.

The boats are the people in life, and most of the boats are silent. They paddle within the areas they know to be safe and always are cautious not to upset the life that they have established for themselves. Hemingway is explaining that most people don't raise a commotion; they just allow life to happen to them. The old man is testing his limits; he is challenging the ocean, and rowing where he wants to go not where the ocean wants to take him. Hemingway believes that in life, the farther person stays from the observers, the more free and exhilarated they will be.

If there is a hurricane, you always see the signs of it in the sky for days ahead, if you are at sea. They do not see it ashore because they do not know what to look for, he thought. The land must make a difference too, in the shape of the clouds. But we have no hurricane coming now. Hemingway theorizes that in life there are going to be unexpected collisions. Just as the sea creates storms life creates storms. Those who live life to the fullest will be the least affected by these storms because they have the strength and the knowledge to handle them, but the observers or those on land will be destroyed because they do not have the power to handle the destruction that the storms will cause.

The individuals who are far out to sea have the knowledge that the ocean will test them with momentous storms, and this is why they go so far out to sea. The people who Hemingway thinks face life head-on are represented by lions in the novel. Hemingway uses the metaphor of the lion to depict the participants in life. When Santiago is a child he visits Africa, and tells Manolin of the lions he sees. "When I was your age I was before the mast on a square-rigged ship and that ship ran to Africa and I have seen lions on the beaches in the evening."

Hemingway uses the lions on the beach as a metaphor, because most lions would never be found on a beach. The only lions that would ever be found on a beach are the lions who are equivalent to the humans who are participants. The lions on the beach are going where most lions would never dare go. These lions are testing their boundaries, seeing just how far they can go, just like participants. This line also hints at Hemingway's belief that age impairs, but does not extinguish one's ability to be participants in their own lives.

Santiago realizes that all of his glories were in his youth, and strongly relates the power that the lions in his dreams have to his youth. He no longer dreamed of storms, or of women, or of great occurrences, or of great fish, nor fights, nor contests of strength, nor of his wife. He only dreamed of places now and of the lions on the beach. The played like young cats in the dusk and he loved them as he loved the boy. He never dreamed about the boy. Santiago is slowly losing his ability to be an effective participant in his life because of the limitations that are associated with aging. Hemingway also experiences inabilities that he has never known and which brings him into a depression.

Santiago is beginning to believe that he is not a participant in his life so he doesn't depress himself by dreaming of anything other than the lions, who are participants. In hi dreams, Santiago are living vicariously through the lions. The lions represent all that

Hemingway ever was, and what he wishes he still could be. The tourists in the novel are metaphors for what Hemingway isn't. The tourists are metaphors for the people Hemingway believes live their lives as passive observers. The tourists appear only briefly but the statement that Hemingway makes through them is profound.

That afternoon there was a party of tourist at the Terrace and looking down in the water among the empty beer cans and dead barracudas a woman saw a great long white spine with a huge tail at the end that lifted and swung with the tide while the east wind blew a heavy steady sea outside the entrance to the harbor. 'What's that?' she asked a waiter and pointed to the long backbone of the great fish that was just now garbage waiting to go out with the tide. 'Tiburon,' the waiter said, 'Eshark.' He was meaning to explain what dare grapple happened.

'I didn't know sharks had such handsome tails.' 'I didn't either,' her male companion said. These two tourists who speak are hardly differentiated from the group to which they belong. They are all metaphors for individuals who are spectators of the human scene rather than participants in its activity. They see, but they see without fully comprehending. They are only faintly curious, only passingly interested, only superficially observing, they have not been initiated into the mysteries that Santiago understands. These tourists live their lives as tourists, skimming the surface of life, without resolution or clarity.

Their life reflects that of all people who live their lives ashore, who dare not grapple with the mysteries of the ocean, or of life. This is the type of life that Hemingway always tried to avoid, to the point of his taking his own life. Hemingway uses metaphors to reflect his opinions of life and the people that he has met in life. The metaphor of the sea symbolizes all of life and the roles that people must choose to have in life. The lions are a metaphor for the people Hemingway respects and the type of person Hemingway is. The tourists are a metaphor for the individuals who choose to live their life as onlookers but never participants. Through Hemingway's use of penetrating metaphors in his novels, readers gain an understanding of Hemingway's life and or their own. Through his novels Hemingway challenges every member of society to admit that most people are observers and through his novels dares them to head out to sea and catch their marlin.

## Chapter 14

# Critical Analysis of "Soldier's Home"

Before, During, and After the War Many of the titles of Ernest Hemingway's stories are ironic, and can be read on a number of levels; Soldier's Home is no exception. Our first impression, having read the title only, is that this story will be about a old soldier living out the remainder of his life in an institution where veterans go to die.

We soon find out that the story has nothing to do with the elderly, or institutions; rather, it tells the story of a young man, Harold Krebs, only recently returned from World War I, who has moved back into his parents' house while he figures out what he wants to do with the rest of his life. And yet our first impression lingers, and with good reason; despite the fact that his parents' comfortable, middle-class lifestyle used to feel like home to Harold Krebs, it no longer does. Harold is not home; he has no home at all. This is actually not an uncommon scenario among young people (such as college students) returning into the womb of their childhood again. But with Harold, the situation is more dramatic because he has not only lived on his own, but has dealt with and been traumatized by life-and-death situations his parents could not possibly understand.

Hemingway does not divulge why Krebs was the last person in his home town to return home from the war; according to the Kansas City Star, Hemingway himself "left Kansas City in the spring of 1918 and did not return for 10 years, [becoming] 'the first of 132 former Star employees to be wounded in World War I,' according to a Star article at the time of his death". Wherever he was in the intervening time, by the time Harold gets home, the novelty of the returning soldier has long since worn off.

All the other former soldiers have found a niche for themselves in the community, but Harold needs a while longer to get his bearings; he plays pool, "practiced on his clarinet, strolled down town, read, and went to bed". What he is doing, of course, is killing time. The problem, of course, has to do with Harold's definition of who he has become. He recognizes he has changed, and this change is played out dramatically against the backdrop of a town where nothing else has changed since he was in high school.

His father parks his car in the same place; it's still the same car; the girls walking down the street look like the same girls, except more of them have short hair now. Imamura comments, "Krebs admires them, yet he protects himself from the danger of sexual involvement as if he were still suffering from a previous affair". And Daniel Slaughter observes that "One gets the sense while reading 'A Soldier's Home' that watching the girls was a healing process" (Slaughter, hemingway 1.html). What has happened here, really? Why is Krebs unable to adjust to life back in Oklahoma? Why can't he talk to girls, or manage to do anything productive with his time? These answers can be found in a careful examination of what Krebs was doing before the war and what happened while he was in Europe.

Prior to the war, Hemingway tells us in the very first paragraph, Krebs attended a Methodist school in Kansas. He was not out of place then; Hemingway says "There is a picture which shows him among his fraternity brothers, all of them wearing exactly the same height and style collar" (Hemingway, 145). There is a tremendous poignancy in this detail; at least one of these young men, so concerned about his appearance, would soon be shipped overseas to the most horrific war the world had ever known. The fact that his college was a religious institution is also significant, for it shows that he was, at that time, in synch with his mother's religious values.

At least, he did not have any reason to doubt them, or

not enough strength to resist them (or her). Hemingway tells us before the first paragraph is over that Krebs "enlisted in the Marines in 1917" (Hemingway, 145). The Marines are an elite fighting force who today advertises they are looking for "a few good men" indicating that if the prospective soldier is not out of the ordinary, he need not apply. However, was Krebs a good Marine?

J.F. Kobler observes that there is at least some indication in "Soldier's Home" "that Krebs did not fight bravely in the war. Krebs admits to himself that he has lied in public about his military experiences, but he cannot stop lying to himself about the real extent and the psychological effect of his lying" (Kobler, 377). We know for sure that he was "badly, sickeningly frightened all the time" (Hemingway, 146).

Certainly his war experiences were not glamorous, and he brings home quite a collection of battle-scarred baggage, not the least of which is his guilt over having to live a lie. Krebs even connects the politics of courting with "lying", which he has already told us makes him feel "nauseated". As Lamb points out, "The shadow that renders Krebs incapable of action and that lies at the crux of the story is stated in three sentences that follow immediately after his first statement that young women are not worth it: 'He did not want any consequences. He did not want any consequences ever again. He wanted to live along without consequences.'

His desire to avoid consequences is his single overriding motivation. He fondly recalls the French and German women because relationships with them were uncomplicated and without consequence; there was no need even to talk. He wants the hometown women but does not act on these desires because they are too complicated and not worth the consequences. He is attracted to his little sister because he can shrug off her demands and she will still love him. But his mother repels him because her demands are complex and unavoidable".

But it is not until his mother confronts him over breakfast about his future that he realizes that he cannot continue to live at home any more. Robert Paul Lamb observes that before

Harold's mother begins her lecture, she takes off her glasses; "this gesture seems to imply that she either can not, or does not want to 'see' him". His mother, in other words, does not want to be distracted by Harold's point of view while she is expounding on hers. This somewhat echoes his earlier observation that "Later he felt the need to talk but no one wanted to hear about it".

Essentially, no one wants to recognize Harold's unique identity. His mother pressures him to get a job by arguing that "There are no idle hands in [God's] Kingdom," to which Harold significantly observes, "I'm not in His Kingdom". And he's not. The world he discovered during World War I had no hand of God in it. His mother then observes that all the other boys "just your age" are settling down and becoming "really a credit to the community". This hearkens back to the first paragraph of the story, in which Harold observes a picture of himself with his fraternity brothers, all sporting identical haircuts and collars.

Harold is no longer like everybody else; he's not sure who he is, but he's sure of that. Finally, his mother asks whether he loves her. He replies quite truthfully that he does not. We know that this is because his entire worldview has been turned upside down by his traumatic experiences in the war, and the ability to genuinely love requires an emotional balance he does not have right now. But his mother does not understand this, because she cannot identify with his experiences; as Tateo Imamura observes, "Krebs' small-town mother cannot comprehend her son's struggles and sufferings caused by the war.

She devotes herself to her religion and never questions her own values". So he lies to please her, and kneels down as she prays to please her and then he knows he has to go away. Harold lies out of an inability to force a painful issue and take a stand. He may feel that he acquiesces out of compassion, but in fact he is not secure enough in his own self to risk a confrontation that could be painful or guilt-inducing. Harold veers onto the edge of self-revelation with his straight-forward answers about the Kingdom of God and his lack of ability to love, but when his mother begins to cry he waffles; she will never see that he isn't the boy he was in high school — or perhaps, the boy she thought he was. Young Goodman Brown: Going Home.

My home is my haven and the place that I feel the safest and most comfortable at. It is where many good memories and feelings arise and I am able to be myself with no false pretenses. It is my "Home Sweet Home" yet the stories "Young Goodman Brown," by Nathaniel Hawthorne, and "Soldier's Home," by Ernest Hemingway show a different attitude about home going and the effects it has on the main characters.

In Hawthorne's story, "Young Goodman Brown," Goodman Brown ventures on a journey into the forest and refuses the temptations of the devil. Unfortunately though, throughout the night, Brown finds out more than he ever wanted to know about how his fellow Puritan townsmen, including his wife, have betrayed their faith by giving into their dark desires. In utter despair, Goodman Brown returns at dawn to his Salem village "staring around him like a bewildered man."

He doesn't believe it is the same place as it was the night before and he no longer feels at home. Whether his experiences were real or not, his faith is gone and he feels as though he is the only pure one. He suffers tremendous guilt and discomfort and trusts no one. His excessive pride is evident when he takes a child away from a blessing given by Goody Cloyse, his former catechism teacher, as if he were taking the child "from the fiend himself."

His distrust and resentment towards his townsmen is apparent when he sees his wife, Faith. She is overwhelmed with joy to see him arrive home yet he looked "sternly and sadly into her face and passed on without a greeting." All that he learned in the night was too much for him, and it changed a devoted husband with bright hopes and a wife whom he loved, to a tired, beaten, questioning and almost faithless man.

Harold Krebs in Hemingway's "Soldier's Home," returns from World War I to a society that he no longer feels a part of and receives no welcome for his heroic deeds. He resents being home which is largely due to the fact, that during the war he led a very simple lifestyle and upon returning home is thrust back into a complicated domestic life. He tries to seek refuge by withdrawing from society and engages himself in individual activities.

His faith in religion appears to have diminished because of experiences during the war. Before the war he attended a Methodist college but upon returning home, he is unwilling to pray. His belief in God has faltered and he no longer feels that he is "in His Kingdom." Krebs's views of women and love also changed significantly. In Europe during the war, he experienced obligation free relationships and found it easier to be intimate with French and German girls.

"It was simple and they were friends." He was disgusted by the prospect of returning home to a complex relationship. He felt that the girls in America were "too complicated," and "he did not want any consequences ever again." Harold Krebs lost himself in the war and comes home as a cold, selfish, and unloving person. He even went, as far as to lie to his mother about loving her when in truth he loves no one. Whether Goodman Brown's experiences were real or perhaps a dream, his feelings towards his home were never the same again. Had he followed his heart, he may have lived a good life. Instead he followed his head and excommunicated himself from the community and therefore died a lonely and depressed man.

Harold Krebs found himself in place he did not want to be. He regards his home life as a complicated situation and yearns for a more simplistic life. He no longer believes in society, love, or faith and lies to himself, his community, and his family. It's a shame that these characters did not truly appreciate what they had at "home." Ernest Hemingway is noted for having made many contributions to the literary world and one of his most notorious contributions is the Code Hero. The birth and growth of the Code Hero can be easily observed simply by watching the growth and development of Nick Adams throughout Hemingway's writing.

In Our Time contains a various assortment of Nick Adam stories at various stages of his life and also shows the Code

Hero at various stages of its development. In Our Time was the second book Hemingway had published. His first contained only three short stories and ten poems and had little to do with the Code Hero, making In Our Time the first time Hemingway revealed the Code Hero to the rest of the world. The technique and characterization contained in In Our Time is consistent with most of Hemingway's later writings, setting up In Our Time as a model of Hemingway's style and the Code Hero According to Professor Paul Totah of St.Ignatius, Hemingway defined the Code Hero as "a man who lives correctly, following the ideals of honour, courage and endurance in a world that is sometimes chaotic, often stressful, and always painful." The Code Hero measures himself by how well they handle the difficult situations that life throws at him. In the end the Code Hero will lose because we are all mortal, but the true measure is how a person faces death.

The Code Hero is typically an individualist and free-willed. Although he believes in the ideals of courage and honour he has his own set of morals and principles based on his beliefs in honour, courage and endurance. Qualities such as bravery, adventuresome and travel also define the Code Hero. A final trait of the Code Hero is his dislike of the dark. It symbolizes death and is a source of fear for him. The rite of manhood for the Code Hero is facing death. However, once he faces death bravely and becomes a man he must continue the struggle and constantly prove himself to retain his manhood (Totah).

The Code Hero is present in the majority of Hemingway's novels. Even the young man in Hills Like White Elephants contained many of the characteristics of the Code Hero such as free-willed, individualist, and travel. The individualism comes out in his desire to not have a child. It would solidify the group aspect of a family between him and the lady. The travel trait is obvious by the mention of the stickers on the luggage denoting the many places they had been. His free will comes out also in his desire not to be a father. If he were a father he would have to begin making decisions for his child and family, not just for himself.

The first Nick Adam story, Indian Camp shows Nick as a young boy and also shows Nick as he experiences the main characteristic of the Code Hero, facing death bravely. Nick's witnessing of the Indian's suicide introduces him to death for the first time. Instead of being frightened or sickened by the experience, Nick stays strong and asks his father questions about it instead. The fear of darkness is also touched upon in Indian Camp. When Nick first goes to the camp it is dark and he sits in the boat with his father's arm around him, providing a sense of security.

When Nick leaves the camp it is light outside. Nick runs his hand through the water, which is described as warm and provides the sense of security that his father had to provide during the night. The light shining on the water and warmth that Nick feels is also mentioned along with Nick's thought that he would never die. Nick draws strength and sanctuary from the morning as opposed to the night before. Nick's feeling that he would never die shows this as an early stage in his development into a Code Hero. He has not accepted the inevitability of death, yet.

The Doctor and the Doctor's Wife also shows Nick developing into the Code Hero, although in a very subtle way. Nick is only involved in the end of the story but the few sentences that Hemingway writes about him are enough to show development. Nick is described as sitting in the woods reading. This shows him as someone who enjoys the outdoors. From this it can be derived that he enjoys traveling. He doesn't like being tied down to civilization; he'd rather be out exploring and setting his own path. This shows the free will and individualism of Nick. The description of him reading shows that he's expanding his knowledge. It's unimportant what he's reading; it just shows that he's expanding his knowledge of the world.

From this he will form his opinions and beliefs, helping him create his own value and belief system. His parents' contradicting religious views reinforce this. Since he does not have one religion exposed to him he has to examine both. From this he will pick and chose the ideals he believes in. The End of Something and The Three-Day Blow show the development of Nick's individualism. Although his age is not mentioned, it can be assumed he has passed through adolescence and is becoming a young man. He feels that his relationship with Marjorie is becoming too close.

He is losing his individuality as they become more of a couple, although he doesn't realise it. All he knows it that the relationship wasn't fun any longer and it was over for some reason he didn't know. Bill articulates the reason when he describes what married life would have been like for Nick. Nick would have had to settle down and get a job and raise a family. Bill also points out that Nick would have been marrying her whole family, not just her. Nick would have no longer been an individual; he would have been part of a group. He also would have lost his free will.

He would not have been able to do whatever he wanted whenever he wanted. He would have had to factor in the family into his decisions. Bill further points out that Marjorie's mother would have been around all the time telling them how to do things and act. Nick's desire to travel is illustrated when he thinks about how he and Marjorie had talked of going to Italy and all the places they would go and see. Another characteristic revealed is honour. Bill states that Nick did the right thing by breaking up with Marjorie now while she still has a chance to meet someone else and settle down with him.

It is implied that by Nick stopping things he actually helped both of them avoid a life that would have made them miserable. In The Battler Hemingway has Nick face death for the first time since that day at the Indian camp as a young boy. Nick is older now and is becoming a young man. Although death is not openly visible in the story, Nick does face it in two ways. The first is symbolic in the fact that although it is dark outside, Nick walks up to the fire and the stranger and begins a conversation. Nick bravely faced death in this instance.

He didn't let the fact that it was dark, he was not near anyone that could help him, or that he didn't know the man stop him. The other way Nick faced death was his encounter with Ad. Ad said he was going o give Nick a beating but a man that could snap in and out of reality the way Ad did could easily beat Nick to death. Nick is aware that he is in a dangerous situation, but he remains calm and doesn't show cowardice. He slowly backs away from Ad while trying to talk him out of the fight.

Although he backed away, he didn't turn and run or begin crying and begging for mercy. He recognized the fact that he couldn't win a fight against Ad and used his intelligence to try and find another solution. The Battler also shows Nick as a traveller. He is train hoping his way from town to town. Cross-Country Snow again shows the travel aspect of the Code Hero. Nick talks of wanting t travel all over Switzerland and Europe to ski and mentions having traveled a lot in the United States. The story also shows Nick being unhappy about giving up his free will and individualism.

He has a baby on the way and it will change everything. He knows he will have to return to the U.S. He says he is happy now that he will be a father but he still emits regret at not being able to ski anymore. This is symbolic of more than skiing, though. It symbolizes his regret at not being able to just bum around Europe or travel around the States. It symbolizes a loss of his free will. His decisions will no longer affect just him. This tie in with his loss of individualism. He now has a family to think about and provide for. He is part of a small group and not just an individual. Despite all this, he faces it bravely. He says he is happy to become a father. In this way he faces the death of his free will and individualism bravely.

Big Two-Hearted River shows Nick as a man and also reveals that he has acquired many of the qualities of the Code Hero. He is out in the woods and camping along the river alone, depicting his individualism. His camping and fishing show his adventuresome personality. His reminiscing of other fishing trips at various places reveals his love of traveling. Nick is always respectful of nature and the river. There is an aspect of Nick's fear of the dark as well. When he speaks his voice sounds strange in the darkness and he doesn't speak again. Despite this fear he is brave and camps out alone near the river.

By this point Nick has nearly matured into the full Code Hero and fully into a man. Chapter IV is the conclusion of the growth of the Code Hero and Nick Adams. Nick is in a war, most likely WWI.

He has been shot and he is staring into the face of death. He is also smiling. In this short one paragraph sketch, Nick shows his bravery, courage and endurance to face an extremely difficult situation and face death. At this point Nick proves his manhood and shows the final evolution of the Code Hero. The fact that Nick is a soldier fighting in a war reinforces his bravery and courage. His survival during the war displays his ability to endure and persevere through tough situations.

Although it is a collection of short stories, Hemingway's In Our Time presents his famous Code Hero in various stages of its development through the development of one of his most famous characters, Nick Adams. Characteristics such as bravery, courage, endurance, free will, individualism, a desire to travel, a fear of the darkness and the ability to face death and the difficulty of life are prevalent in Nick as he grows from a young boy in Indian Camp into a man in Chapter VI. The Nick Adams stories contained in In Our Time do a great job of showing Nick at various stages of his life and in various stages of his development into the Code Hero, making the book a model of the Code Hero.

## Chapter 15

# A Case of Identity

The recognition of Hemingway as a major and representative writer of the United States of America, was a slow but explosive process. His emergence in the western canon was an even more adventurous voyage. His works were burnt in the bonfire in Berlin on May 10, 1933 as being a monument of modern decadence. That was a major proof of the writer's significance and a step toward world fame. To read Hemingway has always produced strong reactions. When his parents received the first copies of their son's book In Our Time (1924), they read it with horror. Furious, his father sent the volumes back to the publisher, as he could not tolerate such filth in the house. Hemingway's apparently coarse, crude, vulgar and unsentimental style and manners appeared equally shocking to many people outside his family. On the other hand, this style was precisely the reason why a great many other people liked his work. A myth, exaggerating those features, was to be born.

### HEMINGWAY IN OUR TIME

After he had committed suicide at Ketchum, Idaho, in 1961, the literary position of the 1954 Nobel Laureate changed significantly and has, in a way, even become stronger. This is partly due to several posthumous works and collections that show the author's versatility - A Moveable Feast (1964), By-Line (1967), 88 Poems (1979), and Selected Letters (1981). It is also the result of painstaking and successful Hemingway research, in which The Hemingway Society (USA) has played an important role since 1980. Another result of this enduring interest is that many new aspects of Hemingway's life and works that were previously obscured by his public image have now emerged into the light. On the other hand, posthumously published novels, such as Islands in the Stream (1970) and The Garden of Eden (1986), have disappointed many of the old Hemingway readers. However, rather than bearing witness to declining literary power, (which, considering the author's declining health would, indeed, be a rather trivial observation even if it were true) the late works confront us with a reappraisal and reconsideration of basic values.

They also display an unbiased seeking and experimentation, as if the author was losing both his direction and his footing, or was becoming unrestrained in a new way. Just as modern Hemingway scholarship has added immensely to the depth of our understanding of Hemingway - making him more and more difficult to define! - these works reveal and stress a complexity that may cause bewilderment or relief, depending on what perspective one adopts.

## THE "HARD-BOILED" STYLE

The slang word "hard-boiled", used to describe characters and works of art, was a product of twentieth century warfare. To be "hard-boiled" meant to be unfeeling, callous, coldhearted, cynical, rough, obdurate, unemotional, without sentiment. Later to become a literary term, the word originated in American Army World War I training camps, and has been in common, colloquial usage since about 1930.

Contemporary literary criticism regarded Ernest Hemingway's works as marked by his use of this style, which was typical of the era. Indeed, in many respects they were regarded as the embodiment and symbol of hard-boiled literature. However, neither Hemingway the man nor Hemingway the writer should be labeled "hard-boiled" - his style is the only aspect that deserves this epithet, and even that is ambiguous. Let us get down to basics, concentrate on one main feature in his literary style, and then turn to the alleged hard-boiled mind behind it, and his macho style of living and speaking.

## A HARD-BOILED MIND

An unmatched introduction to Hemingway's particular skill as a writer is the beginning of A Farewell to Arms, certainly one of the most pregnant opening paragraphs in the history of the modern American novel. In that passage the power of concentration reaches a peak, forming a vivid and charged sequence, as if it were a 10-second video summary. It is packed with events and excitement, yet significantly frosty, as if unresponsive and numb, like a silent flashback dream sequence in which bygone images return, pass in review and fade away, leaving emptiness and quietude behind them.

The lapidary writing approaches the highest style of poetry, vibrant with meaning and emotion, while the pace is maintained by the exclusion of any descriptive redundancy, of obtrusive punctuation, and of superfluous or narrowing emotive signs:

In the late summer of that year we lived in a house in a village that looked across the river and the plain to the mountains. In the bed of the river there were pebbles and boulders, dry and white in the sun, and the water was clear and swiftly moving and blue in the channels. Troops went by the house and down the road and the dust they raised powdered the leaves of the trees.

The trunks of the trees too were dusty and the leaves fell early that year and we saw the troops marching along the road and the dust rising and leaves, stirred by the breeze, falling and the soldiers marching and afterwards the road bare and white except for the leaves. At the end of the sixteenth chapter of Death in the Afternoon the author approaches a definition of the "hard-boiled" style:

"If a writer of prose knows enough about what he is writing about he may omit things that he knows and the reader, if the writer is writing truly enough, will have a feeling of those things."

Ezra Pound taught him "to distrust adjectives" (A Moveable Feast). That meant creating a style in accordance with the esthetics and ethics of raising the emotional temperature towards the level of universal truth by shutting the door on sentiment, on the subjective.

## THE UNWRITTEN CODE

Later biographic research revealed, behind the macho façade of boxing, bullfighting, big-game hunting and deep-sea fishing he built up, a sensitive and vulnerable mind that was full of contradictions. In Hemingway, sentimentality, sympathy, and empathy are turned inwards, not restrained, but vibrant below and beyond the level of fact and fable. The reader feels their presence although they are not visible in the actual words. That is because of Hemingway's awareness of the relation between the truth of facts and events and his conviction that they produce corresponding emotions.

"Find what gave you the emotion; what the action was that gave you the excitement. Then write it down making it clear so the reader will see it too and have the same feeling as you had." That was the essence of his style, to focus on facts. Hemingway aimed at "the real thing, the sequence of motion and fact which made the emotion and which would be as valid in a year or in ten years or, with luck and if you stated it purely enough, always" (Death in the Afternoon). In Hemingway, we see a reaction against Romantic turgidity and vagueness: back to basics, to the essentials. Thus his new realism in a new key resembles the old Puritan simplicity and discipline; both of them refrained from exhibiting the sentimental, the relative. Hemingway's sincere and stern ambition was to approach Truth, clinging to an as yet unwritten code, a higher law which he referred to as "an absolute conscience as unchanging as the standard meter in Paris".

## NEAR-DEATH EXPERIENCE

Though Hemingway seems to have seen himself and life in general reflected in war, he himself never became reconciled to it. His mind was in a state of civil war, fighting demons inwardly as well as outwardly. In the long run defeat is as revealing and fundamental as victory: we are all losers, defeated by death. To live is the only way to face the ordeal, and the ultimate ordeal in our lives is the opposite of life. Hence Hemingway's obsession with death. Deep sea fishing, bull-fighting, boxing, big-game hunting, war, all are means of ritualizing the death struggle in his mind it is very explicit in books such as A Farewell to Arms and Death in the Afternoon, which were based on his own experience.

Modern investigations into so-called Near-Death Experiences (NDE) such as those by Raymond Moody, Kenneth Ring and many others, have focused on a pattern of empirical knowledge gained on the threshold of death; a dream-like encounter with unknown border regions.

There is a parallel in Hemingway's life, connected with the occasion when he was seriously wounded at midnight on July 8, 1918, at Fossalta di Piave in Italy and nearly died. He was the first American to be wounded in Italy during World War I. Here is a case of NDE in Hemingway, and I think that is of basic importance, pertinent to the understanding of all Hemingway's work. In A Farewell to Arms, an experience of this sort occurs to the ambulance driver Frederic Henry, Hemingway's alter ego, wounded in the leg by shellfire in Italy. (Concerning the highly autobiographical nature of A Farewell to Arms, see Michael S. Reynolds's documentary work Hemingway's First War: The Making of A Farewell to Arms, Princeton University Press 1976). As regards the NDE, we can note the incidental expression "to go out in a blaze of light" (letter to his family, Milan Oct. 18, 1918), and the long statement about what had occurred: Milan, July 21, 1918 (Selected Letters, ed. Carlos Baker, 1981).

Hemingway touched on that crucial experience in his life what he had felt and thought - in the short story "Now I Lay Me" (1927): "my soul would go out of my body I had been blown up at night and felt it go out of me and go off and then come back" and again, briefly, in In Our Time in the lines on the death of Maera. It reappears, in another setting and form, in the image of immortality in the African story The Snows of Kilimanjaro, where the dying Harry knows he is going to the peak called "Ngàje Ngài", which means, as explained in Hemingway's introductory note, "the House of God".

## THE COYOTE AND THE LEOPARD

Hemingway's seeming insensitive detachment is only superficial, a compulsive avoidance of the emotional, but not of the emotionally tinged or charged. The pattern of his rigid, dispassionate compressed style of writing and way of life gives a picture of a touching Jeremiad of human tragedy. Hemingway's probe touches nerves, and they hurt. But through the web of failure and disillusion there emerges a picture of human greatness, of confidence even.

Hemingway was not the Nihilist he has often been called. As he belonged to the Protestant nay-saying tradition of American dissent, the spirit of the American Revolution, he denied the denial and acceded to the basic truth which he found in the human soul: the will to live, the will to persevere, to endure, to defy. The all-pervading sense of loss is, indirectly, affirmative. Hemingway's style is a compulsive suppression of unbearable and inexpressible feelings in the chaotic world of his times, where courage and independence offered a code of survival. Sentiments are suppressed to the boil.

The frontier mentality had become universal - the individual is on his own, like a Pilgrim walking into the unknown with neither shelter nor guidance, thrown upon his own resources, his strength and his judgment. Hemingway's style is the style of understatement since his hero is a hero of action, which is the human condition. There is an illuminating text in William James (1842-1910) which is both significant and reminiscent, bridging the gap between Puritan moralism, its educational parables and exempla, and lost-generation turbulent heroism.

In a letter written in Yosemite Valley to his son, Alexander, William James wrote: "I saw a moving sight the other morning before breakfast in a little hotel where I slept in the dusty fields. The young man of the house had shot a little wolf called coyote in the early morning. The heroic little animal lay on the ground, with his big furry ears, and his clean white teeth, and his jolly cheerful little body, but his brave little life was gone.

It made me think how brave all these living things are. Here little coyote was, without any clothes or house or books or anything, with nothing but his own naked self to pay his way with, and risking his life so cheerfully - and losing it - just to see if he could pick up a meal near the hotel. He was doing his coyote-business like a hero, and you must do your boy-business, and I my man-business bravely, too, or else we won't be worth as much as a little coyote." (The Letters of William James, ed. Henry James, Little, Brown and Co.: Boston 1926.)

The courageous coyote thus serves as a moral example, illustrating a philosophy of life which says that it is worth jeopardizing life itself to be true to one's own nature. That is precisely the point of the frozen leopard close to the western summit of Kilimanjaro in Hemingway's famous short story. That is the explanation of what the leopard was seeking at that altitude, and the answer was given time and again in the works of Ernest Hemingway.

## JEOPARDIZING LIFE ITSELF TO BE TRUE TO ONE'S OWN NATURE

But what about the ugliness, then? What about all the evil, the crude, the rude, the rough, the vulgar aspects of his work, even the horror, which dismayed people? How could all that be compatible with moral standards? He justified the inclusion of such aspects in a letter to his "Dear Dad" in 1925:

"The reason I have not sent you any of my work is because you or Mother sent back the In Our Time books. That looked as though you did not want to see any. You see I am trying in all my stories to get the feeling of the actual life across - not to just depict life - or criticize it - but to actually make it alive. So that when you have read something by me you actually experience the thing. You can't do this without putting in the bad and the ugly as well as what is beautiful. Because if it is all beautiful you can't believe in it. Things aren't that way. It is only by showing both sides 3 dimensions and if possible 4 that you can write the way I want to.

So when you see anything of mine that you don't like remember that I'm sincere in doing it and that I'm working toward something. If I write an ugly story that might be hateful to you or to Mother the next one might be one that you would like exceedingly."

## MERGING GENDER IN EDEN

Like many others of his works, True at First Light was a blend of autobiography and fiction in which the author identified with the first person narrator. The author, who never kept a journal or wrote an autobiography in his life, draws on experience for his realism, slightly transforming events in his life. In this sense, the posthumous novel Islands in the Stream is in some places neither fictional nor fictitious. The Garden of Eden, however, a book brimming with the author's vulnerability just as A Farewell to Arms is, treats intimate and delicate matters. It is a story told in the third person, as are all his major works. Thus we get to know the writer David Bourne, assuredly an explorer like Daniel Boone, on his adventurous Mediterranean honeymoon.

The anti-hero's wife in The Garden of Eden, Catherine Bourne, is one of the most persuasive and lively heroines in Hemingway's works. She is depicted with fascination and fear, like Marcel Proust's Albertine and, at least in name, she reminds us of the strong and attractive Catherine Barkley (alias the seven-year-older Agnes Von Kurowsky), the Red Cross heroine in A Farewell to Arms. The former character is much more complex and difficult to define, however, and her ardor and the fire of marital love prove consuming and transmogrifying.

Living at the Grau ("canal") du Roi, on the shores of the stream that runs from Aigues-Mortes straight down to the sea, the newly wedded couple in The Garden of Eden live in a borderland where "water" and "death" are key words, and where connotations like L'eau du Léthe present themselves: Eros and Thanatos, love and death, paradise and trespass.

In this innocent borderland, moral limits are immediately extended, and conventional roles are reversed. Sipping his post-coital fine à l'eau in the afternoon, David Bourne feels relieved of all the problems he had before his marriage, and has no thought of "writing nor anything but being with this girl," who absorbs him and assumes command. Then the blond, sun-tanned Catherine appears with her hair "cropped as short as a boy's," declaring: "now I am a boy You see why it's dangerous, don't you? Why do we have to go by everyone else's rules? We're us Please understand and love me I am Peter You're my beautiful lovely Catherine."

From that moment the tables are turned. David-Catherine accepts and submits, and Catherine-Peter takes over the man's role. She mounts him in bed at night, and penetrates him in conjugal bliss:

"He had shut his eyes and he could feel the long light weight of her on him and then lay back in the dark and did not think at all and only felt the weight and the strangeness inside and she said: 'Now you can't tell who is who can you?"

## THE FATHER IN THE GARDEN

Women with a gamin hairstyle, lovers who cut and dye their hair and change sexual roles, are themes that, with variations, occur in his novels from A Farewell to Arms, For Whom the Bell Tolls, to the posthumous Islands in the Stream. They culminate in The Garden of Eden. When writing The Garden of Eden he appeared as a redhead one day in May 1947.

When asked about it, he said he had dyed his hair by mistake. In that novel, the search for complete unity between the lovers is carried to extremes. It may seem that the halves of the primordial Androgyne of the Platonic myth (once cut in two by Zeus and ever since longing to become a complete being again) are uniting here. Set in a fictional Paradise, a Biblical "Eden", the novel is perhaps even more a story about expulsion, the loss of innocence, and the ensuing liberation, about knowledge acquired through the Fall, which is the basis of culture, about the ordeals and the high price an author must pay to become a writer worthy of his salt.

Against a mythical background, the voice of Hemingway's father is heard, challenging his son, as did the Father in the Biblical Garden. Slightly disguised, Hemingway's dear father, who haunted his son's life and work even after he had shot himself in 1928, remained an internalized critic until Ernest also took his life in 1961. Hemingway's père pressed his ambivalent son to surpass himself and produce a distinct and lively multidimensional text, - "3 dimensions and if possible":

"He found he knew much more about his father than when he had first written this story and he knew he could measure his progress by the small things which made his father more tactile and to have more dimensions than he had in the story before." After they had committed honeymoon adultery with the girl both spouses equally love passionately, David exclaims: "We've been burned out Crazy woman burned out the Bournes."

This consuming and transforming fire of love and its subsequent trials and transgressions, in the end has a purging effect on the writer, who finally, as if emerging from a chrysalis stage, rises like the Phoenix from his bed and sits down in a regenerated mood to write in a perfect style:

"He got out his pencils and a new cahier, sharpened five pencils and began to write the story of his father and the raid in the year of the Maji-Maji rebellion David wrote steadily and well and the sentences that he had made before came to him complete and entire and he put them down, corrected them, and cut them as if he were going over proof. Not a sentence was missing He wrote on a while longer now and there was no sign that any of it would ever cease returning to him intact."

## MAJI-MAJI AND MAU MAU

But why is Maji-Maji so important to the author when he has attained perfection? When Tanzania gained independence in 1961-62, President Julius Nyerere proclaimed that the new republic was the fulfillment of the Maji-Maji dream. The Maji-Maji Rebellion had been a farmers' revolt against colonial rule in German East Africa in 1905-1907. It began in the hill country southwest of Dar es-Salaam and spread rapidly until the insurrection was finally crushed after some 70,000 Africans had been killed.

The farmers challenged the German militia fearlessly, crying "Maji! Maji!" when they attacked, believing themselves to be protected from bullets and death by "magic water". Maji is Swahili for "water" – one of the key words in Hemingway's novel. The conviction and purposefulness of the Maji-Maji in The Garden of Eden, corresponds to the Kenyan Mau-Mau context of the novel True at First Light, which Hemingway started writing after his East African safari in 1953. Mau Mau was an insurrection of Kikuyo farm laborers in 1952.

It was led by Jomo Kenyatta, who was subsequently held in prison until he became the premier of Kenya in 1963 (and the first President of the Republic in 1964). For Kikuyo men or women (and there were several women in the movement), to join Mau Mau meant dedicating their lives to a cause and sacrificing everything else, it meant taking a sacred oath that definitely cut them off from decorum and ordinary life. In Hemingway's vision, Maji-Maji and Mau Mau blend with his notion of the ideal committed writer, a man who is prepared to die for his art, and for art's sake.

In the private library of Dag Hammarskjöld, who was awarded the Nobel Peace Prize after his death in the Congo (Africa) in 1961, the year Hemingway died, a copy of the beautiful original edition of A Farewell to Arms (Charles Scribner's Sons, 1929) may still be seen (now in the Royal Library, Stockholm). In a way it is significant that the Secretary-General of the United Nations, who was dedicated to peacemaking, should have been a Hemingway reader.

## Chapter 16

# Ernest Hemingway and World War I

Combatting recent psychobiographical reassessments, restoring the war "Napoleon taught Stendahl how to write." - Ernest Hemingway

To ask whether or not the First World War had a profound effect upon Ernest Hemingway would, not so long ago, have been considered a rhetorical question. It can no longer be considered so, since the influential critics Kenneth S. Lynn and Frederick Crews have sought to dismiss the importance of World War I from Hemingway's life and fiction.'

The mainstream interpretation, which held sway well into the 198xOs, had been advanced in most detail by Philip Young, whose breadth of analysis and psychoanalytical bent amplified the theory of the wound first advanced by Edmund Wilson. Although he did not speak as extensively of the wound theory, Malcolm Cowley had already marked out Hemingway's First World War experiences as a turning point in his life as early as 1945.

Following Cowley and Young, many a teacher taught many a student that Hemingway was badly wounded at the war-wounded inside as well as outside. The war left him with a fear of night, a fear said to relate to his abrupt confrontation with his own mortality. It gave him insight into the fragility of the world, and it fostered a deep skepticism towards the grand abstractions that the First World War rendered bitterly ironic. For a generation of critics, the war was not only the obvious subject matter, the sine qua non, of certain stories and novels, it also undergirded the entire oeuvre, and lurked below the surface of certain important stories that never mentioned the war.

But times have changed, and as Susan Beegel puts it in her recent bibliographic essay on Hemingway criticism, in the 1980s "it became clear that the `wound' and the `code' were about to be muscled off the stage of Hemingway studies". Because the psychobiographical version elaborated by Lynn and supported by Crews inaccurately reappraises Hemingway's life and work in relation to the war, and because this erroneous version has gained considerable currency indeed, much outright acceptance-among general readers and academics alike, I would like to consider anew the importance of the First World War in Hemingway's life and work.

I am not concerned here with clarifying the events surrounding Hemingway's wounding at Fossalta di Piave, for Robert W. Lewis, Michael Reynolds, and, most skeptically, Jeffrey Meyers have thoroughly examined this episode. In a study co-credited to Henry S. Villard, James Nagel has constructed the most convincing say on this matter, countering to a degree the more skeptical scholarly opinions.

They have shown the necessity of questioning biographical sources and interpretations that have hardened into "facts," and, more importantly, their discussions of Hemingway's war experiences rid this portion of his life of a critical one-dimensionality that may have begun to cling to it. But Lynn and Crews have subsequently substituted one sort of unidimensionality for another. They make it seem as if the war slid off Hemingway like water off a duck's back and have asked us to understand that some of his most admired war stories are not really war stories after all.

Such stories as "Now I Lay Me" and "Big Two-Hearted River," they argue, do not have a wounding nor even the generalized trauma of war at their centre, perhaps not even at their periphery. From the demythification of Hemingway's own wound, these critics have extrapolated a Hemingway profoundly unchanged by what he experienced in Italy. Thus Frederick Crews on Hemingway: "Nothing in his subsequent conduct suggests that he returned from Italy with a subdued temper, much less a revulsion against killing or a grasp of the issues and ironies behind the war".

Thus Kenneh S. Lynn on "Now I Lay Me," a story set seven kilometers from the front in Italy and whose two main characters are hospitalized soldiers: "What counts supremely in the story is not the northern Italian frame that has made so many readers regard it as a tale of war, but the childhood memories within the frame" Writing on the publication of Hemingway's Selected Letters in 1981, Lynn argued that the war played no part in "Big TwoHearted River," a story he describes as "a sun-drenched, Cezannesque picture of a predominantly happy fishing trip" ("Private War" 26). In the process of laying out his surprising version of Hemingway's famous story, Lynn rakes Malcolm Cowley over the coals.

Attaching anti-American motives to Cowley, he excoriates his introduction to The Portable Hemingway, wherein he sees Cowley "shoveling much more war-victim material into `Big Two-Hearted River"` ("Private War" 25). In 1984 Cowley responded to Lynn's attack, reiterating his belief in the importance of Hemingway's war experience and offering as new testimony a previously unpublished letter from 1948 in which Hemingway directly states that Cowley was correct about the war wound: "Big Two Hearted River [sic] is a story about a man who is home from the war". In 1985, R. W. B. Lewis thought that the argument had been put to rest, with Cowley winning the day.

Not so, however. In his subsequently published biography, Lynn devotes over four pages to refuting the war-trauma interpretation of "Big Two-Hearted River" and asserts that Hemingway's letter was one of several posthumously published pieces which that Hemingway to be "a master manipulator making fools of [critics] from beyond the grave". Thereafter Frederick Crews joined ranks with Lynn, specifically countering both Cowley and Lewis and asserting the wholesale claim that Hemingway returned from the war unchanged. The rest of this essay will be a direct refutation of the revisionists' interpretation of the war's influence on both

Hemingway's life and fiction, using "Big Two-Hearted River" as a case in point.

Crews in particular make much of the cheery, jocular tone found in the young Hemingway's letters home from the Italian hospital where he was recuperating. These letters prove, he claims, that Hemingway couldn't have been much hurt: "the adeptness of his sprightly rhetoric sits poorly with the conventional idea of his thoroughly unnerved, shell-shocked condition". Setting aside the caricature of "the conventional idea" as holding that Hemingway was immediately and absolutely psychically altered by his wounding, what Crews too easily dismisses is the rhetorical context of these letters home.

Very likely Hemingway did as millions of war veterans have done and adopted the uncomplaining, kidding stoicism expected of him under the circumstances. The manly thing, the adult thing, the heroic thing was not to let on to those at home. Besides putting on the brave and happy face, the later letters could well constitute a bid for public attention, as James R. Mellow has asserted. Hemingway's early letters were delivered to the local press by his parents, and Hemingway's subsequent letters were surely written under the apprehension that they might well find a public audience. No doubt Hemingway did find things in his wounding and in his hospital stay in which he could take comfort.

Even this sort of ordeal, with all its attendant pains and fears, had its compensations in social status and new experience. But about his wounding and convalescence, several facts are not in dispute. He underwent surgery, he picked many pieces of shrapnel from his legs, and, thanks largely to his drinking, he was hit with a case of jaundice. Hemingway was, by several accounts, the life of the party on the hospital floor, full of still adolescent vigour, and his letters home are indeed chipper, but he was not a fool incapable of comprehending the gravity of his situation or of feeling his injuries.

Crews and Lynn do not mention Agnes von Kurowsky's statement that, while hospitalized, Hemingway "was worried about his leg. He was afraid they'd amputate") nor that as late as 22 April 1920, he straight forwardly explained to his parents that although his leg was in pretty good shape, it still bothered him after a hard day-a long recovery time for a young and active man. An early attempt at a fictionalized version of his wounding develops a decidedly unspritely rhetoric. Writing longhand on Milan Red Cross stationery, Hemingway sketches the downfall of Nick Grainger of Petoskey, Michigan.

Like Hemingway, Nick has been struck in the legs by a mortar on the Italian front. Yet, his case is worse than Hemingway's in that he apparently has lost both his legs and his left arm to amputation. The war over, peace celebrants noisy in the streets, Nick bitterly fingers his medals and remains uncomforted by the florid citation that accompanies them. The sketch ends before he swallows the poisonous bichloride solution he has filched for the clear purpose of committing suicide. As a piece of fiction-corny dialogue, unrealized ironic potential-this sketch provides a baseline from which to measure Hemingway's growth as a writer during his subsequent Paris apprenticeship.

And the sketch is an early instance of the suicide theme that would become central in Hemingway's life and fiction. Most to the point here, this particular piece of writing directly refutes the revisionists' thesis that the war contained no dark dimension for the young Hemingway.

And nowhere in the revised version of Hemingway does one see mention of his confidences to his wife Hadley about his recurrent battle nightmares-this in 1923, five years after his wounding. Rather than recognize the mixed nature of Hemingway's wounding, Crews and Lynn insist on depicting a sort of dumb (but cheerful) ox, all the while ignoring the cultural context of his behaviour as well as much evidence that would necessitate a less one-dimensional portrait of Hemingway. There is indeed a great deal more evidence that indicates Hemingway was profoundly influenced by the war.

Both his life and his fictions show that the wounding had its serious effects. Members of Hemingway's family who observed him upon his return from the war would agree. His brother Leicester has written that "not all of Ernest's wounds were physical. Like hundreds of thousands of other soldiers before and since, he had received some psychic shock. He was plagued by insomnia and couldn't sleep unless he had a light in his room" could be argued that Leicester, a young boy when Hemingway returned from Italy, must be judged a second-hand source in regards to this event, perhaps even that he is only giving a version of events fed to him at some later date by brother Ernest.

However, Leicester was actually an early debunker of some of Ernest's Italian war tales, and in regards to this particular portion of his brother's life is not gullible. Furthermore, Marcelline, who was twenty one at the time, also relates her brother's troubled mental state in her memoirs. "In between [his] extrovert activities Ernie had quiet, almost depressed intervals," she writes. But she actually proceeds to betray her protect the-family name use of the word almost, for she describes her brother as staying in bed for long periods of time, drinking on the sly to ease his pain, retreating from family activities and showing little inclination to forge an adult identity for himself.

Reading of Hemingway's letters also reveals a change in his state of mind after the war. With an oddly narrow selectivity and tendentious emphasis, Crews examines Hemingway's 1948 letter to Cowley, wherein Hemingway states, "In the first war, I now see, I was hurt very badly; in the body, mind and spirit; and also morally". Crews emphasizes the clause 1 now see to declare that Hemingway "belatedly claimed to have adopted this poignant" war-wound reading.

As I have already shown, there is a great deal of evidence apart from this one letter with which to counter Crews's mis-emphasis, but a different reading of the letter also presents itself as plausible. It is more tenable to emphasize the words very badly, so that we see the older Hemingway not belatedly claiming a wound he never felt, as Crews would have it, but better understanding the dimensions and profundity of that wound.

This interpretation is bolstered when the next sentence from the letter is not omitted from consideration: "The true gen is I was hurt bad all the way through". All the way through, Hemingway particularizes, and, more tellingly, he uses a favourite phrase of his at the time-the true gen-which he used to signify the transcendent, core truth adhering to an event.

The gen, the mere fact, had always been that Hemingway was wounded; the true gen was that he had been wounded deeply, quite probably so deeply that his trauma found itself in his stories in a way that he was only partially conscious of and only partially but not totally in control of as an author. Such slowly arrived-at self understanding, the gradual (or eventual) coming to terms with the sort of trauma suffered by Hemingway should not be difficult to imagine.

Lynn and Crews undermine their arguments by staging false dilemmas. Either Hemingway immediately and constantly showed the profound effects of the war upon him, or he came out of the war untouched. Either the psychic germ of "Big Two-Hearted River" is World War I or it is Hemingway's conflicts with his mother, but not both. But those who have known or worked with veterans know that the effects of trauma may surface only after the passage of time, sometimes gradually, sometimes by fits and starts, sometimes all at once upon actuation by a particular stimulus, sometimes after the passage of many seemingly trouble-free years.

Likewise, understanding the effects of one's wounding is a process, often one that transpires over many years, even decades. There is no single, exclusive paradigm that invariably governs the effects of traumatic experience.' It is certainly reasonable to conclude that Hemingway suffered the effects of his wounding to a degree at first (and I wish to re-emphasize to a greater degree than acknowledged by Crews or Lynn), and that with the passage of time he came to a deeper awareness and a better understanding of the war's effects upon him.

It is reasonable to accept that the reaction to a wounding need not come in a simple either/or form, that a wounding survived can leave victims feeling alternatively vulnerable and indestructible, and that the balance between these two feelings is quite capable of shifting over the course of one's life. Avoid It is true that in the 1950s Hemingway actually denied the war-wound interpretation of his work as put forth by Philip Young. But Hemingway's objections in this instance were partly strategic.

He wished to hold prying biographers and critics-of whom there were beginning to be a substantial number-at bay, and he was not about to encourage any public version of himself that did not conform to the hairy-chested hero regularly depicted in the pages of national magazines. In his letters of the period he repeatedly asserts his desire to retain his privacy and to have his fictions read on their own terms, without reference to facts from his own life.

In part these assertions stem from sincere beliefs about his art and in part they stem from Hemingway's heavy investment in the macho myth that adhered to his life in the fifties. On the subject of his own biography, Hemingway had mixed feelings and was capable of combining subtle encouragement with openly expressed discouragement in his letters to would-be biographers and critics. In Young's particular case, Hemingway does not deny that he was traumatized in WWI, but rightly sees the critic as oversimplifying the oeuvre and overplaying his critical thesis.

There had been "plenty [of] trauma in 1918," he admitted to Harvey Breit, complaining that Young dwells on the trauma, rather than the fact that he had managed to overcome it. By this time, too, the public Hemingway, "`fraid o' nothing," had firmly seized hold of a large segment of the casual public's imagination and of its subject's own self conception as well. The truths Hemingway told in his fictions battled with the Life-magazine myth, which was to a large extent of his own making. Hemingway's letters do demonstrate his ability to prevaricate, pose, and manipulate.

They also show him to be sincere and straightforward in many instances. Hemingway's 1948 assertion of war trauma to Cowley should be taken at its word. For one thing, what he says in his letter runs counter to the public persona he had participated in building, and, as we shall see, there is a great deal of evidence to be gathered from his statements and fictional works of the twenties that supports his retrospective self assessment. In his quest to prove that Hemingway's "`post war disillusionment', such as it was, proved to be a belated and derivative manifestation," Crews ignores a great deal of very early evidence, including a 1926 letter to Maxwell Perkins.

Writing twenty-two years earlier than the letter to Cowley that Crews picks at, Hemingway complains that Allen Tate has been unfair to him by creating a sort of critical dipstick with which to measure the depth of his alleged hard boiledness: "As a matter of fact I have not been at all hard boiled since July 8 1918-on the night of which I discovered that that also was Vanity" (sic) (Selected Letters 240). The date Hemingway mentions, of course, is that of his wounding at Fossalta di Piave. It is difficult to posit a motivation for Hemingway to lie gratuitously to Perkins in 1926 about his reaction to being wounded.

Neither are Hemingway's early war poems taken into account by the revisionists, including one entitled "Killed Piave July $ -1918," in which a female speaker expresses her longing for her dead lover, who appears metaphorically as "A dull, cold, rigid bayonet" (Complete Poems 35). Written in Paris (all before 1923), the war poems offer little by way of literary achievement but do comprise more evidence that Hemingway thought seriously about the war and felt its wasteful, destructive nature early on, not belatedly. Lynn makes nothing of the poems but chooses to summarize Hemingway's many later assertions that the war had injured him as an obdurate old man's "effort[s] to account for his imperiled sense of himself, as well as to preserve his macho reputation".

Finally neither Crews nor Lynn adequately deals with the imposing fact that so many of Hemingway's protagonists including those in his earliest stories-are men wounded in war: Nick Adams, Jake Barnes, Frederic Henry, Robert Jordan. Sticking with his posthumous psychoanalysis, insistently returning to the sites of supposed childhood trauma, positing Hemingway as always and ever the victim of himself, Lynn ignores the recurrent presence of fictional protagonists wounded by war.

This is not to say that Lynn does not delve into the psyches of these characters; rather, it is to say that he fails to come to terms with the fact that out of an infinite number of causes available with which to wound his main characters, Hemingway consistently chose war. It is obviously impossible to disprove the centrality of the war in stories set at the front, such as "Now I Lay Me"; therefore Lynn's and Crews's arguments need be discussed no further in relation to these stories. However, both men have also examined "Big Two-Hearted River," and this story's relationship to the war is admittedly much more indirect.

Predictably they have found that this story is not concerned with the war either, though many readers have seen it as depicting a war-traumatized Nick Adams returning to familiar territory for camping, fishing and psychic, perhaps spiritual, recovery. Not so, says Lynn. The story is really about Hemingway's rebellious squabbles with his mother Grace. For two consecutive summers after returning from the war, Hemingway and his mother fought an escalating series of battles that culminated in his banishment from the family summer home in July of 1920.

Lynn deduces that this familial acrimony is the true psychic germ of Hemingway's famous story: Perhaps, then, the "other needs" Nick feels he has put behind him include a need to please his mother, while his talk of his tent as his home may represent a reaction to being thrown out of his parents' summer cottage. Perhaps, too, the burned-over country and the grasshoppers that have turned black from living in it constitute tacit reminders to him of his mother's penchant for burning things. And finally, the activity of his mind that keeps threatening to overwhelm his contentment could be his rage [towards his mother).

This argument is consistent with a dominant tendency in Lynn's study: that the conflicts in Hemingway's stories have their source in his own psychic turmoil, that he had little understanding of, often little awareness of, the nature of his rages and inner torments. Lynn's method is at once subtle and mechanical. It is subtle in that it combines detailed biographical research with sophisticated readings of the works and exhibits the critic's high powers of inference.

Yet Lynn too often uses his subtle insights less than responsibly. Lynn's conditional rhetoric here ("perhaps," "may," "perhaps," "could be") would seem to indicate that his reading of this enigmatic story is as speculative as any other, as indeed it is. But in the course of his argument, Lynn actually treats his speculation as if it were a fact beyond dispute-witness his excoriation of those whose speculations are not in line with his own. Lynn's method becomes mechanical in that it insists upon the equation inner torment equals content of the story, while assertive, consciously controlled, fictive imagination is relegated to the end of the bench.

In light of the vitriolic opinions expressed about his mother by Hemingway as an older man, it is perhaps difficult to judge his 1920 fights with her as merely typical of a twenty year-olds desire to be granted autonomy and adult status. Lynn clearly does not judge them so, but rather presents them as being manifestations of a mind already abnormally conflicted in regards to his mother. But surely the war itself was an integral part of Hemingway's conflict with the old-fashioned, sanctimonious, emotionally coercive Grace. Surely it was doubly difficult in his particular situation to be treated like a kid.

It was the summer of his coming of age, a stage of life when the final thrust towards independence and adult status is normal and necessary. But also, as a young man who had been at the war and one-time city beat reporter in Kansas City, he had already seen much more than someone his age would usually see, and he had experienced things far beyond the ken of his suburban, essentially Victorian parents. The same mother who had initially doted on her son's war-hero status overlooked the deeper changes his experiences had caused in him.' In an unpublished letter to Charles Poore, Hemingway relates that after being home from the war for some time "I was having a pretty bad time and my mother started to eat me out for drinking and not taking things seriously etc. and I told her that I had had a sort of bad time some of the time in the war and that if she would leave me alone I would work out of it okay."

In his description of Hemingway's summers of familial discontent, Lynn again presumes a false dilemma-it was either the war (wrong interpretation) or his mother (correct interpretation) that was at the root of Hemingway's-and hence Nick's-restlessness and moodiness. That the two problems could be mixed together, as they skillfully are in fictional form in "Soldier's Home," for example, is an idea that Lynn never entertains.

# Chapter 17

# Criticism by Arnold A. Markley

Markley is an assistant professor at the Penn State University, Delaware County campus. In the following essay he examines Hemingway's distinctive writing style, use of his own war experiences, and examination of themes of identity as they appear in A Farewell to Arms.

Ernest Hemingway is known for his distinctive writing style, an unusually bare, straightforward prose in which he characteristically uses plain words, few adjectives, simple sentences, and frequent repetition. Nevertheless his powers of description are not diminished by his taking care to choose such simple language.

Take a look, for example, at the opening paragraph of A Farewell to Arms:

In the late summer of that year we lived in a house in a village that looked across the river and the plain to the mountains. In the bed of the river there were pebbles and boulders, dry and white in the sun, and the water was clear and swiftly moving and blue in the channels. Troops went by the house and down the road and the dust they raised powdered the leaves of the trees. The trunks of the trees too were dusty and the leaves fell early that year and we saw the troops marching along the road and the dust rising and leaves, stirred by the breeze, falling and the soldiers marching and afterward the road bare and white except for the leaves.

This beautifully written paragraph exemplifies the simplicity of Hemingway's language, and his tendency towards both vivid description and repetition. Hemingway worked hard to write in such a way as to give his readers highly descriptive passages without distracting them with "big words," and he hoped that his writing would leave his readers with distinct visual impressions, without their being able to recall anything unusual or memorable about the language itself.

Despite the simplicity of the language in a paragraph such as the one above, the effect is quite complex. Not only does the author provide a vivid description of the geographical setting for the novel, but he also achieves a sense of the passing of time. The season gradually passes from summer into fall as the paragraph progresses, and likewise the sense of time passing is emphasized by the repeated detail of the soldiers marching by, signalling the reader to the fact that this novel is set in a time of war.

A Farewell to Arms was first published in 1929, and Hemingway had to be persistent in convincing his editor, Maxwell Perkins at Charles Scribner's Sons, not to censor language that the publishing house felt was "indecent." In addition, some contemporary readers found the novel's frank depiction of pre-marital sex to be distasteful, and the book was banned for a time in Boston due to a particular police chief's feeling that it was "salacious." Nevertheless, the novel was immediately popular, and it has enjoyed a warm reception from literary critics throughout the twentieth century.

The novel was Hemingway's first big success, and it cemented his growing reputation as an author of great talent. The novel is narrated by the central character, Frederic Henry, an American who is serving in an Italian ambulance unit during the First World War. Hemingway's style is very effective in his development of Frederic's character. Because the novel is written as if it were Frederic's autobiography, or memoirs, the events of the novel are filtered through Frederic's own consciousness.

The simple style and plain language contribute to the realistic nature of Frederic's voice and his thoughts; at times it even seems as if the reader has been given access to the inner workings of Frederic's mind, as in the excerpt included in the plot summary. The fact that all of the events are seen through

Frederic's eyes also means that the reader's impressions of the other characters in the novel must also come through Frederic's impressions. In fact, Hemingway relies heavily on his highly realistic dialogue in sketching portraits of the other characters, and in revealing how Frederic relates to them, and what each character experiences in the way of feelings, concerns, and motivations.

As a novel of war, based on Hemingway's own experiences in World War I, one of the work's major concerns lies in its critique of the concept of war. At the beginning of the novel Frederic Henry is nonchalant about the war that is going on around him. He is, after all, an American fighting in the Italian army, and he feels a sense of displacement and detachment as a result. Moreover, other characters, particularly Catherine Barkley, comment on the peculiarity of his being an American in the Italian army.

Initially Frederic does not feel that he will be affected by this war — it has nothing to do with him, he says. He lives a hedonistic lifestyle, focusing on his pleasures — drinking and sex. Even after meeting Catherine and getting to know her, he does not initially feel that he will fall in love with her. He merely wishes to become involved with her as if in a game like bridge, but a game in which one makes moves by making statements rather than with caids.

Nevertheless, Frederic is changed by the war. When he is wounded and falls in love with Catherine over the long summer of his recuperation, he returns to the front to find conditions much changed. Things have not been going well for the Italians during his absence, and he notices a distinct difference in the attitudes of his peers — they are much more depressed and anxious about the war, even his usually carefree friend Rinaldi.

The war has become darker and more threatening, and when Frederic is caught up in the chaotic retreat of the Italians from Caporetto, he is confronted with the grimmest realities of war for the first time; he watches as a companion is downed by a sniper, and he himself has a narrow brush with death when he approaches the carbinieri, or military police, as they are executing Italian officers at the bridge over the Tagliamento.

Enough is enough. This isn't my war anyway, Frederic says to himself, and he makes his "farewell to arms" with no reservations about deserting his post in a war that has turned into a horrible nightmare. Like many of Hemingway's main characters, Frederic Henry is a man who is in search of something to believe in. Robert Penn Warren called his search a search for truth and for ethical standards. Frederic detests words that are separated from actions words like "glory" and "courage" were disgusting to him; for Frederic, it is only in one's actions that such concepts have any value or meaning.

A religion, or any organized system of beliefs, has to be tried and tested before Frederic will be able to accept it, and as yet, he has found no system of beliefs or values to which to commit himself entirely. Early in the novel when his companions bait and tease the priest, Frederic nevertheless respects the humble man. Even though he doesn't agree with many of the priest's beliefs concerning Christianity, he admires the priest for believing in his religion and for loving his country so strongly.

As the war progresses, Frederic is better able to decide what he does not believe in he cannot be involved with the horror of war any longer, and instead he devotes himself to his love for Catherine Barkley. And Catherine devotes herself to Frederic, even telling him that he is her religion at one point. Frederic's search is also a search for home a place where he can be comfortable and safe. Throughout the novel he finds it difficult to sleep at night, frightened by the sense of nothingness he feels then. With Catherine, he finally finds a kind of home, first in the hospital in Milan and later in their mountain chalet in Switzerland.

Frederic seems to have found what he has been looking for in his love for Catherine, until Catherine suddenly and unexpectedly dies, just as they are beginning plans for their new life together. Some critics, such as Ray B. West, Jr. and E. M. Halliday, have chosen to read Hemingway's title as ironic, interpreting Hemingway's message that one cannot actually make a "farewell to arms." Frederic may have escaped the brutality and cruelty of war, but ultimately there is no way to escape pain, and solitude, and the difficult aspects of life. There is only entrapment, wherever one turns. Gerry Brenner has written that A Farewell to Arms, which involves an ambulance driver and a nurse and situates a number of its key scenes in hospitals, is less a novel about war or about love than it is a novel about wounds.

Hemingway makes use of some very important symbolism in this novel. Even as early as the first paragraph, he sets up two major symbols the plains and the mountains which will be in conflict throughout the story. Hemingway represents the plains as dangerous, miserable, dry, and barren. The mountains, on the other hand, represent safety, happiness, and good health. The military action that Frederic Henry witnesses takes place on the plains, and his escape, through the cleansing, baptismal ritual of jumping into the river, reaches its end in the secluded mountain chalet with Catherine. But when Frederic must take Catherine out of the mountains and back down to the city below to the hospital where she is to give birth, disaster strikes again.

Rain is another important symbol throughout the novel. Often the rain suggests impending doom; there is a storm the night that Frederic learns he must leave Italy at once to avoid being arrested, Catherine dreams that she is dead in the rain, and indeed at the conclusion of the novel, it is raining when Frederic returns to his hotel. The critic Carlos Baker's essay, "The Mountain and the Plain," is an excellent source for studying these aspects of Hemingway's use of symbolism.

A Farewell to Arms is a very dramatic book. Many scholars, such as Ray B. West, Jr., have compared its five-book structure to that of the traditional English five-act play. There are similarities to be drawn between the structure of the novel and tragic drama: the first book, like the first act in a play, introduces the characters and the situation of the story, and in the second book the romantic plot is developed. Book III provides a climactic turning point: Frederic's desertion of his post in the army and his decision to return to Catherine.

In Book IV it looks as if Frederic and Catherine have successfully escaped the threats of the past, only to meet a tragic end to their love in the final book, which brings the drama to a close like the last act of a tragedy. Moreover, Hemingway's heavy reliance on dialogue between his characters to develop both character and the story line makes the novel similar to a dramatic piece. Hemingway even called the novel his version of Romeo and Juliet.

Like Romeo and Juliet, Frederic and Catherine are lovers who are kept from finding a permanent happiness together, but unlike the world view of William Shakespeare in which there is a foolish family feud to blame for the lovers' deaths, in Hemingway, there is no one to blame for Catherine's fate and Frederic's ultimate solitude. Frederic is left alone in a world in which nothing is permanent, all is subject to chance, and the best one can do, ultimately, is to face that world with acceptance. The story, like Hemingway's style of writing, is bare-boned and realistic, simple and stark.

## Chapter 18

# Brief Review of all of his Works

The old man and the sea by Ernest Hemingway (Book)

Santiago is a Cuban fisherman who encounters a giant marlin in the Gulf Stream and the battle for his catch becomes one of survival against a band of marauding sharks.

A farewell to arms by Ernest Hemingway (Book)

441 editions published between 1900 and 2007 in 41 languages and held by 5,733 libraries worldwide

By turns romantic and harshly realistic, Hemingway's story of a tragic romance set against the brutality and confusion of World War I cemented his fame as a stylist and as a writer of extraordinary literary power. A volunteer ambulance driver and a beautiful English nurse fall in love when he is wounded on the Italian front. The best American novel to emerge from World War I, A Farewell to Arms is the unforgettable story of an American ambulance driver on the Italian front and his passion for a beautiful English nurse. Hemingway's frank portrayal of the love between Lieutenant Henry and Catherine Barkley, caught in the inexorable sweep of war, glows with an intensity unrivaled in modern literature, while his description of the German attack on Caporetto – of lines of fired men marching in the rain, hungry, weary, and demoralized – is one of the greatest moments in literary history. A story of love and pain, of loyalty and desertion, A Farewell to Arms, written when he was 30 years old, represents a new romanticism for Hemingway.

For whom the bell tolls by Ernest Hemingway (Book)

452 editions published between 1940 and 2007 in 35 languages and held by 5,561 libraries worldwide

In 1937 Ernest Hemingway traveled to Spain to cover the civil war there for the North American Newspaper Alliance. Three years later he completed the greatest novel to emerge from "the good fight," For Whom the Bell Tolls. The story of Robert Jordan, a young American in the International Brigades attached to an antifascist guerilla unit in the mountains of Spain, it tells of loyalty and courage, love and defeat, and the tragic death of an ideal. In his portrayal of Jordan's love for the beautiful Maria and his superb account of El Sordo's last stand, in his brilliant travesty of La Pasionaria and his unwillingness to believe in blind faith, Hemingway surpasses his achievement in The Sun Also Rises and A Farewell to Arms to create a work at once rare and beautiful, strong and brutal, compassionate, moving, and wise. "If the function of a writer is to reveal reality," Maxwell Perkins wrote Hemingway after reading the manuscript, "no one ever so completely performed it." Greater in power, broader in scope, and more intensely emotional than any of the author's previous works, it stands as one of the best war novels of all time.

The sun also rises by Ernest Hemingway (Book)

294 editions published between 1926 and 2007 in 31 languages and held by 5,480 libraries worldwide

Published in 1926 to explosive acclaim, The Sun Also Rises stands as perhaps the most impressive first novel ever written by an American writer. A roman Òclef about a group of American and English expatriates on an excursion from Paris's Left Bank to Pamplona for the July fiesta and its climactic bull fight, a journey from the center of a civilization spiritually bankrupted by the First World War to a vital, God-haunted world in which faith and honor have yet to lose their currency, the novel captured for the generation that would come to be called "Lost" the spirit of its age, and marked Ernest Hemingway as the preeminent writer of his time.

The complete short stories of Ernest Hemingway by Ernest Hemingway (Book)

161 editions published between 1900 and 2007 in 23 languages and held by 4,458 libraries worldwide

"Set in the varied landscapes of Spain, Africa, and the

American Midwest, this definitive audio collection traces the development and maturation of Hemingway's distinct and revolutionary storytelling style— from the plain bald language of his first story to his mastery of seamless prose that contained a spare, eloquent pathos, as well as a sense of expansive solitude"—Container.

A moveable feast by Ernest Hemingway (Book)

169 editions published between 1964 and 2007 in 20 languages and held by 4,253 libraries worldwide

A Hemingway memoir recounting stories of himself, his wife, and his literary friends during their early years in Paris.

Islands in the stream by Ernest Hemingway( Book )

86 editions published between 1970 and 2006 in 22 languages and held by 4,039 libraries worldwide

First published in 1970, nine years after Ernest Hemingway's death, Islands in the Stream is the story of an artist and adventurer — a man much like Hemingway himself. Rich with the uncanny sense of life and action characteristic of his writing — from his earliest stories (In Our Time) to his last novella (The Old Man and the Sea) — this compelling novel contains both the warmth of recollection that inspired A Moveable Feast and a rare glimpse of Hemingway's rich and relaxed sense of humor, which enlivens scene after scene. Beginning in the 1930s, Islands in the Stream follows the fortunes of Thomas Hudson from his experiences as a painter on the Gulf Stream island of Bimini, where his loneliness is broken by the vacation visit of his three young sons, to his antisubmarine activities off the coast of Cuba during World War II. The greater part of the story takes place in a Havana bar, where a wildly diverse cast of characters — including an aging prostitute who stands out as one of Hemingway's most vivid creations — engages in incomparably rich dialogue. A brilliant portrait of the inner life of a complex and endlessly intriguing man, Islands in the Stream is Hemingway at his mature best.

To have and have not by Ernest Hemingway (Book)

157 editions published between 1932 and 2006 in 20 languages and held by 3,596 libraries worldwide

First published in 1937, To Have and Have Not is one of Hemingway's most entertaining novels. This realistic adventure tale and subtle portrait of an unlikely love affair demonstrates "Hemingway's gift for dialogue, for effective understatement, and for communicating such emotions as the tough allow themselves"

The garden of Eden by Ernest Hemingway (Book)

54 editions published between 1986 and 2007 in 18 languages and held by 3,576 libraries worldwide

A young American couple vacations in Europe, where the husband explores his bisexuality and the wife becomes increasingly vindictive and obsessed with a dangerously erotic game.

Death in the afternoon by Ernest Hemingway (Book)

93 editions published between 1932 and 2007 in 14 languages and held by 3,322 libraries worldwide

Publisher's description: Still considered one of the best books ever written about bullfighting, Death in the Afternoon reflects Hemingway's belief that bullfighting was more than mere sport. Here he describes and explains the technical aspects of this dangerous ritual, and "the emotional and spiritual intensity and pure classic beauty that can be produced by a man, an animal, and a piece of scarlet serge draped on a stick." Seen through his eyes, bullfighting becomes an art, a richly choreographed ballet, with performers who range from awkward amateurs to masters of great grace and cunning. A fascinating look at the history and grandeur of bullfighting, Death in the Afternoon is also a deeper contemplation on the nature of cowardice and bravery, sport and tragedy, and is enlivened throughout by Hemingway's pungent commentary on life and literature.

Across the river and into the trees by Ernest Hemingway (Book)

138 editions published between 1950 and 2006 in 22 languages and held by 3,270 libraries worldwide

Hemingway's reacquaintance with Venice, a city he loved, provided the inspiration for Across the River and into the Trees, the story of Richard Cantwell, a war-ravaged American colonel stationed in Italy at the close of the Second World War, and his love for a young Italian countess. A poignant, bittersweet homage to love that overpowers reason, to the resilience of the human spirit, and to the worldweary beauty and majesty of Venice, Across the River and into the Trees stands as Hemingway's statement of defiance in response to the great dehumanizing atrocities of the Second World War.

The snows of Kilimanjaro, and other stories by Ernest Hemingway (Book)

109 editions published between 1927 and 2007 in 20 languages and held by 3,234 libraries worldwide

The ideal introduction to the genius of Ernest Hemingway, these stories are beautiful in their simplicity, startling in their originality, and unsurpassed in their craftsmanship, the stories in this volume highlight one of America's master storytellers at the top of his form.

Green hills of Africa by Ernest Hemingway (Book)

115 editions published between 1935 and 2007 in 21 languages and held by 3,089 libraries worldwide

Hemingway's well-documented fascination with big-game hunting is magnificently captured amidst rich descriptions of the beauty and strangeness of East Africa, where he and his wife, Pauline, journeyed in December of 1933. An impassioned portrait of the glory of the African landscape, this immediate and deeply felt account has all of the hallmarks of the most evocative travel writing.

The dangerous summer by Ernest Hemingway (Book)

50 editions published between 1960 and 2006 in 13 languages and held by 3,033 libraries worldwide

True at first light by Ernest Hemingway( Book )

48 editions published between 1999 and 2007 in 12 languages and held by 2,937 libraries worldwide

A fictional memoir of an African safari based on a manuscript edited by the author's son. The action centers on wife Mary's desire to kill a lion and her jealousy of a beautiful African woman Hemingway is eyeing.

By-line: Ernest Hemingway; selected articles and dispatches of four decades by Ernest Hemingway( Book )

14 editions published between 1967 and 2003 in English and held by 2,907 libraries worldwide

The Nick Adams stories by Ernest Hemingway( Book )

33 editions published between 1955 and 2007 in 8 languages and held by 2,771 libraries worldwide

Hemingway thought of himself as Nick Adams. Enjoy these stories as Hemingway shares his life as Nick living in Michigan.

In our time : stories by Ernest Hemingway( Book )

29 editions published between 1925 and 1990 in English and held by 2,542 libraries worldwide

Ernest Hemingway, cub reporter; Kansas City Star stories by Ernest Hemingway( Book )

108 editions published between 1923 and 2004 in 21 languages and held by 2,225 libraries worldwide

The Snows of Kilimanjaro, the protagonist perishes of gangrene alone out in the bush, recognizing his failure as a writer: a writer who never had the nerve to write. He dies with stoic acceptance and a view of the famous summit unseen by any alive. In the Short happy Life of Francis Macomber, Francis is too wimpy to face down a wounded lion, let alone satisfy his wife in bed.

The fifth column, and four stories of the Spanish Civil War by Ernest Hemingway (Book)

43 editions published between 1938 and 1999 in 9 languages and held by 2,177 libraries worldwide

Drama about the Spanish Civil War.

## Chapter 19

# Hemingway on War and Its Aftermath

Researchers come to the Hemingway archives at the John F. Kennedy Presidential Library primarily to examine Ernest Hemingway's original manuscripts and his correspondence with family, friends, and fellow writers. But upon entering, it is hard not to notice the artifacts that ornament the Hemingway Room—including a mounted antelope head from a 1933 safari, an authentic lion-skin rug, and original artwork that Hemingway owned.

Though not as conspicuous, one object on display is far more consequential: a piece of shrapnel from the battlefield where Hemingway was wounded during World War I. Had the enemy mortar attack been more successful that fateful night, the world may never have known one of the greatest writers of the 20th century. Conversely, had Hemingway not been injured in that attack, he not may have fallen in love with his Red Cross nurse, a romance that served as the genesis of *A Farewell to Arms,* one of the century's most read war novels.

Hemingway kept the piece of shrapnel, along with a small handful of other "charms" including a ring set with a bullet fragment, in a small leather change purse. Similarly he held his war experience close to his heart and demonstrated throughout his life a keen interest in war and its effects on those who live through it.

No American writer is more associated with writing about war in the early 20th century than Ernest Hemingway. He experienced it firsthand, wrote dispatches from innumerable frontlines, and used war as a backdrop for many of his most memorable works.

Scholars, including Seán Hemingway, the author's grandson and editor of the recent anthology, Hemingway on War, continue to use documents and photographs in the Hemingway Collection to educate others about Hemingway and his writings on war. The topic of war has also been central to Hemingway forums and conferences organized by the Kennedy Library, including a recent session entitled "Writers on War." And at the Hemingway centennial, held at the library in 1999, many speakers referenced Hemingway's experience in war and his observations on its aftermath as an abiding element of his literary legacy.

## HEMINGWAY AND WORLD WAR I

During the First World War, Ernest Hemingway volunteered to serve in Italy as an ambulance driver with the American Red Cross. In June 1918, while running a mobile canteen dispensing chocolate and cigarettes for soldiers, he was wounded by Austrian mortar fire. "Then there was a flash, as when a blast-furnace door is swung open, and a roar that started white and went red," he recalled in a letter home.

Despite his injuries, Hemingway carried a wounded Italian soldier to safety and was injured again by machine-gun fire. For his bravery, he received the Silver Medal of Valor from the Italian government—one of the first Americans so honored.

Commenting on this experience years later in *Men at War,* Hemingway wrote: "When you go to war as a boy you have a great illusion of immortality. Other people get killed; not you. . . . Then when you are badly wounded the first time you lose that illusion and you know it can happen to you. After being severely wounded two weeks before my nineteenth birthday I had a bad time until I figured out that nothing could happen to me that had not happened to all men before me. Whatever I had to do men had always done. If they had done it then I could do it too and the best thing was not to worry about it."

Recuperating for six months in a Milan hospital,

Hemingway fell in love with Agnes von Kurowsky, an American Red Cross nurse. At war's end, he returned to his home in Oak Park, Illinois, a different man. His experience of travel, combat, and love had broadened his outlook. Yet while his war experience had changed him dramatically, the town he returned to remained very much the same.

Two short stories (written years later) offer insights into his homecoming and his understanding of the dilemmas of the returned war veteran. In "Soldier's Home," Howard Krebs returns home from Europe later than many of his peers. Having missed the victory parades, he is unable to reconnect with those he left behind—especially his mother, who cannot understand how her son has been changed by the war.

"Hemingway's great war work deals with aftermath," stated author Tobias Wolff at the Hemingway centennial celebration. "It deals with what happens to the soul in war and how people deal with that afterward. The problem that Hemingway set for himself in stories like 'Soldier's Home' is the difficulty of telling the truth about what one has been through. He knew about his own difficulty in doing that."

After living for months with his parents, during which time he learned from Agnes that she had fallen in love with another man, he decamped with two friends to his family's Michigan summer cottage, where he had learned to hunt and fish as a young boy. The trip would be the genesis of *Big Two-Hearted River*—a story that follows one of Hemingway's best known fictional characters, Nick Adams, recently returned from war, on a fishing trip in northern Michigan.

In the story, Hemingway never actually mentions the war and the injuries Nick has sustained in it—they simply loom below the surface. In this and other stories in his first major collection, *In Our Time,* Hemingway does more than advance a narrative; he also debuts a new style of writing fiction.

"The way we write about war or even think about war was affected fundamentally by Hemingway," stated Harvard Professor Henry Louis Gates, Jr., another speaker at the Hemingway centennial. In the early 1920s, in reaction to their experience of world war, Hemingway and other modernists lost faith in the central institutions of Western civilization. One of those institutions was literature itself. Nineteenth-century novelists were prone to a florid and elaborate style of writing. Hemingway, using a distinctly American vernacular, created a new style of fiction "in which meaning is established through dialogue, through action, and silences—a fiction in which nothing crucial—or at least very little—is stated explicitly."

"Hemingway was at the crest of a wave of modernists," noted fellow centennial panelist and book critic Gail Caldwell, "that were rebelling against the excesses and hypocrisy of Victorian prose. The First World War is the watershed event that changes world literature as well as how Hemingway responded to it."

## RETURN TO POSTWAR EUROPE

Hemingway returned to Europe after marrying his first wife, Hadley Richardson. His 1923 passport contains a photograph of him as a young, though serious, man. Initially working as a correspondent for the *Toronto Star,* while living in Paris he grew into a novelist with the encouragement of such Left Bank notables as Gertrude Stein, Ezra Pound, and F. Scott Fitzgerald.

Nobel laureate Nadine Gordimer described Hemingway's motivation to return to Europe as an expatriate this way. After the war, "Hemingway never really came home again." Yet unlike other expatriate writers who were forced to leave their native lands in the face of political persecution, he left the United States of his own volition fueled, in Gordimer's words, by "the beginnings of a broader human consciousness beyond nationalistic operatives, good or bad. And he made his choice of one of the causes in particular—of justice that was threatened in the cultural Mecca of Europe."

As a correspondent, Hemingway chronicled the outbreak of wars from Macedonia to Madrid and the spread of fascism throughout Europe. Although best known for his fiction, his war reporting was also revolutionary. Hemingway was committed above all else to telling the truth in his writing. To do so, he liked being part of the action, and the power of his writing stemmed, in part, from his commitment to witness combat firsthand.

According to Seán Hemingway, his grandfather's war dispatches "were written in a new style of reporting that told the public about every facet of the war, especially, and most important, its effects on the common man, woman, and child." This narrative style brought to life the stories of individual lives in warfare and earned a wide readership. Before the advent of television and cable news, Hemingway brought world conflicts to life for his North American audience.

In 1922, for example, Hemingway covered the war between Greece and Turkey and witnessed the plight of thousands of Greek refugees. In a sight that has become common to our time, Hemingway documented one of the hidden costs of war—the postwar displacement of whole peoples from their native lands. His vivid dispatches brought this and other stories to the attention of the English-speaking world.

Hemingway often used scenes that he had witnessed as well as his own personal experience to inform his fiction. Explaining his technique 20 years later, he wrote, "the writer's standard of fidelity to the truth should be so high that his invention, out of his experience, should produce a truer account than anything factual can be. For facts can be observed badly; but when a good writer is creating something, he has time and scope to make of it an absolute truth."

*In Our Time* was published in 1925. It was followed by Hemingway's first major novels, *The Sun Also Rises* and *A Farewell to Arms,* which chronicle, in reverse order, Hemingway's experiences in war and postwar Europe.

*The Sun Also Rises* features Jake Barnes, an American World War I veteran whose mysterious combat wounds have caused him to be impotent. Unlike Nick Adams and Howard Krebs, who return stateside after the war, Barnes remains in Europe, joining his compatriots in revels through Paris and Spain. Many regard the novel as Hemingway's portrait of a generation that has lost its way, restlessly seeking meaning in a postwar world. The Hemingway Collection contains almost a dozen drafts of the novel, including four different openings—examples of a burgeoning, hardworking, and exceptionally talented young novelist.

His second novel, *A Farewell to Arms,* is written as a retrospective of the war experience of Frederic Henry, a wounded American soldier, and his doomed love affair with an English nurse, Catherine Barkley.

Hemingway rewrote the conclusion to *A Farewell to Arms* many times. Among the gems of the Hemingway Collection are the 44 pages of manuscript containing a score of different endings—which are often used today by visiting English teachers to provide their students with a glimpse of Hemingway the writer at work.

At a recent Kennedy Library forum, author Justin Kaplan noted the number of delicate changes Hemingway made to the novel's last paragraphs. When asked once why he did so, Kaplan recounted, Hemingway responded "I was trying to find the right words."

After reading an early draft, F. Scott Fitzgerald suggested Hemingway end the book with one of its most memorable passages: "The world breaks everyone and afterward many are strong at the broken places. But those that will not break it kills. It kills the very good and the very gentle and the very brave impartially. If you are none of these you can be sure that it will kill you too but there will be no special hurry." Scrawled at the bottom of Fitzgerald's 10-page letter in Hemingway's hand is his three-word reaction—"Kiss my ass"—leaving no doubt of his dismissal of Fitzgerald's suggestions.

Though World War I is more backdrop than cause to this tragedy—Catherine's death in the end is brought about through childbirth not warfare—the novel contains, as seen in the following passage, a stark critique of war and those who laud it:

I was always embarrassed by the words sacred, glorious, and sacrifice. . . . We had heard them, sometimes standing in the rain almost out of earshot, so that only the shouted words came through, and had read them, on proclamations that were slapped up by billposters over other proclamations, now for a long time, and I had seen nothing sacred, and the things that were glorious had no glory and the sacrifices were like the stockyards at Chicago if nothing was done with the meat except to bury it. There were many words that you could not stand to hear and finally only the names of places had dignity. Certain numbers were the same way and certain dates and these with the names of the places were all you could say and have them mean anything. Abstract words such as glory, honor, courage, or hallow were obscene beside the concrete names of villages, the numbers of roads, the names of rivers, the numbers of regiments and the dates.

Much of the literature decrying World War I came from British poets, many of whom perished in battle. In *A Farewell to Arms,* Hemingway added his voice to the chorus, expanding the message to an American audience whose citizenry had not suffered nearly the level of war losses as its European allies. To appreciate the stance that Hemingway took, according to Gail Caldwell, one has to understand how revolutionary it was in light of the Victorian understanding of patriotism and courage. "If you look at Hemingway's prose and the writing he did about war, it was as radical in its time as anything we have seen since."

Commenting on the days and months he spent writing the novel, Hemingway wrote his editor, Max Perkins, that during this time much had occurred in his own life, including the birth of his second son, Patrick, by Caesarian section and the suicide of his father.

"I remember all these things happening and all the places we lived in and the fine times and the bad times we had in that year," Hemingway wrote in a 1948 introduction to *A Farewell to Arms.* "But much more vividly I remember living in the book and making up what happened in it every day. Making the country and the people and the things that happened I was happier than I had ever been. . . . The fact that the book was a tragic one did not make me unhappy since I believed that life is tragedy and knew it could only have one end. But finding you were able to make something up; to create truly enough so that it made you happy to read it; and to do this every day you worked was something that gave a greater pleasure than any I had ever known. Beside it nothing else mattered."

## THE SPANISH CIVIL WAR

Hemingway had an enduring love affair with Spain and the Spanish people. He had seen his first bullfight in the early 1920s, and his experience of the festivals in Pamplona informed his writing of *The Sun Also Rises*. The Hemingway Collection contains the author's personal collection of bullfighting material, including ticket stubs, programs, and his research material for his 1931 treatise on bullfighting, *Death in the Afternoon*. So it is not surprising that as fascism spread throughout Europe, Hemingway took special interest when civil war broke out in Spain.

Hemingway first encountered fascism in the 1920s when he interviewed Benito Mussolini, a man he described as "the biggest bluff in Europe." Although others initially credited Mussolini for bringing order to Italy, Hemingway had seen him for the brutal dictator he was to become. In fact, Hemingway dated his own antifascism to 1924 and the murder of Giacoma Matteotti, an Italian Socialist who was killed by Mussolini's Fasciti after speaking out against him.

In Spain, Francisco Franco, with support from Germany and Italy, used his Nationalist forces to spearhead a revolt against the government and those loyal to the Republic. When civil war broke out, Hemingway returned to Spain as a correspondent for the North American Newspaper Alliance, serving, at times, with fellow journalist Martha Gellhorn, who would become his third wife.

While in Spain, Hemingway collaborated with famed war photographer Robert Capa. Capa's photographs of Hemingway during this period are now part of the Hemingway Collection's extensive audiovisual archives of more than 10,000 photographs.

Hemingway's coverage of the war has been criticized for being slanted against Franco and the Nationalists. In a 1951 letter to Carlos Baker, Hemingway explained it this way. "There were at least five parties in the Spanish Civil War on the Republic side. I tried to understand and evaluate all five (very difficult) and belonged to none . . . . I had no party but a deep interest in and love for the Republic. . . . In Spain I had, and have, many friends on the other side. I tried to write truly about them, too. Politically, I was always on the side of the Republic from the day it was declared and for a long time before."

"It is the duty of a war correspondent to present both sides in his writing," contends Seán Hemingway, and in this instance, Hemingway "failed to do so siding as he did so strongly with the Republic against the Nationalists." Yet his dispatches provide a vivid accuracy of how the war was fought—and his experience would later inform his writing of *For Whom the Bell Tolls*. Despite his sympathies for the Loyalist cause, he is credited for documenting in this novel the horrors that occurred on both sides of that struggle.

The novel's protagonist, Robert Jordan, an American teacher turned demolitions expert, joins an anti-fascist Spanish guerrilla brigade with orders from a resident Russian general to blow up a bridge.

For author Gordimer, what is remarkable about the novel (which she describes as a cult book for her generation) is that Jordan takes up arms in another country's civil war for personal, not ideological, reasons. In the novel, Hemingway suggests that Jordan has no politics. Instead, his dedication to the Republic is fueled, in Gordimer's words, by a "kind of conservative individualism that collides in self-satisfaction with the claims of the wider concern for humanity." Jordan dedicates himself to a cause and is willing to risk his own life for it.

The bridge gets destroyed, his compatriots flee, and Jordan is left behind, injured, to face certain death at the hands of the approaching fascist troops. It is perhaps because of his commitment to action that Jordan became such a cult figure for his times. In his own words from the novel: "Today is only one day in all the days that will ever be. But what will happen in all the other days that ever come can depend on what you do today. It's been that way all this year. It's been that way so many times. All of war is that way."

## WORLD WAR II AND ITS AFTERMATH

In 1942 Hemingway agreed to edit *Men at War,* an anthology of the best war stories of all time. With the United States now at war, Hemingway remarked in the introduction: "The Germans are not successful because they are supermen. They are simply practical professionals in war who have abandoned all the old theories . . . and who have developed the best practical use of weapons and tactics. . . . It is at that point that we can take over if no dead hand of last-war thinking lies on the high command."

Not one to sit about or practice the "dead hand of last-war thinking," Hemingway, living in Cuba when the war broke out, took it upon himself to patrol the Caribbean for German U-boats. The Hemingway Collection contains many entries in the day log of his boat *Pilar* and his typewritten reports to local military commanders indicating how carefully he recorded his sightings and passed them on to American intelligence officials.

In 1944 he returned to Europe to witness key moments in World War II, including the D-day landings. He was 44 at the time and, comparing his photograph on his Certificate of Identity of Noncombatant to the portrait of the young 19-year-old who volunteered in World War I, one notices how distinguished the internationally renowned author had become in those 25 years.

Hemingway accompanied American troops as they stormed to shore on Omaha Beach—though as a civilian correspondent he was not allowed to land himself. Weeks later he returned to Normandy, attaching himself to the 22nd Regiment commanded by Col. Charles "Buck" Lanham as it drove toward Paris (whose liberation he would later witness and write about). Before doing so, Hemingway led a controversial effort to gather military intelligence in the village of Rambouillet and, with military authorization, took up arms himself with his small band of irregulars. According to World War II historian Paul Fussell, "Hemingway got into considerable trouble playing infantry captain to a group of Resistance people that he gathered because a correspondent is not supposed to lead troops, even if he does it well."

On June 23, 1951, Hemingway wrote to C. L. Sulzberger of the *New York Times* with his own explanation: "Certain allegations of fighting and commanding irregular troops were made but I was cleared of these by the Inspector General of the Third Army. . . . For your information, I had an assignment to write only one article a month for *Colliers* and I wished to make myself useful between those monthly pieces. I had a certain amount of knowledge about guerilla warfare and irregular tactics as well as a grounding in more formal war and I was willing and happy to work for or be of use to anybody who would give me anything to do within my capabilities."

Hemingway remained in Europe for 10 months traveling with the Allied infantry into the Hürtgenwald forest as they "cracked" the Siegfried Line. At war's end, Hemingway was back in Cuba. In light of American use of the atomic bomb, he reminded his fellow countrymen that "For the moment we are the strongest power in the world. It is important that we do not become the most hated." To avoid such a fate, he said, "we need to study and understand certain basic problems of our world as they were before Hiroshima to be able to continue, intelligently, to discover how some of them have changed and how they can be settled justly now that a new weapon has become the property of the world. We must study them more carefully than ever now and remember that no weapon has ever settled a moral problem. It can impose a solution but it cannot guarantee it to be a just one."

In a small ceremony in June 1947 at the U.S. embassy in Cuba, Hemingway was awarded a Bronze Star for his service as a war correspondent for having circulated "freely under fire in combat areas in order to obtain an accurate picture of conditions. Through his talent of expression, Mr. Hemingway enabled readers to obtain a vivid picture of the difficulties and triumphs of the front-line soldier and his organization in combat."

Hemingway wrote one novel with World War II as its backdrop. *Across the River and Into the Trees* is set in Venice at the close of the war and tells the story of an aging American colonel who falls in love with a young Italian countess. The book was not as well received as his earlier novels—not meeting the expectation that it might capture the essence of World War II the way *A Farewell to Arms and For Whom the Bell Tolls* had done for World War I and the Spanish Civil War.

Nor did his short stories published in this period capture the public's imagination concerning the most recent world war. One story that has garnered attention in recent anthologies, *Black Ass at the Cross Roads,* was never published in Hemingway's lifetime (the original manuscript remaining instead as part of the papers of the Hemingway Collection). According to Fussell, this "masterpiece," which tells the story of an ambush of German soldiers by an American infantryman who suffers great remorse for what he has done, "is so realistic and so inexplicable in any other way than to believe that Hemingway was there and that perhaps it was never published because it was too incriminating."

In 1952 Hemingway redeemed his reputation as one of the century's great writers with the publication of *The Old Man and the Sea,* which also helped earn him the 1954 Nobel Prize for Literature. When Fidel Castro swept into power in 1959, Ernest and Mary Hemingway left their home in Cuba, moving to the outskirts of Ketchum, Idaho. During the next few years, Hemingway experienced serious health problems and committed suicide on July 2, 1961.

## AN ENDURING LEGACY

It is often difficult to separate the public Hemingway from his art—and his literary achievements have, at times, been overshadowed by his mythic persona. Much of that myth stems from Hemingway's own hand. For example, in a public flap with writer William Faulkner after Faulkner suggested that Hemingway had not been a courageous writer,

Hemingway asked Gen. "Buck" Lanham to respond on his behalf. Lanham did so, outlining Hemingway's feats at his side during World War II and concluded that he was "without exception the most courageous man I have ever known, both in war and peace. He has physical courage, and he has that far rarer commodity, moral courage."

Gordimer suggests that in assessing the legacy of Hemingway and his insights on war that we leave such arguments alone. "I'm not concerned with what Ernest Hemingway did or did not do in his own body, his own person, out of his own courage in wars. . . . Let us leave his life alone. It belongs to him as he lived it. Let us read his books. They are his particular illumination of what our existence has been, his gift to us that belongs to us all."

Professor Gates concluded the centennial celebration similarly—noting that Hemingway was "one of the finest prose stylists in English. He captured in stunning stories and novels the uncomfortable realities of his age and forced into public consciousness a realization of the brutalities of war and their lingering psychological affects. His stories of Nick Adams depict the adolescent agonies of a generation. His best novels record for all time the emotional turmoil of modern warfare and modern life. It is the integrity of his craft, a richness beyond legend, that will forever endure."

Hemingway's legacy is inexorably tied to his books, stories, and dispatches. Those who visit the Hemingway Collection—be they scholars conducting research or students experiencing Hemingway for the first time—are most drawn to the letters and manuscripts written in the author's own hand. To see each word, deletion, and edit is to witness a master craftsman at work.

Hemingway dedicated himself to writing "truly" on all topics including and especially the subject of war and its effect on his times. He dedicated the anthology *Men at War* to his three sons so that they might have a book "that will contain the truth about war as near we can come by it. . . . It will not replace experience. But it can prepare and supplement experience. It can serve as a corrective after experience." The same can be said of Hemingway's own work. It cannot replicate the experience of those who lived through the war-torn years of the first half of the 20th century, but it offers the truth about those wars as near we can come by it.

Quotations from Nadine Gordimer, Tobias Wolff, Gail Caldwell, and Henry Louis Gates, Jr., were taken from remarks given at the Hemingway centennial celebration at the John F. Kennedy Library on April 10–11, 1999. Audiotapes of those proceedings and other Hemingway forums are available at the Kennedy Library. Inquiries can be made directly to the author.

The quotations from Paul Fussell are taken from remarks at the forum "Writers on War" at the John F. Kennedy Library on March 21, 2004.

The quotation from Justin Kaplan is taken from remarks given at a forum, "Dear Papa; Dear Hotch," at the Kennedy Library on November 28, 2005.

Quotations from Seán Hemingway come from his introduction to *Hemingway on War* (New York: Scribner, 2003). The quotation from *Mussolini, Europe's Prize Bluffer* is also from that anthology.

Correspondence such as the letter from F. Scott Fitzgerald and the letter to C. L. Sulzberger are from the Hemingway Collection.

The logbook to the *Pilar*, Hemingway's fishing boat, and Hemingway's memorandums on his U-boat sightings to U.S. military intelligence officials are from the Hemingway Collection.

Letters between Hemingway and Carlos Baker are from the Hemingway Collection. Background material and references also come from Baker's biographies, *Hemingway: Writer as Artist* (Princeton, N.J.: Princeton University Press, 1952) and *Ernest Hemingway: A Life Story* (New York: Scribner, 1969). The Hemingway Collection as a whole was discussed in Megan Floyd Desnoyers, "Ernest Hemingway: A Storyteller's Legacy," *Prologue: Quarterly of the National Archives* 24 (Winter 1992): 334–350.

# Chapter 20

# The Common Conceit

It is a common conceit that Fidel Castro and Ernest Hemingway were friends. The photograph of the two together after a sail fish fishing competition May 12 to 15th of 1960 at the Miramar Yatch Club which Castro "won" is usually cited as evidence of this. This is the official Cuban government take on the matter, and all other opinions are suppressed. Cuban archives are only commonly made available to those believed to be sympathetic to that government. One notes that the present Cuban government achieves a considerable profit from the Hemingway trade.

Castro had never fished sailfish before and he was accompanied by Ernesto Ché Guevara, Celia Sánchez, the boat's captain Julio Arocha, Manuel Bell Gorgas (commonly known as Blakamán), a game fishing instructor from the Industria Nacional de la Industria Turistica (INIT), who was a member of the Castro team. This last source reports that some experienced fishermen were "amazed" at Castro's beginner's luck. Hemingway's sail-fishing boat "Pilar" was usually kept in the tiny bay of Cojima which is east of Havana. This implies that the Pilar either was sailed to the western Havana suburb of Miramar or it went by road, most probably via the new tunnel under Havana Bay and then along the best traffic route, on the shore line four-lane, high-speed, Malecón avenue. The possible significance of this route is discussed later in this article.

It is widely stated that Mary Hemingway, Hemingway's fourth wife and widow, donated his property to Cuba in 1962. However, exile sources declare that Hemingway met with the

Cuban leader at the fishing competition primarily trying to convince Castro not to confiscate his property.

Meyers states that Hemingway's property was officially confiscated after his death. However, Meyers also notes that Hemingway long feared that this would happen, despite the support that he had given Castro. Myers, seemingly over looks the story "The Shot" and its significance in this regard, although he does mention others of similar title.

These fears of confiscation were very rational. Hemingway left Cuba in July 1960 while the massive confiscations were beginning but before the October 14th 1960 "La Ley de la Reforma Urbana." However even as early a February 7, 1959 expropriations of land without cash payments, were authorized, and the death penalty legalized. Castro, almost immediately after arriving in Havana on January 8th 1959, started the process of confiscating all property on the Island. Although remaining residents were granted usufruct, all residences belonged to the state and use of such property was dependent on the residents' obedience to the mandates of the Cuban state. This left private property rights in great jeopardy as the Cuban authorities became more and more aggressive and greedy. It slowly became clear that the Castro government, following its own interpretation of marxist guidelines wanted possession of everything. All this is consistent with the fact that Hemingway left most of his property, books and papers in Cuba. This was usual in such confiscations because household items were inventoried and held on site by the Cuban government agency "Ministerio de Recuperación de Bienes Malversados."

As Hemingway must have known before he left Cuba, his putative plea to retain his property would prove hopeless. One of the dictator's marxist supporters admiringly states; Fidel Castro even took his mother's lands. This same supporter lauds the "benevolence" of Raul Castro, in that despite Lina Ruz's armed resistance she was "allowed" to stay under the protection of eldest sibling Ramón who was charged by the "Revolución" with general oversight of the agriculture of the region.

Hemingway's professional code was not always ethical. And much of what Hemingway wrote, often horrendous in its callousness and betrayal, is taken from real life. For instance: Jesus Enrique Lister Forján is one of the three "peasant leaders" referred to by the character "Robert Jordan" in Ernest Hemingway's for "For Whom the Bell Tolls."

Strangely enough Spanish and USSR personnel including this same general Enrique Lister, as he is commonly known, had shown up again in Cuba at that time. Lister had gone to Cuba in 1927 during the Machado Dictatorship and joined the Cuban Communist Party. In late 1959 Castro's intelligence chief Ramirito Valdés had contacted the KGB in Mexico City. The Soviets sent one hundred mostly Spanish-speaking advisors, including Enrique Lister, to organize the Committees for the Defense of the Revolution in Cuba. Later many more were sent. The founding of this committee is officially dated September 28, 1960 which means Lister must have arrived in Cuba before that date, thus it could be that Hemingway's final departure from Cuba in July 1960 and Lister's arrival overlapped.

Arrozarena's date for the arrival of a Basque contingent in Cuba, June 31 1961, does not mean that Hemingway would not have met Lister again, since the Arrozarena cite refers only to a small of Basque's among the far larger numbers of the "International Brigades." Lister most probably had arrived far earlier (as indicated in by Fernandez see cite 25). Personal memories recall such personal in public view at the FOCSA building in April of 1961. Given the circumstance of gossip of the time news of Lister's arrival almost certainly would have reached Hemingway who was always "well connected," and the presence of Lister plus the 4th of March 1960 explosion of La Coubre (e.g. see Haverty, citation) must certainly have alerted him to what was going on.

One notes with interest that this Hemingway novel's protagonist "Robert Jordan's" grandfather is said to have fought in the U.S. Civil War. This may well refer to the Confederate General Thomas Jordan, a former U.S. Army officer who became a Confederate colonel, and started an embryonic spy network in Washington. Thomas Jordan was also general of Mambí forces in the Cuban Ten Year's War, who used almost suicidal assault tactics that grandfather Calixto Enamorado wrote so critically about in his 1917 novel "Tiempos Heróicos. Persecución."

The suicide of "Robert Jordan's" father, as well as that of Hemingway's own father, resembles that of great grandfather Major General Calixto Garcia's (Calixto Enamorado's father) own attempt at suicide to avoid capture. In support of this one notes Hemingway's familiarity with Cuba where General Garcia Iñiguez was, and to some extent still is, a major national hero.

General Garcia's magnificent, twice life size and then new, equestrian statue showing the scar of the general's attempted suicide to escape capture, was commissioned to US sculptor Felix Weldon and architect Elbert Peets; construction was completed in Batista's time but it was inaugurated in 1959. This large monument placed at Malecón and Calle 6 could not have escaped Hemingway's routes in Havana and its observation and must have impinged on his memory.

Dramatic monument not only has twenty-four bronze plaques around the statue narration Garcia's 30-year struggle for Cuban independence, but it is located on the water front main highway close to the former Plaza de la República now known as La Plaza de la Revolución. Thus if Hemingway ever went to Miramar by road he must certainly have seen it. Contemplation of this statue, even in brief passing, surely found sad resonance in Hemingway's unfortunate family history of war and suicide..

The Hemingway story "The Shot," as pointed out previously by others, has hallmark descriptions of killings attributed to Fidel Castro. This short story seems to be amalgamation of several of these killings certainly including that of Manuel (Manolo) Castro del Campo, a government official unrelated to Fidel Castro Ruz, and probably that of Oscar Fernández Caral. Fernández Caral, who had proclaimed himself as witness to the Manolo Castro murder was promptly murdered by Castro and his colleagues.

Although Manolo Castro had a violent past Hemingway was no stranger to violence and violent people, and found such people sources of inspiration. Thus, Hemingway found such as some of his friends and fellow authors descriptions of Kenneth Tynman's disgust at visit to his restaurant table by executioner Herman Marks merely amusing.

Manolo Castro, had been close enough to Hemingway to allow this author to referee a boxing match held President Grau's time in the main arena of Havana the old Palacio de los Deportes. In addition, Hemingway, like Manolo Castro, was partial to ideologies of the left, and was given to support these even in his journalistic reports and behaviors.

Hemingway, although offering public support to Castro, privately feared the loss of his property and was loyal to the U.S. Hidden in Hemingway's complex personality was a long enduring dislike of Castro dating back to the killing of Manolo Castro. It would be illogical to propose that these two enormous egos were not rivals at some level. This dislike of Fidel Castro can be illustrated by the first paragraphs of Hemingway's "The Shot." Apparently this dislike was mutual since Fidel Castro likewise disliked Hemingway considering him to be a "yanqui cagón."

This Hemingway short story starts:

"We were finishing lunch by the swimming pool. It was a hot day for Cuba because the breeze had fallen off, but the pool was cool where the trees had made shade over it and it was cool and next to cool if you went deep enough into it at the deep end."

"I didn't see these two Negroes until they were by the table where it was set under the arbor to be in the shade. I had been watching the reflection of the bamboos and the Alamo trees in the pool and when I looked up and saw these two by the table I knew that I was slipping. They had come up a piece of dead ground but I should have seen them come around the corner of the shower house."

"One was very big and tough with a face I remembered. The other was his *guardaspaldas*. That is the man who keeps you from being shot in the back. He doesn't have to big, very big and he is always a little behind and he turns his head like a pitcher watching a man on first with no one out. Guardaspaldas, it is usually shortened to that, get the same kind of neck that pitchers get and that fighter pilots are afflicted with if they stay alive if there is a real fighter opposition in the air."

"This man, who looked like an oversized Joe Walcott, had a letter to me. It was from himself. He was a little hot, it seemed, and he needed to go to a certain South American Republic very fast. He was unjustly accused of being in the second of two cars which had killed two and wounded five in what is known as the old one-two. The first car comes by the house of friends whom they have checked are there and wish to surprise.

They shoot the house up as a gesture. The friends swarm out, unhurt and bearing arms and full of defiance, and the second car comes by with the mains and wipes them out. This man was falsely accused, he explained to me, of being one of the mains. He had been falsely accused many times. But he claimed to be a friend of a friend of mine who was shot dead in the street with thirty-five cents in his pocket, and never a nickel stolen and no personal fortune, while he held a government post. I suppose you know gentlemen, what that means in these times."

"This friend who had been shot had been a beautiful backfield man on the local university team. He was a fine quarterback and he could play halfback. He (Manolo Castro) was director of sports of the republic when he died. No one has ever been punished for the killing. This friend of mine was supposed to be a little triggery; but I never heard of him killing the wrong people. Anyway, when they killed him he had thirty-five cents, no money in any banks, and he was unarmed."

"So what this man, who claimed to be his friend, and whose face I remembered, needed was $500. I told him it was two. I hope he doesn't get falsely accused of anything before he emigrates."

"So with a background of this sort of shooty-shooty, I'm

going to write 2,000 words about an antelope hunt where you kill one antelope that can't shoot back. ..."...

Unfortunately for Hemingway, Castro apparently recognized himself, despite the "blackface," in the story and being an unforgiving long long memoried sort, probably enjoyed taking the house at La Vigia. However, Castro always cautious never revealed publicly anything in this regard. Whether this loss of Hemingway's beloved residence, manuscripts and papers contributed to his suicide can only be speculated.

Castro's propagandists continue to cover up the confiscation of La Vigía, alleging the Hemingway residence was a "donation to the revolution." The basis for this claim is that Hemingway's widow Mary was forced to sign papers in this regard in return for being allowed to gather a few items from the house.

Agencia de Noticias Xinhua de China 2006 (accessed 12-4-06) Celebran en Cuba aniversario de Comités de Defensa de la Revolución, Patrimonio Cultural y Natural de China September 29, 2006. "Constituidos el 28 de septiembre de 1960, los CDR surgieron en respuesta al reclamo popular de unirse para enfrentar los continuos ataques, sabotajes e intentos por detener la revolución que triunfó el 1 de enero de 1959"

Aguila, Arnoldo 2003 (accessed 11-3-06) Fidel explica porqué asesinó y condenó."...según otros testigos de una parte que no pude oír, se refirió a los fusilados como "tres negritos"..."

Andrew, Christopher and Oleg Gordievsky 1990. KGB: The Inside Story. HarperCollins, New York ISBN 0060166053. p. 467. "In July 1959, Castro's Intelligence Chief, Major Ramiro Valdes, began secret meetings with the Soviet Ambassador and KGB residency. The KGB dispatched over a hundred advisers to overhaul Castro's security and Intelligence system, many drawn from the ranks of *los niños,* the children of Spanish Communist refugees who had settled in Russia after the Civil War. One Spanish Republican veteran, Enrique Lister Farjan, organized the Committees for the Defense of the Revolution, a Cuban neighborhood watch system to keep track of counter revolutionary subeversion. Another, General Alberto Bajar, set up a series of guerrilla training schools."

Anonymous (accessed 10-24-06) Biografía concisa del tirano Fidel Alejandro Castro Ruz Historia de Cuba (Datos adicionales) Circuito Sur "Ya asentado en la Universidad, participa en cuantas protestas callejeras se producen siendo presidente Grau, y pasado un tiempo se une a uno de los llamados grupos "gatillo alegre". Estos grupos de "gatillo alegre" peleaban entre si por el control de la Federación Estudiantil Universitaria (FEU), y Fidel Castro se unió a uno llamado Unión Insurreccional Revolucionaria, dirigido por Emilio Tró. Aquí es donde comienza ha definir el actual tirano su espíritu pandillero, gangsteril."...."Al pasar este episodio de Cayo Confite, los grupos gangsteriles recrudecen sus acciones, y así vemos como el jefe del grupo al que pertenecía Fidel Castro, Emilio Tró cae abatido por las balas junto a cuatro de sus colaboradores en el Municipio de Marianao.

Después Manolo Castro, el líder de la Federación Estudiantil Universitaria (FEU) y opositor de Tró, y Fidel, al estar parado en la acera del "Cinecito" de La Habana es asesinado de varios disparos. En el entierro de Manolo Castro dos oradores Alfredo Yabur, y Eduardo Corona acusaron de la muerte del líder estudiantil entre otros a Fidel Castro, y Oscar Fernández Caral policía de la Universidad interrumpió varias veces gritando que Fidel era el asesino. Después los dos oradores en el entierro de Manolo Castro se hicieron súbditos de Fidel Castro, y al triunfo de la revolución, bajo la presidencia de Dorticós el Tirano nombra a Yabur Ministro de Justicia, y a Corona representante ante la UNESCO.

Corona acompañaba a Manolo Castro cuando el atentado en "El Cinecito", y por milagro salió ileso. Otro de los conocidos hechos gangsteril en los que participó el actual Tirano, fue cuando asesinaron a Justo Fuentes Clavel, vicepresidente de la FEU, y miembro de la Unión Insurreccional Revolucionaria al salir de una emisora de radio, y que por casualidad ese día no lo acompañaba el también miembro de la UIR Fidel Castro. En represalia por este asesinato, Fidel Castro se parapeta en el techo de la Facultad de Ingeniería de la Universidad portando una escopeta, y cuando ve a Leonel Gómez, dirigente del Instituto de La Habana, y señalado como el que baleó a Justo Fuentes, le hace varios disparos, los cuales no hirieron a Fuentes. Debido a ese hecho de la muerte de Fuentes, Fidel Castro en compañía de Rafael del Pino le hicieron un atentado al entonces Senador Rolando Masferrer Rojas, en las calles de La Habana, cuando este viajaba en su automóvil, a lo que Masferrer respondió haciendo que Fidel y del Pino salieran corriendo para refugiarse en el convento de las Ursulinas.

El otro suceso conocido, es el asesinato de Oscar Fernández Caral, masacrado a tiros frente a su hogar, y que aun con vida, le dijo a los presente que Fidel Castro fue el que le disparó. Al siguiente día 5 de julio de ese año 1948, la prensa se hacia eco del hecho, y el periódico "El Crisol" de La Habana, destacaba las palabras de Fernández Caral en su titular. Oscar Fernández Caral fue el que vio a Fidel Castro en las inmediaciones "Del Cinecito", cuando asesinaron a Manolo Castro de la FEU, y que después lo acusó públicamente en la despedida de duelo."

Arencibia Cardoso, Pedro Pablo 2005 (accessed 10-24-06) ¡Fidel, el peor de todos! Cuba Democracia y Vida 20-10-2005. "Una digresión: yo no comparto el criterio de que Fidel estaba en el grupo ejecutor que mató a Manolo Castro, que ya no estaba en la Universidad y era un alto funcionario vinculado al Deporte, aunque sí es muy posible que haya estado vinculado a esa acción. El crimen del sargento de la policía universitaria, por ser un testigo indeseado de ese asesinato, y el intento de matar a Leonel Acosta, que había sido presidente del Instituto de Segunda Enseñanza de La Habana, al que le disparó por la espalda, son solo algunas misiones que, a mi entender, llevó a cabo el muchachón teniendo detrás a la banda a la que pertenecía y en la que él era sencilla y solamente un sicario; a su vez el usó a la banda para ganarse el respeto y la fama de un tipo de ACCION (¡un tipo duro!, diríamos hoy, pero esa era la palabra que se usaba en esa época) así como tener cuidada sus espaldas. Sobre el asesinato de Manolo Castro y del sargento de la policía universitaria (asesinato ocurrido delante del hijo de la víctima) y otras acciones" ..." El otro suceso conocido, es el asesinato de Oscar Fernández Caral, masacrado a tiros frente a su hogar, y que aun con vida, le dijo a los presente que Fidel Castro fue el que le disparó."

Arrozarena, Cecilia 2003 El Roble y la Ceiba, Historia de los Vascos en Cuba. Editorial Txalaparta, Tafalla, "Nafarroa" Spain ISBN 848136357X p. 366 "Poco después triunfar de la revolución de Fidel Castro el pidió a Enrique Lister, en el mas estricto secreto, el envío de técnicos españoles. Éramos 24 quienes formábamos aquella primera (sic) y singular expedición, la mayoría matrimonios de niños de guerra. El 31 de junio de 1961 llegamos a las isla tras pasar por Praga, donde nos dieron documentos y identidades falsas, como si fuésemos turistas cubanos..."

Ash, Paul 2006 Communication to Army talk. Date: Sun, 3 Dec 2006 03:38:42 -0800 (PST) [ArmyTalk] Re: Cuba Dustup on BBC World Service Today ....Ja, my great uncle lived in Cuba from the early Thirties and rose to quite a senior position on the Cuban railways....When he retired in 1954, he invested his pension and savings into a motel at a place called Gaspar, midway between Havana and Santiago de Cuba. Life was pretty good for him and his Cuban wife, and their little herd of cows.....When Castro took over, the first thing the government took was the motel (they let him and Caterina live on in one of the rooms).

Then they took his cows, except one, and most of the land. Finally they confiscated his Toyota Land Cruiser, so he bought a horse and named it "Toyota"....In the end he was reduced to relying on my grandfather here in Jo'burg for monthly supplies of Oxo stock tablets, writing paper, powdered soup, glaucoma medicine, eye ointment, toothpaste ... The parcels would take months to arrive and were routinely pillaged before they got to him....He bore this with great humour and loved Cuba until the day he died ... two days after he relented to pressure from his daughter in Miami who had arranged an exit permit for him and Caterina....Amidst all of this, he was stupified that South Africa had a legally-sanctioned system of discrimination. He just could not understand it. Cheers Paul

Bianchi Ross, Ciro 2005 (accessed 12-3-06) Palmacristazo Juventud Rebelde Domingo, "El monumento a Calixto García, a la entrada de la calle, frente al Malecón, es de mucho realce. Sobre un pedestal de granito negro de Los Andes se alza su estatua ecuestre, en bronce, y el héroe, en traje de campaña y descubierta la cabeza, aparece en actitud de arengar a su tropa. Frente al pedestal se aprecia el escudo de la República. El lugar donde se emplaza imita una antigua fortaleza. Lo rodea un muro de piedra que en su parte interior, y a lo largo de 36 pies, lleva 24 bajorrelieves de bronce con representaciones de los episodios culminantes de la vida de Calixto, y entre ellos, el mapa con sus campañas militares. La estatua del General es de doble tamaño del natural. El monumento es obra de los norteamericanos Weldon y Peets y se inauguró en 1959. Su primera piedra se colocó dos años antes. Costó unos 300 000 pesos."

Cabrera Infante, Guillermo interviewed by Marie-Lise Gazarian Gautier 1980 and 1984, in New York (accessed 10-24-06) An Interview with Guillermo Cabrera Infante. Interviews with Latin American Writers by Marie-Lise Gazarian Gautrier. Dalkey Archive Press, This is a typically violent episode from that capitalist democratic period, 1947 and 1948, involving various so-called revolutionary student groups. It is an extraordinary occurrence because the head of the Federación de Estudiantes Universitarios (FEU) (Federation of University Students), Manolo Castro, was killed. This assassination is recounted by Hemingway in one of his famous articles.

He used it as the beginning of a piece in which he went on to relate how he hunted antelopes in Idaho or something like that. Hemingway said (Manolo) Castro had been a very honest man because he had died with thirty-two cents in his pocket. He was indeed an honest person, but he had also engaged in violent acts. The group who decided to kill him was the same to which Fidel Castro belonged, the UIR. So there is a great probability that one of the men who murdered Manolo Castro was Fidel Castro, because the leader of the UIR had a very macabre sense of humor.

For instance, if the UIR had been after someone for years, they would leave a note on the dead body saying, "Justice is slow, but it comes." This was the trademark of the UIR. So the fact that one Castro should kill another probably appealed to the dark sense of humor of the UIR's leader, although it was never conclusively proven that Fidel Castro was one of the killers, only that he knew when the murder was going to occur, and that he was a member of that group. And the reference to "he who had to die" indicates that Manolo Castro had been on the UIR's death list for quite some time."

Calvo, Ricardo E. 2002 (accessed 10-5-06) Pensamientos sobre la propiedad privada en la reconstruccion de Cuba. Guaracabuya. "En Mayo de 1959 se creo el INRA (Instituto Nacional de Reforma Agraria) al firmarse la Ley de Reforma Agraria a traves de la cual solo se permite "poseer" (lease usufructo) un maximo de 30 caballerias de tierra. Cualquier cantidad por encima de esa cifra paso a manos del Estado sin compensacion..... La inviolabilidad del domicilio paso a las paginas de la historia ya que toda y cada una de las residencias eran propiedad del Estado."

CIA 1961 (accessed 9-11-6) Report on Cuban military potential and internal conditions in Cuba by 30th of n Abstract: Pages:0010 Pub Date: 11/28/1961 Release Date8/31/2001 Case Number: F-1982-00782 By November , although there was strong resistance in Escambray, Castro army and militia strength (exceeds 200,000) and number of repression operatives (50,000) including 25,000 members of "International Brigades", had increased enormously

Coca, César 2005 (accessed 10-31-06)La historia más triste de Hemingway. Panorama La Verdad Digital 5/05/2005, "Luego, con Mary, se (Valerie Danby-Smith) fue a Cuba, con objeto de catalogar y recuperar cuanto de valor había en Finca Vigía. La casa había sido cedida por el escritor al pueblo cubano. Mary recurrió a Castro para conseguir los permisos para llevarse a EE UU los cuadros y objetos de gran valor que había en la casa. El comandante le dijo que no habría problema, pero pocos días después llegó una funcionaria que les comunicó que todo era propiedad del Estado cubano y ni siquiera Castro podía cambiar la ley. Así que tuvieron que sacar todo de allí de forma ilegal."

Cuban Government 1959 (accessed 11-3-06) Ley Fundamental de 1959 (7 de febrero de 1959) "En los casos de expropiaciones forzosas que se realizaren para llevar a efecto la Reforma Agraria y el consiguiente reparto de tierras, no será imprescindible que el pago previo de las indemnizaciones sea en efectivo. La Ley podrá establecer otros medios de pago, siempre que reúnan las garantías necesarias...Artículo 25.- No podrá imponerse la pena de muerte. Se exceptúan los casos de los miembros de las Fuerzas Armadas, de los cuerpos represivos de la Tiranía, de los grupos auxiliares organizados por ésta, de los grupos armados privadamente organizados para defenderla y de los confidentes, por delitos cometidos en pro de la instauración o defensa de la Tiranía derrocada el 31 de diciembre de 1958. También se exceptúan las personas culpables de traición o de subversión de orden constitucional o de espionaje en favor del enemigo en tiempo de guerra con nación extranjera"

Hemingway paper Robert: Again thank you, again an important detail (Killings by Manolo Castro L.D).....That helps make my point that Hemingway did not pass moral judgment on his friends. I still think that Hemingway and (Fidel) Castro did not get along; and that Fidel Castro, even if he had been friends with Hemingway would never let mere friendship stand in the way of getting something he wanted. Remember the Stalinist (see reference to Stalin L.D.) statement, "gratitude is a vice of dogs." take care be well Larry Daley

Fernandez, Frank (interviewed by Larry Gambone) 1997 An interview with a Cuban Anarchist. In: ANY TIME NOW 6, 7, "At the beginning of the Revolution, 1959-60, some were detained and let go. Augustin Souchy was in Havana in those days and in a conversation with Abelardo Iglesias, Manuel de la Mata Manuel de la Mata and Salvador Garcia, all members of the CNT-FAI during the Spanish Revolution, told his comrades of the recent visit to Cuba by "old friends" from the Spanish and Italian Communist Party, Enrique Lister and the infamous Vittorio Vidale, invited by the Castro regime. Souchy warned them of the inevitable persecution from the new secret police in which Lister and Vidale were involved. The CNT comrades were involved in certain "counter-revolutionary" activities and with the experience of Spain behind them, they knew how to escape on time - with the protection of a Latin American embassy.."

FOIA Log Freedom of Information 2005 (accessed 10-24-06) "18-Oct-05 F-2006-00056 Manuel de Castro (Del Campo) Aka Manolo Castro; Fidel Castro with the Insurrectional Revolutionary Union (UIR); Miguel Murciano and other Cubans "

Furiati, Claudia (Rosa S. Corgatelli, translator) 2003 Fidel Castro La historia me absolverá. Barcelona, Spain Plaza y Janes ISBN 140008346X This book is at one time a series of justifications for Castro's ruthless deeds, a guide book for apologists: but it is also a source of interesting information if one reads, with great care, for Castro's self-serving voice can be heard between the lines.

García Márquez, Gabriel (accessed 12-4-06) Hemingway, el nuestro. Prolog to Norberto Fuentes "Hemingway en Cuba" "Pero la obra mayor iba a ser el esperpento neoclásico del Capitolio Nacional —copiado piedra por piedra del Capitolio de Washington—, en cuya cantera trabajaba un picapedrero llamado Enrique Lister, que años más tarde sería uno de los generales legendarios de la Guerra Civil Española."

Gatti, José María 2002 Tantas veces me mataron Radar | Domingo, 17 de Marzo de 2002 "Zoé Valdés, la narradora cubana que escribió toda su obra en el exterior de la isla, sintetiza así la relación: "Hemingway odiaba a Batista y Castro le era poco simpático. A Castro, Hemingway le parecía un buen escritor, pero se cansó de decir que era un yanqui cagón". Más allá de lo anecdótico, es sabido que Hemingway guardaba por Castro un marcado rencor por la muerte de Manolo Castro, su amigo personal desde la época de la Guerra Civil Española. La historia se remonta al año 1946. Por entonces Fidel era un joven estudiante que buscaba apoyo para convertirse en líder de la Escuela de Leyes de La Habana. Tratando de lograr un acercamiento con Manuel Castro, se pelea con Leonel Gómez, un dirigente estudiantil de las Escuelas Secundarias opositor a Manolo Castro. Fidel hiere a Leonel de un balazo en el abdomen, pero éste milagrosamente se salva. Y Manolo Castro, lejos de apoyar el gesto, le manda un mensaje a Fidel a través de José de Jesús Ginjaume: "Dile a ese tipo que no voy a apoyar a un mierda para presidente de Derecho".

Sin sustento de Manolo Castro y Rolando Masferrer, otro veterano de la Guerra Civil Española, Castro veía desvanecer su intención de incorporarse al Movimiento Socialista Revolucionario (MSR), por eso se acerca a José de Jesús Ginjaume (anticomunista y paracaidista durante la Segunda Guerra Mundial) y a Emilio Tro, otro personaje siniestro que lo protege y perdona por su malograda pelea con Rolando Masferrer. Poco después ocurriría el asesinato de Emilio Tro (el 15 de setiembre de 1947) y la muerte de Manolo Castro (el 22 de febrero de 1948), cuando un grupo de malhechores de la UIR serían los encargados de acribillarlo a balazos en una calle de La Habana Vieja. Lo concreto es que Fidel no mató a Manolo, pero Hemingway siempre le atribuyó la autoría intelectual.

Nunca pudieron aclarar el entredicho. Lo más probable es que ninguno de los dos hubiera dado el brazo a torcer. A Castro no le pareció oportuno tratar el tema en el único encuentro que tuvieron y "Papa", reconocido soberbio, jamás hubiera tomado la iniciativa. Pero como respuesta a su descreimiento, Hemingway escribió "The shot", un relato donde recurre a su conocida técnica de utilizar a personas de la vida real y enmascararlas literariamente (en este caso, el asesino del cuento era fácilmente reconocible como Fidel)."

Gente Magazine Staff 1958 (accessed 12-9-06) Havana's New Tunnel Gente Magazine American Edition, Havana, January 5, 1958, 1(1) 66A, taken from Cuban Information Archives

Gonzalez Echevarria, Roberto 1980 The Dictatorship of Rhetoric/the Rhetoric of Dictatorship: Carpentier, Garcia Marquez, and Roa Bastos. Latin American Research Review, Vol. 15, No. 3 (1980), pp. 205-228 "For example, the assassination of Manolo Castro is retold by alluding to Hemingway's "The Shot,...""

Gorry, Conner and David Stanley 2004 Cuba. Lonely Planet Publications; 3rd edition (January 2004) ISBN 1740591208 p. 82 "Another impressive memorial is the Monumento a Calixto García (1959, Malecón and Calle 6) of the valiant Cuban general...Twenty-four bronze plaques around the equestrian statue provide a history of Garcia's 30-year struggle for Cuban independence."

Haverty, Claire 2006 Memories of the revolution in Cuba. The Day, (New London, CT) August 13, 2006 p. 3E "In the spring of 1960, ..."You're next." My husband knew it was time to get his family out of the country...There is the memory of the sound of the French ship, La Coubre, which was delivering munitions for Castro's regime, exploding in Havana Harbor (March 4, 1960 L.D.) and rushing to my children's school to get them out before something happened.... Recollections of hearing the Russian troops singing at the intelligence camp across the Almendares River; turning out the lights to shield the person who had escaped from that same camp; overhearing a short-wave radio;"

Hemingway, Ernest 1938 The denunciation. In: The complete short Stories of Ernest Hemingway1987. Charles Scribner's Sons, New York. ISBN 0684186683 pp. 420-428.

Hemingway, Ernest 1940 Reprint edition (July 1, 1995) For Whom the Bell Tolls. Charles Scribner's Sons, New York ISBN 0684803356

Hemingway, Ernest 1951 The Shot. True the men's magazine. April 1951. pp. 25-28.

Kowalski, Daniel (accessed 9-5-06) Stalin and the Spanish Civil War Chapter 12. Command Structure and Advisory Apparatus in Spain. I. The Republic Requests Advisors. "The first Soviets to arrive in Spain after the war began, not counting Comintern agents, were journalists, filmmakers, members of the newly established Soviet diplomatic mission, and a handful of military and economic specialists. The first advisors on the scene included the military attaché V. E. Gorev, the naval attaché Nikolai Kuznetsov, 25 the chief military advisor Jan

Berzin, the economic (or trade) attaché Artur Stachevskii, and Aleksandr Rodimtsev, who served largely as advisor to Enrique Lister, commander of the Quinto Regimento. 26 This skeletal team arrived ahead of the main influx of Soviet advisors and technicians, and was charged with overseeing Operation X on the Spanish end."

La Pipa De Hemingway Tuesday, August 01, 2006 Comandante Hemingway, "Papá" Castro 2006 (accessed 10-24-06) "Castro comenzó a mirar su sombra. Después de cuarenta y siete años en el poder debió ceder el mando. Los opositores llaman a esto "solución biológica". Los amigos "un malestar temporario a causa del stress". Fidel Castro y Ernest Hemingway nunca fueron amigos. La historia se ha encargado de resaltar las afinidades entre ambos, pero lo cierto es que solamente se encontraron una vez: el 15 de mayo de 1960.

Ese día Fidel fue invitado al Torneo Anual de Pesca de La Habana. Debía ser el juez, pero insistió en competir. Resultado: ganó el trofeo. En el momento en que lo fotografiaron juntos, le confesó a Hemingway su admiración. La fotografía recorrerría todo el mundo como ícono de la revolución. Pero la realidad es otra. Hemingway guardaba por Castro un marcado rencor por la muerte de Manolo Castro, su amigo personal desde la época de la Guerra Civil Española. El 22 de mayo de 1948, un grupo de matones acribilló a balazos en una calle de La Habana Vieja a Manolo Castro. Lo concreto es que Fidel no mató a Manolo, pero Hemingway siempre le atribuyó la autoría intelectual. En privado, Hemingway culpaba a Fidel del asesinato. En cuanto a Fidel, admiraba la literatura de Hemingway, pesó se cansó de decir que era un yanqui cagón. Hoy Hemingway pertenece a la historia.

León, Ismael 2001 (accessed 11-3-06) Hemingway navega de nuevo El primer ministro compite y gana (1960) Punto de Vista Places contest between May 12 to 15th of 1960 at the Club Náutico Internacional de La Habana but the prize was awarded at the Miramar yatch Club. "Lo acompañaban a bordo sus antiguos compañeros de la guerrilla, Ernesto Ché Guevara y Celia Sánchez, el patrón Julio Arocha y Manuel Bell Gorgas (commonly known as Blakamán), a funcionario del departamento de Caza y Pesca del INIT y compañero de equipo del Primer Ministro. Como las reglas de entonces exigían que los competidores fueran miembros de un club, el Cristal fue adscrito a la flota de la Asociación de los Amigos del Mar....En la prueba de apertura, el Premier ganó -con dos agujas- el trofeo concedido por el Miramar Yacht Club al segundo lugar en puntuación individual.

Lo superó ese día M. A. Escoto y lidereó por equipos el Club Náutico Internacional de La Habana. Después de una jornada de receso, reanudan la competencia el sábado 14 y Castro engancha otras dos agujas. Algunos concursantes de larga trayectoria se asombraban de que el jefe de gobierno, un principiante en la pesca mayor, pudiera usar indistintamente las líneas del número 15 y las más finas, del número 9, y tuviera con ambas el mismo éxito."

"Algunos concursantes de larga trayectoria se asombraban de que el jefe de gobierno, un principiante en la pesca mayor, pudiera usar indistintamente las líneas del número 15 y las más finas, del número 9, y tuviera con ambas el mismo éxito.... Después de la premiación, el Primer Ministro cubano y el escritor Ernest Hemingway tuvieron en Barlovento la única conversación de su vida."

Longacre, Edward G. 2002 (accessed 12-2-06) Espionage in the Civil War. Shotgun's Home of the American Civil War. Source: "Historical Times Encyclopedia of the Civil War" Edited by Patricia L. Faust, Article by Edward G. Longacre.... "By the outbreak of the war, neither the Union nor the Confederacy had established a full-scale espionage system or a military intelligence network. The South, however, was already operating an embryonic spy ring out of Washington, D.C., set up late in 1860 or early in 1861 by Thomas Jordan. A former U.S. Army officer, now a Confederate colonel, Jordan foresaw the benefits of placing intelligence agents in the North's military and political nerve center."

Lozano Moreno, Susana 2001 (accessed 10-31-06) Textos e imágenes de la generación perdida. La adaptación cinematográfica: de Hemingway a Furthman, Faulkner y Hawks. "Memoria"Universidad Departamento de Filología

Inglesa, Facultad de Filología Complutense de Madrid. PhD Thesis. p. 300

Mascareñas, Dolly 2006 The Raúl I know. Time 168 (7) August 16, 2006 pp. 40-43. "she (Lina Ruz, Fidel Castro's mother L.D.) met the revolutionaries at the door..."

Matacena, Orestes (accessed 11-4-06) Orestes Ferrara's Florentine Mansion Havana, Cuba

Matos, Orlando 2006 Cuba: Hemingway's famed fishing Boat is getting a facelift.

Millman, Joel, 2006 Hemingway's ties to Havana bar help sell mojitos. The Wall Street Journal Friday, December 08, 2006 taken from the Post Gazette (Pittsburgh, Pa.) Saturday, December 09, 2006 "In 2001, Cuba's state-owned tourism conglomerate, El Gran-Caribe SA, began licensing La Bodeguita del Medio franchises abroad, although not in the U.S., where it can't do business because of the U.S. trade embargo imposed in 1962. Charging licensing fees of up to $100,000, plus 5 percent of gross revenues, the Castro regime today takes in at least $500,000 a year through the franchises, according to estimates from franchisees and others in the restaurant industry. Turempleo SA, a state employment agency, sends licensees Cuban waiters, bartenders, cooks and musicians, who jump at the chance to work overseas and earn good tips."

Montaner, Carlos Alberto 1999 Viaje al corazón de Cuba Journey to the Heart of Cuba. Plaza & Janés Spanish at English translation Algora Publishing, New York; 1 edition (March 15, 2001) ISBN 1892941619 "Fidel pudo, sin muchas dificultades, probar su coartada. Hemingway no lo creyó y escribió un cuento, The shot, sobre su amigo muerto, en el que el asesino está inspirado en Fidel Castro."

Montenegro, Luisa 2005 (accessed 10-31-06) Once again, Hemingway's Cuban ghost. Cubanow May, 2005

Meyers, Jeffrey 1999 Hemingway: A Biography. Da Capo Press; 1 Da Capo edition ISBN 0306808900 "p. 1 Both of Hemingway's grandfathers fought in the Civil War and the family was proud of its military traditions"...p. 20 "After his father's suicide Hemingway—who always portrayed himself as a victim and had to find a scapegoat for all his problems".

Reese, James 2003 (accessed 10-31-06) Publishers synopsis of Hemingway House in Cuba: Finca Vigia- Fictionwise eBook

Rodríguez García, José A. 1905 (accessed 12-3-06) Croquis histórico. Mauricio Casanova, Habana Calixto + Garcia + statue + OR + monumento + OR + statue&psp=9#PRA1-PP14,M1 p. 12 "... queriendo antes morir que caer en manos de sus enemigos, como hizo el general Calixto García (el cual fué maravilla quo no quedara en el sitio,..."

Ros, Enrique 2003 Fidel Castro y El Gatillo Alegre: Sus Años Universitarios (Colección Cuba y Sus Jueces) Ediciones Universal Miami ISBN 1593880065 p. 13 "...El joven (Fidel Castro) que se opone a que se integre el equipo de pelota de la Universidad el mejor jugador por que es negro y la Liga Amateur no le permitiría, entonces, el equipo universitario participar en el campeonato. ..." The author discusses the matter in greater length on page 46.

Sanders, Tom 2002 (accessed 11-3-06) Pilgrimage to Cuba - In Search of Hemingway's Ghost. Hemingway Resource Center "In fact, when he left Cuba in July 1960 on an ill-fated trip to the USA then on to Spain, Hemingway could not have known he would never return."

Simon, Joel 2006 (accessed 12-3-06) Muzzling the Media: How the New Autocrats Threaten Press Freedoms. World Policy Journal, Summer 2006, 23 (2), 51-61. Posted Online August 11, 2006. "In Cuba, Burma, and Eritrea, dozens of journalists are in jail and the press is a essentially a functional arm of the state."

Solera, Robert 2006 personal communication Re: Hemingway and Castro hated each other? Larry: I cannot find my comments to your sketch. Nevertheless it is: There are incongruous statements that might confuse the reader. Sometimes you don't who is saying what. You should make clear what you say and what somebody else does, using different types of letters or fonts of diverse size. One person is saying that Leonel Gomez was not hurt.

The others say (Gomez was L.D). Also his surname is altered in one of the instances. Some others say that Fidel was involved and others that he was not, although it is a proven fact he was in the surrounding area —btw in a cafe sitting with former FEU president —his name escapes my mind now— the one that went to Bogotá in 1948 when the Bogotazo. Fidel insisted to the waiter to look intensely to his face so he will — the waiter— remember later on if he was asked about it. The former FEU president said so in a radio interview before he died —he was an architect.

Also it has been mentioned that a godson of Paulina Alsina was involved. Also it mentions Manolo Castro as a member a FEU —which he was not at the time and say he was involved in sports when in fact he was Manolo Castro the Head of the Direccion de Deportes and promoter of Cayo Confites —mentioned without the 's'. My suggestion would be that if it does not clarify the story it should be deleted —I mean the quotation from other sources most if based in hearsay. For example Fidel could not veto anyone for been a negro from participating in sports at the University or in the amateur organization —he would not have been blackballed for his race because it was against the law and besides Fidel Castro was a nobody at the time to have the necessary clout to do so.

La Liga Amateur de Beisbol had many black people playing in any of the organizations that were part of it. Also MSR is identified as the R standing for something else instead of Movimiento Socialista Revolucionario. How Hemingway could have been asking Fidel to spare him his la Vigia home in early 1960 if he was at the time still in Cuba and very famous and close to Fidel —btw the photo was taken in Miramar Yacht Club. Americans came and went from the States to Cuba and viceversa which was very normal at the time. In the story it is not mentioned that Manolo Castro was a co-owner of Cinecito. I think it is almost impossible that he was shot by people walking because those were by driving shoot outs.

More or less that is what I remember of my comments. I am not too sure that. Manolito —Manolo's son which I met— was present at the time of his death. The other owner of Cinecito was an Spaniard exiled that I met back in 1960 at his home in Havana's outskirts. Also San Rafael and Consulado where Cinecito was it is not Old Havana. Take care! Life is too brief to waste it! Date: Sat, 4 Nov 2006 18:17:16 -0500 From: nellsol1 nellsol1@bellsouth.net To: daleyl@peak.org Subject: Re: Hemingway paper Larry never heard about that institute Fish and Game Tourism Institute (INIT) . Besides INIT means Industria Nacional de la Industria Turistica, led at the time by Bilito Castellanos and being his second in command Jesus "Chucho" Montane Oropesa (corr by R.S), later right hand man to Fidel Castro, second in command to Raul Castro at the MINFAR and Minister of Communications, already deceased/ More. Manolo Castro himself killed Raul Fernandez Fiallo, Catedratico at the Havana University. When he was killed, Carlos Puchol was also killed. According to Mario Rieras' Cuba Libre' Fidel Castro was exonerated from the process by Judge Jose Mario Gispert who received orders "de arriba" to do so. Remember that Gustavo Ortiz Faez —godson to Paulina Grau Alsina— was involved in the killing. page 164. Life is too brief to waste it!

Stalin, Joseph birth name Iosif Vissarionovich Dzhugashvili (accessed 11-4-06) "Gratitude is a sickness suffered by dogs.- Joseph Stalin" Basic Quotations

Time staff 1959 The Hemisphere. Chief Executioner Monday, Apr. 13, 1959 immediate source Jose Luis Fernandez. After taking Holy Week off, Captain Herman Marks, 37, an ex-convict from Milwaukee who fought with Fidel Castro's rebels, got back on the job one night last week. Consulting his written orders, he marched with an armed guard to the death row of Havana's gloomy Cabana Fortress, brought out three former policemen, all convicted in military courts on charges of murder. A short ride in a bus and a jeep brought Marks, the guards, a priest and the prisoners to within 200 feet of an old moat, 20 feet deep and surrounded on three sides by high stone walls.

A six-man firing squad waited on a spot worn bare of grass. Under the glare of three floodlights, Marks marched former Batista Police Lieut. Eloy Contreras to a bullet-scarred wall, 36 feet from the firing squad. "Atención!" yelled Marks at 1:13 a.m. "Preparen . . . apunten . . . fuego!" After the volley,

Marks stepped up to Contreras' writhing body, fired the coup de grâce with his .45 automaticá had to shoot two more times before his man finally died. Guards took off Contreras' shoes, fingerprinted him, placed him in a plain wooden coffin, and loaded him aboard a hearse for delivery to waiting relatives. By 1:55 a.m., all three prisoners were dead, and Marks's work was ended for the night. "Execution is not a pleasant task," says Castro's chief executioner, "but a necessary one."

Later in the week, firing squads through the island shot 13 more men, raising the execution toll that week to 475. "War crimes" courts worked around the clock to clean up "hundreds of pending cases." Marks is no newcomer to unpleasantness. His U.S. police record includes 32 arrests, from Long Beach, Calif. to Bangor, Me. on charges ranging from drunkenness, vagrancy and assault to auto theft and draft dodging. He escaped from a Wisconsin reform school in 1938, from an Ohio jail in 1946, from a California industrial farm in 1950. Finally, he did 3½ years in the Wisconsin pen for raping a 17-year-old girl. Warden John C. Burke remembers him as "a real stinker." Behind this sordid record lies the soul of a romantic. On his left arm Marks wears a tattooed double heart inscribed "Love, Nellie." On his right is an eight-inch snake coiled about a dagger stuck through the top of a skull and bearing Marks's motto, which happens to be "Death Before Dishonor."

Thomas, Hugh 1977 The Spanish Civil War Harper and Row London revised and enlarged edition ISBN 0060142782 p. 274

University of North Carolina Press 2006 (accessed 12-3-06) publicity "blurb" for: Piero Gleijeses Conflicting Missions. Havana, Washington, and Africa, 1959-1976 "Gleijeses was even able to gain extensive access to closed Cuban archives—this comprehensive and balanced work sheds new light on U.S. foreign policy and CIA covert operations.... Piero Gleijeses is professor of American foreign policy at the School of Advanced International Studies at the Johns Hopkins University. He is author of Shattered Hope: The Guatemalan Revolution and the United States, 1944-1954."

Uría, Miguel 2006 Personal communication in phone

conversation on 10-27-06), José Adán, a very knowledgeable person on this matter and who is now deceased said in President Grau's time (1944-1948) that Manolo Castro allowed Hemingway to referee a boxing match old in Palacio de los Deportes.

Vargas Llosa, Álvaro 2005 (accessed 10-30-06) La máquina de matar: El Che Guevara, de agitador comunista a marca capitalista. The New Republic 11/7/2005

"something that is conceived in the mind; a thought; idea: He jotted down the conceits of his idle hours." (accessed 1-31-06 from)

"La inviolabilidad del domicilio paso a las paginas de la historia ya que toda y cada una de las residencias eran propiedad del Estado" (Calvo 2002).

Here the word marxist in lower case refers to practice and not theory.

This everything includes almost all private property from the magnificent Florentine mansion of Italian Independence fighter Orestes Ferrara (see Matacena, 2006), through the farm residence of my grandfather Mambí Brigadier General Calixto (García-Iñiguez) Enamorado, also an independence general, the old jeep of Uncle Marcos García-Iñiguez Ramírez, to my childhood stamp collection.

Meyers, 1999 discusses the death of Hemingway senior at length, but I could not find mention of General Thomas Jordan nor General Calixto Garcia, who once served under Jordan's command during the Ten Years' War in Cuba.

Solera (2006) states in part: "Manolo Castro himself killed Raul Fernandez Fiallo, Catedratico (Professor) at the Havana University. When he was killed, Carlos Puchol was also killed. According to Mario Rieras' Cuba Libre' Fidel Castro was exonerated from the process by Judge Jose Mario Gispert who received orders "de arriba" to do so."

E.g. a Hemingway's short piece —"the Denunciation' (see Hemingway, 1987) very strongly suggests that Hemingway actively participated betraying victims to the dread execution purges of the communist hatchet man Andre Marty.

Daley to Solera in reference to killings by Manolo Castro,

"That helps make my point that Hemingway did not pass moral judgment on his friends. I still think that Hemingway and Castro did not get along; and that Fidel Castro, even if he had been friends with Hemingway would never let mere friendship stand in the way of getting something he wanted. Remember the Stalinist statement, "gratitude is a vice of dogs."

This description of skin color seems to be a "beard" used to protect the anonymity of the author of these events (Gatti, 2002). This skin color could also be taken as an insult by Fidel Castro citing a baseball conflict at Havana University (Ros, 2003 pp. 13, 46). Others point out that in this case Castro well may not have been in a position to do this due to his low status in the Havana student government at that time and because this was against the law in Cuba (Solera, 2006). Supporting a bias against Blacks by the until recently leader of the Cuban communist government is his 2003 remark "tres negritos" by which he refers to victims of one of his executions (Aguila, 2003).

While supposedly Hemingway did not meet Fidel Castro before (e.g. León, 2001), other reports suggest that Hemingway hated Fidel Castro for killing Manolo Castro who was a long time friend (Gatti, 2002; Uría, 2006). Such hatred suggests that Hemingway, it they had not met at least knew of and recognized Fidel Castro as is described in "The Shot" where Hemingway writes he knew the approaching shooter who was seeking him out as a source of money.

Another allusion de Castro as a base ball pitcher e.g. see Furati, 2003 p.82

In real life Fidel Castro, left Cuba after the murder of Manolo Castro (February 22, 1948). While still in Cuba Fidel Castro stayed in hiding (Ros, 2006 pp. 181-182), he and very anxious to leave (Ros, 2003 p. 250). He negotiated the funding or the trip from Argentine diplomats in the middle of March (Furiati, 2003, p. 122), and also collected $500 dollars from Miguel Angel Quevedo the director of the foremost Cuban magazine "Bohemia." Thus it is entirely possible that Castro really received money from Hemingway as well. Castro left Cuba apparently in an Argentine diplomatic vehicle (Ros, 2003

p. 182) to Venezuela and Panama (Furiati, 2003, p. 122; Ros, 2003 p. 182 and others) and on to Colombia arriving there on April 1st, 1948 (footnote 251 of Ros, 2003 p. 188). Here Fidel Castro participated in the riots of the Bogotazo. The money for this trip was provided by Argentine authorities direct to do so by Juan Peron (Furiati, 2003, p. 122; Ros, 2003 pp. 181-182).

In reality the actual scene apparently was the movie theater e.g. "Cinecito" (Gutiérrez, 2005 )then known as the "Resumen" which was at San Rafael and Consulado and where the Movimiento Socialist Popular (MPS) to which Manolo belonged held meetings (Ros 1963, p. 62); however the murder of Oscar Fernández Caral was, as in the Hemingway story in front of his house (Arencibia, 2005)

According to Ros (pp., 167-170), Manolo Castro was tricked into leaving the theater (of which he was partial owner Solera, 2006) to go outside by a communist believed to have been the "fingerman." According to some the actual attack was done on foot. First the targeted group was fired at and Manolo and the rest dive to the sidewalk. A few moments pass, Manolo stands up. Then the five "main" assassins fire, killing two as in the Hemingway story. The dead were Manolo and a companion. Fidel Castro appears not to have been directly involved, but Hemingway does not seem to believe it. Fidel Castro is known to have wanted Manolo Castro killed (Ros, 2003, p. 170). However, others state Solera (2006) that the attack was done from vehicles as Hemingway describes it.

## ERNEST HEMINGWAY IN CUBA

Born and reared in the suburbs of Chicago, Ernest Hemingway was a product of the American heartland who, once he got out of it, never wanted to have much to do with the American heartland again. Aside from a few of his earliest short stories, which in any case are set in upper Michigan rather than suburban Illinois, Hemingway never published a word about where he came from, nor did he ever go back for long.

There are as many possible explanations for this as there

are biographies of Hemingway. Some have suggested that Hemingway, like others of his generation who lived as expatriates in Europe after World War I, found the provincialism and narrow-mindedness of middle America stultifying. Unlike most of his fellow expats, however, Hemingway never went home. After leaving his birthplace of Oak Park, Illinois in the fall of 1921 with his new bride, Elizabeth Hadley Richardson, Hemingway spent the rest of his life either outside the United States or on the periphery of its life, in places like the Florida Keys, the upper plains states, (he enjoyed Montana and Wyoming for their hunting) the Pacific northwest, specifically Idaho, where he ended his life in 1961...and Cuba.

Given the enormously complex relationship that Hemingway had with his family, particularly with his demanding and overbearing mother, whom he repeatedly and for years denounced as a "bitch" to anyone who would listen, it's possible that Hemingway simply wanted to give the midwest a "wide berth" because that was where his mother was until her own death in 1951. (One of Nietzsche's biographers has suggested that Nietzsche's own passion for climbing high mountains may have stemmed from a desire to get as far away as possible-in this case the direction being up-away from a father as overbearing as Hemingway's mother was reported to be.)

Shortly before Ernest and Hadley were married in September, 1921, Hadley had said to Ernest, "The world's a jail and we're gonna break it together." They were young-he was 22 on their wedding day; she was not quite 30-and deeply in love; in later years, after later marriages, Hemingway would suggest that Hadley was the only woman whom he had ever truly loved. But, although he was at heart a romantic, and conventional enough a midwesterner in his heart to feel that any time he fell in love with a woman, he ought to marry her, Hemingway couldn't be monogamous. His friend and fellow author Scott Fitzgerald (who managed to remain married to the same woman until he died even though his wife, Zelda Sayre, was mentally unstable, he was an alcoholic and their marriage was a stormy melodrama) predicted quite early on that Hemingway was going to require "a new wife for each book." The remark turned out to be quite prescient; it was in fact the course of Hemingway's four marriages that took him to Cuba and lodged him there-he ultimately made Cuba the most permanent home he would ever make of any place.

Hemingway's trek south began in 1927, when he and Hadley divorced over his affair with wealthy Arkansas socialite and magazine journalist Pauline Pfeiffer, who promptly became the second Mrs. Hemingway. One thing Hemingway would never do with his wives, until his fourth and last one anyway, was to subject the new wife to living in the environs of the old. The venue of Ernest and Hadley's marriage had been Paris, where he struggled in the early-to-mid 1920s to get his writing career started.

With the end of his first marriage, Hemingway's affection for Paris declined temporarily, and another friend and fellow novelist, John Dos Passos, suggested to him that Key West, Florida might be a good place for him to relocate. In 1928, when Hemingway and Pauline went to live there in a house that her wealthy Uncle Gus had given them as a wedding present, Key West was a sleepy, run-down fishing village at the end of the Keys southwest of Miami. Prohibition was still in effect, and among Key West's attractions for the notoriously-bibulous Hemingway may well have been that its very position on the periphery of America made prohibition little more than a word there; smuggled liquor from Cuba was easy to get, and the island had plenty of its own sources of bathtub booze as well. Key West was in fact popular with the artistic and literary crowd; poet Wallace Stevens was among those who spent time there. In any case Pauline and Ernest set up housekeeping in Key West and Ernest, who already had one son from his marriage with Hadley, soon had two more.

Every tourist who's ever gone to Key West to take pictures of Hemingway's house there knows that Sloppy Joe's Bar was his favorite Key West hangout. He quickly made friends with its owner, Joe Russell, described by Hemingway biographer Michael Reynolds as "a salty, red-faced bootlegger who was the real thing." Russell had a boat for fishing, the *Anita,* and he and Hemingway often went out on fishing expeditions in it, some of which lasted for days. One such expedition took place in the spring of 1932. Pauline had given birth to Hemingway's third and final son the previous November. Hemingway wasn't pleased about becoming a father again, and the birth put further strain on what was already a strained relationship-Pauline's family's money had been largely responsible for freeing Ernest from the necessity to write journalism, enabling him to devote himself exclusively to fiction, and he was not a man to be comfortable with owing anyone anything. Partly to get away from the strained relationship and partly to get away from the sound of a crying baby, Hemingway went off with Russell in April of that year on another fishing trip. They sailed to Havana for what was supposed to be a two-day stay. They ended up staying four months.

Hemingway had seen Havana once before, when he and Pauline had a stop-off there on their way to Key West from France in 1928. But Havana had new attractions for him now, not the least of which was 22 year-old Jane Mason, the wife of the head of Pan American Airways in Cuba. They began an affair as Hemingway took up extended residence at what would be his base in Havana for the next several years, the Hotel Ambos Mundos. In the spring of the following year, as his second marriage continued to unravel, Hemingway was in Havana for another extended stay, and once again Jane Mason was there. Pauline used the excuse of the annual visit of Hemingway's son Jack, known as Bumby, to come over from Key West as she brought the boy to Havana to spend time with his father. But Hemingway made her feel unwelcome and she soon went back to Key West alone.

Hemingway and Mason talked of getting married, but it didn't happen. Instead, in 1936 back in Key West, he met Martha Gellhorn, a vivacious and attractive blonde and fellow author/journalist with whom he would soon share a hotel room in Madrid while they were both covering the Spanish Civil War as correspondents, and who would become the third Mrs.

Hemingway in 1940 after Pauline, a devout Catholic who did not take divorce lightly, finally agreed to divorce Ernest so he could marry Martha. The divorce became final in November of that year and Hemingway and Gellhorn were married the same month.

The house in Key West had been a gift from Pauline's family; obviously Ernest and Martha weren't going to live there, although he remained generally on good terms with Pauline and they did sometimes visit. The logical place for the newlyweds to settle after their Hawaiian honeymoon was the city that had virtually been Ernest's home away from home since 1932: Havana.

Aside from the fact that he had already established in Havana what's known in the world of bullfighting as a *querencia*-the part of the ring where the bull feels comfortable and at home-there were other reasons for Hemingway to like Havana. During the years of the Grau and Batista regimes that preceded the rule of Fidel Castro, Havana was something of a playground for the wealthy of America's east coast (some have called it "America's brothel.") Havana was a good place to have a good time, and Hemingway liked a good time.

His years in Key West had already given him a taste for tropical ambience. Naturally sloppy in his personal habits, (Martha Gellhorn casually nicknamed him "Pig") he liked a place where he could go around in shorts and loose-fitting shirts all the time. His outings aboard the *Anita* with Joe Russell-who died of a stroke in 1941-had given Hemingway a passion for deep-sea fishing, and the Gulf Stream, adjacent to Cuba, offered the best marlin fishing in the world. Always fond of blood sports, Hemingway discovered and became an enthusiastic follower of cockfighting in Havana, and there was also the less-bloody, but for its human participants more dangerous, sport of Jai Alai, another amusement of which Hemingway became a devoted *aficionado*.

Martha had in fact joined Hemingway in Havana the year before they were married, but she was not about to share a small, dirty room at the Hotel Ambos Mundos with him. Looking in a newspaper, she found a 15-acre estate about 15 miles from downtown Havana called the "Finca Vigia" ("Lookout Farm.") The place was badly dilapidated and Hemingway thought it not even worth trying to renovate, but Martha saw it as a challenge and hired workers at her own expense to knock the Finca into liveable shape. At first they rented the farm for $100 a month; in December 1940 after they were married, Hemingway bought the Finca Vigia for $18,500. It was the first home he had ever owned that hadn't been given to him by someone else, and he "settled" there to the extent that a man as restless as Ernest Hemingway could settle anywhere.

The Finca provided a spacious, quiet place for him to work. It had a swimming pool and tennis court, and Hemingway's myriad cats and dogs wandered freely about the place. Soon he was a regular fixture at Havana's Floridita bar, where he could be seen downing ice-cold dacquiris in his own reserved seat at the end of the bar.

But the Hemingway-Gellhorn marriage was as doomed as his two previous ones. Martha had in fact expressed misgivings to a friend before her marriage to Ernest as to how well things would work out. Both of Hemingway's first two wives had been older than he was, she pointed out, whereas she was nine years his junior. Martha was less than enthusiastic about assuming the role of housekeeper, and Hemingway's mercurial temper, often exacerbated by drinking, increased tensions. Martha later decried her husband's "ceaseless, crazy bullying" of her. There is also some evidence, not surprising perhaps in view of the fact that Martha was the first of Ernest's wives to be younger than he was, that they were sexually incompatible.

Then World War II came along and invaded what was already less than Eden. Hemingway had already been directly or indirectly involved in four wars: World War I; the 1922 war between Greece and Turkey; the Spanish Civil War and, most recently, the Japanese war in China, which he and Martha had gone off to cover as correspondents shortly after their marriage. He was inclined to sit this one out, although in 1943 German U-boats were slipping into the Gulf of Mexico to torpedo American and Venezuelan shipping, and Hemingway saw an opportunity to participate in war without straying too far from home. By now he had his own fishing boat, the *Pilar*, and with the connivance of the American ambassador in Havana, Spruille Braden, Hemingway embarked on a slightly-crackpot "U-boat hunting" scheme-he had the *Pilar* outfitted with machine guns and ammunition, rounded up a crew and made a number of patrols in the Gulf Stream looking for German subs. (They never found one.)

Other than that, Hemingway inclined toward staying home in Cuba as the war in Europe raged. Martha didn't. She was an ambitious writer who loved her work and was not going to be content with sitting around the Finca Vigia being Mrs. Hemingway when the whole world was at war. She went off to cover the war as a correspondent for *Collier's* magazine, and Hemingway was eventually cajoled into doing likewise. In 1944 he went to London, his first stop toward becoming *Colliers'* front-line correspondent after the Normandy Invasion, at which he was present. His marriage to Martha was already in trouble, and the war finished it off-in London he met yet another woman journalist, Mary Welsh, who would become the fourth and last Mrs. Hemingway. In 1946 he brought her to the Finca Vigia, where she became the somewhat-uneasy but increasingly confident mistress of the place.

Mary did, in fact, unlike her predecessor Martha, go to great lengths to make the Finca a "home," although for Hemingway "home" seldom meant much more than a base of operations. Mary put in a great deal of work maintaining flower and vegetable gardens on the property and went to great pains with the upkeep of the decaying house while also having to work around her husband's less-than-fastidious personal habits and coexisting with a menagerie of cats, dogs and other animals on the property. Years earlier, Pauline Pfeiffer had tried to keep Hemingway close by giving him a decent home in Key West; Mary Welsh in the 1940s and '50s made similar efforts in Cuba for a man now in his fifties and aging quickly, with a list of physical-and mental-ailments that would mount and mount over the years, making their life together on the island as stormy as the previous Hemingway marriages.

Hemingway would in fact make Cuba his base of operations for the remaining years of his life, although being naturally footloose and craving audiences as well as excitement, he and Mary and would often leave their somewhat-remote tropical outpost for sojourns in the United States, Europe and Africa. When Castro came to power in 1959 and the Americans who had been in Havana evacuated the place quickly, Hemingway chose to stay on; he had been fully aware of the corruption and abuses of the previous regimes and, naive about Communism, felt he had no reason not to accept Castro as a welcome reformer. He went so far as to wish Castro "all luck" with running the country, an attitude which didn't do much to endear Hemingway to either the U.S. government or the FBI.

FBI director J. Edgar Hoover had in fact been "keeping an eye" on Hemingway ever since the sub-hunting adventure of 1942-43, and Hemingway's mounting paranoia in his later years about FBI surveillance was not entirely without basis in fact. (Castro returned Hemingway's compliment, by the way-since Hemingway's death he has been a much-honored cultural hero in Cuba, the government maintaining his house as a museum and even having his boat the *Pilar* transported overland to be the museum's chief attraction.)

People did sometimes ask Hemingway why he chose to live in Cuba. Late in 1948 he wrote an article for *Holiday* magazine in which he talked about his life there, offering his readers verbal snapshots of cool mornings at the Finca, cockfights and pigeon shoots, but most importantly the incomparable marlin fishing in the Gulf Stream, which he lovingly called "the Great Blue River." In fact it was not only in journalism but in his often less-than-successful later fictions that Hemingway's attractions toward this part of the world are apparent.

In his 1937 "proletarian" novel *To Have And Have Not* Hemingway displayed his affection for the seamy side of Havana life, and on one level his late novella *The Old Man And*

*The Sea* could be read as a lyrical tribute to the Gulf Stream. His posthumous novel *Islands In The Stream,* cobbled together in 1970 from a huge pile of manuscript that he churned out between 1946 and 1950, while it may be unbearably talky in places, is in other places a moving tribute to the Caribbean world-and to Cuba. Hear Hemingway in that novel use his unmatched gift for evoking topography to share with his readers what was, unquestionably, a longstanding love-of-place:

*He got into the car and told the chauffeur to go up O'Reilly to the* Floridita. *Before the car circled the plaza in front of the embassy building and the Ayuntamiento and then turned into O'Reilly he saw the size of the waves in the mouth of the harbor and the heavy rise and fall of the channel buoy. In the mouth of the harbor the sea was very wild and confused and clear green water was breaking over the rock at the base of the Morro, the tops of the seas blowing white in the sun. It looks wonderful, he said to himself. It not only looks wonderful, it is wonderful.*

# Chapter 21

# Chronology

| | |
|---|---|
| 1920 | Hemingway started reporting for the Toronto Star. |
| 1921 | Ernest married Hadley Richardson (his 1st of 4 wives); they moved to Paris, France, on the advice of American playwright Sherwood Anderson, to join the expatriate community of writers there. |
| 1922 | As a correspondent for the Toronto Star, Hemingway covered the Greco-Turkish War. |
| 1923 | Hemingway's Three Stories and Ten Poems was published by Robert McAlmon in Paris; his first son, John, was born. |
| 1924 | In our time, a collection of vignettes, was published in Paris by Three Mountains Press. |
| 1925 | In Our Time, adding fourteen short stories to the earlier vignettes, was published in New York by Boni & Liveright. |
| 1926 | The Torrents of Spring and The Sun Also Rises are published by Charles Scribner's Sons, who became Hemingway's regular publisher. |
| 1927 | Hemingway published a short story collection, Men Without Women, which included "Hills Like White Elephants"; he married Pauline Pfieffer after divorcing Hadley Richardson. |
| 1928 | The Hemingways moved to Key West, Florida, where son Patrick was born. Hemingway's father, Dr. Clarence E. |

Hemingway, committed suicide on Dec. 6th; Hemingway asked his brother to send him the gun that their father had used.

1929 Hemingway's father committed suicide in Oak Park, IL; Hemingway asked for the gun his father used to kill himself to be sent to him. A Farewell to Arms was published after the first manuscript was lost by Pauline and Hemingway had to start over. Commentary on the novel. Background on how the events of the novel parallel Hemingway's own wounding, plus his reactions in poetry to being wounded and in the war.

1931 Gregory, Hemingway's third son, was born.

1932 Death in the Afternoon, a nonfiction study of bullfighting is published.

1933 Hemingway published a short story collection, Winner Take Nothing.

1935 Hemingway published Green Hills of Africa.

1937 Hemingway reports as war correspondent on the Spanish Civil War; To Have and Have Not was published (later made into a movie that starred Humphrey Bogart and Lauren Bacall).

1938 Hemingway collaborated with Joris Ivens on The Spanish Earth, a film espousing the Loyalist cause; he also published The Fifth Column and the First: Forty-nine Stories.

1940 He divorced Pauline Pfieffer and married Martha Gellhorn, also a writer. The Hemingways purchased Finca Vigia to be their home in Cuba; For Whom the Bell Tolls was published. (

1942 Hemingway edited Men at War.

1944 He met Mary Welsh in London, traveled with American troops in France and Germany as a World War II correspondent, and participated in the Allied liberation of Paris.

1945 Hemingway divorced Martha Gellhorn,

supposedly for laughing at him in the hospital after he was involved in a serious car crash.

1946 He married Mary Welsh.

1947 Hemingway received the Bronze Star for his role in the liberation of Paris. (Scroll down to the bottom photo at this link to decide for yourself if his actions were heroic.)

1950 Across the River and into the Trees was published. Hemingway survived a nearly fatal plane crash.

1951 Ernest's mother, Grace Hall Hemingway, died.

1952 The Old Man and the Sea was published (and later made into a movie starring Spencer Tracy).

1953 Hemingway won the Pulitzer Prize for Fiction.

1954 Hemingway was awarded the Nobel Prize for Literature.

1960 The Hemingways moved to Ketchum, Idaho, near Sun Valley. Ernest was hospitalized at the Mayo Clinic for uncontrolled high blood pressure, liver disease, diabetes, and depression. He received shock treatments because he thought the FBI was following him, but he couldn't convince others. These treatments weakened and emaciated Hemingway, along with his diseases, and drained him mentally so that he found it nearly impossible to write. (The FBI was keeping tabs on him because he had lived in Cuba until Castro took over.)

1961 Hemingway committed suicide in Ketchum, Idaho, at about 5:00 a.m. on July 2, by shotgun to the head (his father had used a pistol); he was found by his wife, Mary. He is buried in Ketchum.

1964 A Moveable Feast was published posthumously.

| | |
|---|---|
| 1969 | The Fifth Column and Four Stories of the Spanish Civil War were published as scholars began to find Hemingway's unfinished manuscripts. |
| 1970 | Islands in the Stream was published. |
| 1972 | The Nick Adams Stories, a short story collection, was published. |
| 1985 | The Dangerous Summer was published. |
| 1986 | The Garden of Eden, a novel Hemingway started about a love triange, was completed and published. |
| 1987 | The Complete Stories of Ernest Hemingway: The Finca Vigia Edition was published as the definitive version of Hemingway's best stories. |

# Bibliography


Baker, Carlos. *Hemingway: The Writer as Artist*. Fourth edition, Princeton University Press: Princeton, NJ, 1972.

Bruccoli, Matthew J. (Ed.). *Ernest Hemingway's apprenticeship: Oak Park, 1916-1917*. NCR Microcard Editions: Washington, D.C., 1971.

Bruccoli, Matthew J., and Robert W. Trogdon (Eds.). The Only Thing That Counts: *The Ernest Hemingway-Maxwell Perkins Correspondence 1925-1947*. Charles Scribner's Sons: New York, 1996.

Clifford, Stephen P. *Beyond the Heroic "I": Reading Lawrence, Hemingway, and "masculinity"*. Bucknell Univ. Press: Cranbury, NJ, 1999.

Hemingway, Ernest. By-Line: *Ernest Hemingway. Selected articles and dispatches of four decades*. Edited by William White, with commentaries by Philip Young. Collins: London, 1968.

*Complete poems*. Edited with an introduction and notes by Nicholas Gerogiannis. Rev. ed., University of Nebraska Press: Lincoln, 1992.

*The Complete Short Stories*. The Finca Vigía ed. Charles Scribner's Sons: New York, 1998.

*Death in the Afternoon*. Jonathan Cape: London, 1932.

*Ernest Hemingway: Selected Letters, 1917-1961*. Ed. Carlos Baker. Charles Scribner's Sons: New York, 1981.

*A Farewell to Arms*. Charles Scribner's Sons: New York, 1929.

*Fiesta*. Jonathan Cape: London, 1927.

*For Whom the Bell Tolls*. Charles Scribner's Sons: New York 1940.

*The Garden of Eden*. Charles Scribner's Sons: New York, 1986.

*Green Hills of Africa*. Charles Scribner's Sons: New York 1935.

*In Our Time*. Boni and Liveright: New York, 1925.

*Islands in the Stream*. Charles Scribner's Sons: New York, 1970.

*A Moveable Feast*. Jonathan Cape: London, 1964.

*The Nick Adams Stories*. Preface by Philip Young. Charles Scribner's Sons: New York, 1972.

*The Old Man and the Sea*. Charles Scribner's Sons: New York, 1952.

*Selected Letters 1917-1961*. Ed. Carlos Baker. Panther Books/ Granada Publishing: London 1985(1981).

*The Snows of Kilimanjaro and other stories*, Charles Scribner's Sons: New York, 1961.

*The Sun also rises*. Charles Scribner's Sons: New York, 1928(1926).

*The Torrents of Spring: A Romantic Novel in Honor of the Passing of a Great Race*. Charles Scribner's Sons: New York, 1926.

*Three Stories & Ten Poems: Ernest Hemingway's First Book*. A facsimile of the original Paris Edition published in 1923. Bruccoli Clark Books: Bloomfield Hills, Michigan, 1977.

*True at First Light*. Edited with an Introduction by Patrick Hemingway. Arrow Books/Random House: London 1999.

*Winner Take Nothing*. Charles Scribner's Sons: New York, 1933.

Josephs, Allen. *For Whom the Bell Tolls: Ernest Hemingway's Undiscovered Country*. Twayne: New York, 1994.

Lacasse, Rodolphe. *Hemingway et Malraux: destins de l'homme*. Profils; 6, Montréal 1972.

Lynn. Kenneth S. *Hemingway*. Simon and Schuster: London, 1987.

Mandel, Miriam. *Reading Hemingway: The Facts in the Fictions*. Scarecrow Press: Metuchen, NJ and London, 1995.

Meyers, Jeffrey. *Hemingway: A Biography*. New York, 1985 (Macmillan: London, 1986 (Harper & Row: New York 1985).

Nelson, Gerald B. & Glory Jones. *Hemingway: Life and Works*. Facts On File Publications: New York, 1984.

Palin, Michael. *Hemingway's Travels*. Weidenfeld & Nicolson: London, 1999.

Phillips, Larry W (Ed). *Ernest Hemingway on Writing*. Grafton Books: London, 1986 (1984).

